RAJIV GANDHI'S MODERN INDIA

Development with Science and Technology

Author with Rajiv Gandhi

RAJIV GANDHI'S MODERN INDIA
Development with Science and Technology

Dr. PAWAN SIKKA
M.Sc; Ph.D; D.Sc. (Physics)
V.F. University of Oxford, Oxford, UK
Former Advisor/Scientist-G
Government of India
Department of Science and Technology
(Ministry of Science and Technology)
New Delhi-110001

UPPAL PUBLISHING HOUSE
NEW DELHI - 110002 (India)

UPPAL PUBLISHING HOUSE
3 Ansari Road, Darya Ganj, New Delhi - 110002
Phones: 23273756,23286571, Fax: 91-011-23286571
Email: uppalbooks@vsnl.net

First Published 2007
ISBN: 13: 978-81-7658-042-7
ISBN: 10: 81-7658-042-2

Printed in India

Published by B.S. Uppal for M/s Uppal Publishing House, 3 Ansari Road, Darya Ganj, New Delhi and Typeset by Priyanka Graphics, Laxmi Nagar, Delhi and Printed at Arora Offset Press, Delhi-110092.

To

Shalini

My Life Companion

Akhand Saubhagyavati Bhava

Preface

The modern World is science-based. The development of science and technology in India since Independence has been essentially based on the visionary support by political leadership at the highest level, namely Jawahar Lal Nehru and Indira Gandhi, and to some extent, Rajiv Gandhi, who unfortunately did not have the necessary time span; along with the support of visionaries of science like Homi Bhabha, C.V. Raman, Vikram Sarabhai, S. S. Bhatnagar, D. S. Kothari, Meghnad Saha and P. C. Mahalanobis.

Rajiv Gandhi had a scientific bent of mind. As Prime Minister of India, in 1984-89, he could see that there was a strong nexus between science and technology and the economic development of the society. He said - Where science and technology in concerned, we must keep in mind that nothing but the best will do for the country; and we must work towards that end. He had a vision for the modern India. He gave a clarion call to the nation to take a quantum leap into the 21st century. It was his dream of modernizing India, of bringing her fully technologically, economically and socially into the new millennium. He said – *"We can achieve world leadership in key areas by refocusing our strategies on areas that we feel are more relevant or necessary to us, or areas that we want to go ahead in ....".*

He believed that - Science is a world-wide discipline, not confined by political boundaries or by narrow walls. It cuts across all such boundaries. What is needed is a better interaction, better cross-fertilization of ideas or disciplines... We have to change the basic thinking in our society. Development must relate to science and science must relate to development. This requires the need for the inculcation of scientific temper among people.

He was instrumental in fostering an atmosphere of modernity in the country. His modern outlook, clear vision and abiding faith in science and technology was for eradicating poverty and for providing good quality of life to the people. His speeches delivered during his dynamic years, at many national and international scientific forums, show his mind and ideology and also provide new directions to the application of science and technology for the socio - economic development of India of the new millennium. His clear vision and new agenda navigated India towards progress and prosperity. The present volume is a compilation of his selected speeches to get his major observations on the current state of affairs on science and technology in the country. It was his mission of making India developed, as closed as possible to the world.

This is a companion volume to my earlier book, *Rajiv Gandhi – His Vision of the 21st Century: Science, Technology and National Development* – an in-depth study of his mind and ideology, of employing science and technology for the welfare of mankind and the monumental work done during his dynamic years. He introduced computerization in India, launched technology missions in selected scientific fields with immediate social relevance, such as - Oil Seeds, Mass Immunization, Better Communications, Drinking Water, Supply, Reducation of Illiteracy and Milk production; regarded brain – drain as brain – bank, set up a Ministry of Science and Technology and created five subject-oriented Scientific Departments for the development of Biotechnology, Environment and Forests, Ocean Development, Non-Conventional Energy Sources, and

Scientific and Industrial Research in India; enacted Computer Policy - 1984, New Seed Policy - 1988, National Education Policy-1986, R & D Cess Act-1986, Environment Protection Act-1986, National Forest Policy-1988, New Industrial Policy-1988, (please refer my earlier volume for their full-texts) Ganga Action Plan etc etc during his short tenure of Prime - Ministership. This book belongs to Shri Rajiv Gandhi. You can hear his voice in it.

Today the challenges are many and unless we reach out well-beyond what others are reaching for, we shall not be doing justice to our scientists, to our own people in the country... What we need is an Indian approach to Indian problems. We should not be looking for a Japanese or an American or a German solution to Indian problems. Development means, the development of society and science and technology have a key role in that development... our task in India is to end poverty. The challenge to our scientists is: How can modern scientific and technological knowledge be brought to bear on the task of removing poverty? – said Rajiv Gandhi.

This book, hopefully would aid the science policy planners, social scientists and researchers on the contemporary studies etc. in evolving future management strategies by employing the combined strength of science and socio – economic sectors towards making a strong, modern and vibrant India.

Rajiv Gandhi was about to turn a corner in his life when the tragedy struck. His untimely death, at the prime age of 47, on 21st May 1991, cut short his dreams of building technologically advanced India of the new millennium. In his passing away, we have just not lost a person, but a direction for the future of science and technology in India. He came with a mission to usher in a new technological era in the country.

My sincere thanks are due to:-

- Jawahar Lal Nehru Memorial Fund, New Delhi,
- Rajiv Gandhi Foundation, New Delhi,
- Publications Division, Ministry of Information and Broadcasting, Government of India, New Delhi and
- Indian Science Congress Association , Kolkatta for their kind permission to use the copyright text–materials, in the publication of this book.

Thanks are also due to my wife Dr. Shalini Sikka for her constant encouragement and to our children: Saurabh, Ayushi, Tarun and little master Vayun for their moral support and patience.

7 May, 2007
New Delhi **Dr. Pawan Sikka**

Contents

.....We will have to take a leap forward, get on to the frontline technology. Today, we have no doubt that our technologists, our scientists have the capability for this leap.

It is for us in the Government, for the Departments, for all the organizations that are involved in this exercise to make that leap possible and that will mean a lot of new thinking right down the line, a more aggressive thinking, a more objective thinking, not accepting everything we are given.

— **Rajiv Gandhi**
3 January, 1987

A Tribute to the Visionary Shri Rajiv Gandhi Who Dreamt India of the 21st Century

अथ योगानुशासनम् ॥ १ ॥
योगश्चितवृतिनिरोद्यः ॥ २ ॥
तदा द्रशटुः स्वरूपेऽवस्थानम् ॥ ३ ॥

Never Born, Never Died
Only Visited the Planet Earth
Between
20th August 1944 & 21st May 1991
Envisioned India's Progress & Prosperity, and
Enlightened Humanity to Live with Pride & Dignity

Rajiv Gandhi, as Prime Minister of India, in 1984-89, brought with him dynamism, hope and a new vision of the modern India. He symbclized the new generation of India – bold, energetic and innovative. He like his grandfather Pandit Jawahar Lal Nehru and mother, Mrs. Indira Gandhi, believed that science and technology held the key to India's future, that could transform her into a modern State. He said, on 12 June 1985 that –

> *I am young, and I too have a dream ... I dream of an India – strong, self-reliant and in forefront in the front rank of the nations of the world, in the service of mankind. I am committed to realizing that dream through dedication, hard work and the collective determination of our people.*

Scientist-cum-Politician

Rajiv Gandhi was neither a scientist nor a politician in the conventional sense. He was an innovative mind, attempting to redefine India's role in a changing world environment. It was his vision of making India progressed, as closed as possible to the world, in all spheres of human activity. He had a great fascination for science and technology and its effective utilization for the social transformation. He projected modern scientific outlook and qualities then badly needed to speed up the process for achieving the over all techno - economic development of India.

He realized that the modern science and technology can play a useful role in social uplift, in creating a more open society and in bringing India together. His slogan Mera Bharat Mahan (my India is great) was actually aimed at keeping the country together. It was his dream of a strong, proud and united India, which would march into the 21st century, with courage and confidence. Rajiv Gandhi had soon after assuming the office of Prime Ministership of India, promised the nation a government that will work faster. He also declared that he wanted to lead India, into the 21st century. In his first broadcast to the Nation, on 12 November 1984, he said -

> *As we build today so will be the tomorrow. Together we will build for an India of the 21st century. Together we will transform what needs transform, what needs transformation. Together we will face challenges and obstacles to progress. Together we will create an India that is strong, wise and great – a flame of peace and tolerance.*

He outlined his task ahead – *Our task today is to bring India to the threshold of 21st century – free from the burden of poverty, legacy of our colonial past and capable of meeting the rising aspirations of our people. This will require sustained efforts on our part. How are we going to prepare the nation to meet the challenges of the next century, to meet the challenges of the latest technology, as it comes? ... Development has to mean absorption of the most modern techniques at the most basic levels in our society ...*

He recognized that the relationship between science and society for the development was weak in the country. Scientific activities should accelerate the pace of social change. He stressed upon the need for inculcating scientific temper among the masses for deriving maximum benefits of advancements now taking place in all sectors of science and technology. This futuristic thrust became the *leit-motif* of his agenda for a change. He said – "no scientist, whatsoever his discipline, can escape his social responsibility". He further said - what we need to establish are adequate linkages between science and technology, on the one hand and the economic and productive sectors, on the other. What is needed is a tangible link between the pursuit of science and the welfare of society, especially in developing country like ours, since science costs money.

He was a thorough gentleman with a positive outlook towards future and intended to provide technological solutions to the age-old problems afflicting the Indian society for a long. He was the harbinger of the generational change, not just in Indian politics, but in almost all spheres of national life. An in-depth study of his speeches and writings on science and technology shows his mind and ideology, as well as his sincere zeal for the effective utilization of science and technology towards the welfare of mankind. His thought process, priorities and new action plan of modernizing India with the current developments of modern science and technology is clearly reflected in them. He cultivated the spirit of discovering something new. According to Mrs. Sonia Gandhi –

> His speeches and conversations, many of which have been published, in five volumes of the Publications Division, reflect the breadth of his interests and the depth of his concerns. They outline his vision for the future of India, and the world, his approach to their myriad problems and his potential philosophy. His words are a becon of hope and a symbol of his tireless striving for solutions. They recount his struggles and his achievements. Above all, they reflect his dedication to his work and his country.

Rajiv Gandhi said in Rajya Sabha, on 23 January 1985, that – The *challenges before our country are many. We have to modernize India. We have to change the thinking of the people of India, to look ahead into the future and not to keep dwelling on the past. We have to make India self-reliant in every important sphere. We have to create a dynamic country that is equal to any other country in the world.*

He said in the Lok Sabha on 10 April 1986 that – The foundations of our scientific and technological developments were laid many years ago by Panditji and a major thrust was given to our science and technology by Indiraji. It is on this base, that we are able to use our science and technology to help the poorest people in our country. Indian scientists have shown that they are upto the best in the world when it comes to developing technology and when it comes to taking our nation forward.

A New Aproach

Pandit Nehru had said : "It is science alone that can solve the problems of hunger and poverty, of insanitation and illiteracy, of superstitions and vast resources running to waste of a big country inhabited by starving people. **"This is the prism that encompasses all our needs and aspiration, said Rajiv Gandhi, on 3 January 1987.** He understood well that technology could lift India out of its poverty and backwardness.Therefore he wanted to introduce and induct the latest and most sophisticated technology into the trade, commerce , industry, agriculture and administration. He wanted to reduce the technology gap between India and the developed countries. He wished Indians to develop scientific temper.

He was a crusader of the modern science and technology and enunciated his inspiring vision in clear and confident terms, often contradicting the dominant discourse of his time. He said, ...*the idea today is not to eliminate or destroy the system that has been in practice. The attempt is to modify and guide the system, in particular, specific directions and to try and stop any drift.* He understood the role of technology in meeting the basic human needs. Better technology is for the better future. He frankly expressed –

- India missed the industrial revolution, it cannot afford to miss the computer revolution.
- Mention has been made of brain-drain. This is one of our problems, but I see it differently .... or as I prefer to call it the brain – bank.
- Our scientific and technological institutions do not allow the young minds to come out to the fore. There is an administrative or may be a bureaucratic block and some how this has to be overcome, if we are to really progress.
- We have not gone from a scientific temper to industrialization but we have industrialization leading to a scientific temper. We have to break out of this rut to encourage innovation.
- We start accusing the tribals of doing all sort of things in the forests, forgetting that they have lived in these forests for hundreds and thousands of years ..... Perhaps the problem is not what the tribals do but we ourselves do in their name.
- Although they bear the brunt of environmental damage, the poor are themselves little responsible for any of that damage. For centuries they have lived in harmony with nature in the forests. The problem is caused by large-scale commercial exploitation, which garners the profits but escapes the consequences.

- He ensured that if a particular forest has to be cut to accommodate a project, an equivalent area be replaced at some other location, preferably near the same area.

Rajiv Era -

"We must remember that the primary problem that we face in India is one of removing poverty and keeping in mind that the litmus test for any national activity is how it helps us remove poverty. That applies equally to science and technology " said Rajiv Gandhi. Technology was a passion with him. Technology not for the sake of technology, but in the service of basic developmental tasks. He said - "India can be innovative, that India can show imagination and we can orient science and development of imported technology, or indigenous generation of new technologies and of moving to the frontiers to put Indian science and technology at the front rank in the world." His youthful energies and dedicated efforts for realizing his vision – India, as a progressed, modern, vibrant, and self-reliant nation, manifested in formulating several path-breaking initiatives, flowering of each stage in the developmental pattern is described from the several stand points of transformation of the nation. Technology during the Rajiv Era blossomed more than science. During his dynamic years, he advocated the need for technology management for the overall social transformation of India. During his dynamic years.

- He ushered in a computer revolution in the country. He recognized the tremendous technological changes taking place in the information field, made us aware of its impact and prepared us for this massive development. The first policy he announced, was the Computer Policy for India, on 19 November 1984.
- Realising that science and technology led to the agricultural transformation and the development

of agriculture was the backbone of the Indian economy, he stressed upon the need for faster and even agricultural growth, say in the North – Eastern part of India. He announced in 1988, a New Policy for Seed Development and also set up Krishi Vigyan Kendras in all districts of India.

- He was deeply concerned about the problem of environmental degradation and its catastrophic impact on the human civilization. He enacted an Environment Protection Act, in 1986, which do not allow certain types of industries to come up in certain areas. He introduced a mechanism of assessing the environmental impact of the developmental work so as to harmonize development with environment; besides the implementation of the Ganga Action Plan to prevent the pollution of the river Ganga. He proposed the establishment of a Planet Protection Fund under the aegis of the United Nations to be used for protecting the environment by developing or acquiring conservation-compatible technologies in critical areas which could then be brought into the public domain for the benefit of both the developed and the developing countries. He said that the National Forest Policy, announced in 1986 was aimed at conserving forests, resurrecting our eco-system and restoring the geographical balance, along with economic development.
- In 1986, he introduced a National Education Policy to modernize and expand new educational programmes across India and preserve, nurture and foster excellence. It is looked upon as an instrument for shaping the future of India.
- Rajiv Gandhi was the prime mover of the vitally important Technology Missions in the country, in selected fields like – oil seeds, mass communication, drinking water supply, reduction of illiteracy and

milk production. These missions were assigned to a concerned nodal Ministry, which coordinated all the concerned science and other Departments, who were responsible for the various inputs for the successful implementation of the identified task. He said that – "*We have set up these missions, which start with the frontiers of science and hopefully will end up in the homes of people, in their daily lives*". Technology Missions are directly related to our highest national priority.

Rajiv Gandhi, as a deviation from the past of constituting apex science advisory bodies for the Cabinet, then set up a Science Advisory Council to the Prime Minister, to render him advice on –

- major issues facing science and technology today.
- the health of science in the country and the directions in which it should move, and
- a perspective plan for 2001 A. D.

Further, with a view to providing new thrust to the development of emerging fields like biotechnology, environment, ocean development, industrial research and non-conventional sources of energy, Rajiv Gandhi created separate Departments for each one of these, in 1985-86, under the Government of India. For the first time, he set up a Ministry of Science and Technology, with three scientific departments of: Science and Technology (DST), Biotechnology (DBT) and Scientific and Industrial Research (DSIR). What these measures collectively did was that they created a conducive environment for the overall socio-economic growth of India. Though the opening of the economy happened a few years later, it was this period that laid the foundation of change. These policy directions set the economy on an even keel.

He said – "*Where science and technology is concerned, we must keep in mind that nothing but the best will do for the country, and we must work towards that end. With everybody's support, I believe we will be able to do it.*"He was crystal clear in his approach to the target ... *together we will build an India of the 21st century.*

The 21st Century

He was a good human being and a true democrat. He said in his maiden speech, in the Lok Sabha (Parliament) 22 January 1985 that "I look forward to all the friends in the Opposition, whether they are in this House or the other parties in the Oppositions who are not in this house. if both the Opposition members, as well as of the Ruling parties work together to achieve this aim (of societal progress) much can be done". Further, on the question of providing of conducive environment to the scientists, he said on 3 January 1987 that – "This fight has to be a national fight which must be put up jointly with the help of all our political parties. It is not something which can be made in to a party matter. It is only when we are able to take this challenge. That we shall really start getting results from science and technology relevant to our development programmes."

"The 21st century does not mean just computers, although to an average person, technology means computers and television and fancy data communication links and satellites; advanced technology also means genetic engineering, making seeds better, making them resistant to disease, making them more productive, seeing what else the farmer needs as back up, tractors, implement power, water, fertilizer. That too is technology. We have to give the best so that the farmer can perform his best", said Rajiv Gandhi to a group of children, assembled at his residence on 6 July 1985.

How would you like history to record your own legacy? —asked a British journalist from London, to the Prime

Minister, Rajiv Gandhi, on 4 July 1985. As a modest and soft-spoken person, he replied,

> *"...well as having brought India, into the twenty-first century, paralleled with more advanced countries in the world, out of branding India as a developing country to the status of a developed country.* He further added with his usual humour that – *when India solves problems, it solves the problems of a sixth of humanity.*

Later, when asked by another journalist, to sum up his five years as a Prime Minister of India, 1984-89, - moments he handed over the charge to next incumbent, Rajiv Gandhi said that – *"I think India has never had the sort of development and progress and international standing that it has gained in these five years".*

A Great Visionary

He was Prime Minister of India for five years only, yet his half-decade seems to have left an imprint, which bespeaks a much longer tenure. The Rajiv era brought many new ideas. All of them could not be implemented, yet they gave a new course to the history of modern India. He accelerated the pace of change towards liberalization and brought about new attitudinal changes in government and people. He believed in the growth of the individual, as well as of the nation. He was instrumental in fostering an atmosphere of modernity in the country. India surged ahead with him.

He drew on his experience as a pilot by emphasizing the value of technology and modern business methods for attaining social transformation. The power of technology greatly fascinated him. He increased Government support to S & T and associated industries and reduced import quotas, taxes and tariffs on technology based industries especially computers, aviation, defence & telecommunications. His first major achievement was the introduction of computerization in

India, but perhaps the most significant innovation was the emphasis on modernization of the economy and the economic liberalization.

Rajiv Gandhi gave a new direction of thinking, a new strategy and new approach of managing the vast human, as well as national resource. He gave to the nation a new hope for developing more confidence to become active partner in global progress. His vibrant force of change, brought nearly two decades ago, still continues to nurture, shelter, illuminate, enrich and empowers millions of lives today.

He did not live long enough to see his India of the 21st century, but India lives on to see his dreams. He died tragically, in the prime of his youth, at the age of 47, on 21 May 1991. He lived a short life long. The revolutionary and visionary steps taken by him for strengthening the development of science and technology in India and making it self-sufficient, during his dynamic years will continue to inspire and lead us to a better way of life. He will be remembered for his pioneering efforts of navigating India into the new millennium with the application of science and technology. He was the genre of those great men produced by our country who shone briefly on the firmament but left a brilliance that will continue for years thereafter.

His life was gentle and the elements so mixed in him that nature itself could stand up and say to all the world – "This was a man". Further

A Beautiful Life Full of Kind Deeds
A Helping Hand to All in Needs
Sincere and True in Heart and Mind
What a Magnificent Heritage to Leave Behind.

Rajiv Gandhi was a great visionary who saw the critical role that science and technology could play in making India a leading and a modern nation in the world. A man of vision lives forever. He was really a modernizer who wanted to take India into the 21st Century. He said - *No nation can be built if the people are not willing to sweat, and not willing to put up with difficulties. If we are to build India, we must sacrifice something on our part. This means more hard work in the labs... in the fields.*

He envisioned India's progress by linking research and development (R&D) with humanity. He s[aid - In India today, the prime need is a higher and more sophisticated technology to meet the needs of the poorest sections of our society. There can be no poverty alleviation without technological upgradation... It is necessary that knowledge must surge, quality must improve, and nature must be made more beautiful. Science has played a vital role in the emergence of modern India.

– Dr. Pawan Sikka

RAJIV GANDHI
ON
SCIENCE AND TECHNOLOGY
COMPUTER AND INFORMATION TECHNOLOGY
TECHNOLOGY MISSIONS
AGRICULTURE AND BIO-TECHNOLOGY
ENVIRONMENT AND FORESTS
INDUSTRY AND TECH-INNOVATION
ELECTRONICS AND TELECOM
SCIENCE - ADMINISTRATION & MANAGEMENT
BRAIN-DRAIN, BRAIN-BANK, AND MEDIOCRITY
ALLEVIATION OF POVERTY.

1

The Dawn of Computer Revolution

It gives me great pleasure to be with you today because this is a field that interests me and is critical for India's growth. Electronics is really like the nervous system of a nation. As a nation evolves that nervous system must evolve with it, just as it evolved with the species. In the earliest species, there were barely 250 odd nerve-junctions. The human have 15 billion odd nerve-junctions.

We need a similar network in our country if India is to progress, if India is to move ahead, if we are to keep up with the world. We missed one bus with the industrial revolution. A sudden boost in muscle power, and we were not able to catch up for 300 years. May be, we didn't jump on the second bus on time- and that is the electronic revolution or computer revolution- and now we might have to run behind that bus, catch up to it and jump on it. I think we are capable of doing this.

(You referred Mr. Chairman, to the first wife and the second wife. But we should not be looking at our industries as wives, specially as we have only one wife now anyway! The relationship should be more like the one between brothers and sisters.)

* Seminar on Investment Opportunities in Electronics, All India Manufacturers Organisation, New Delhi, 21 February, 1985.

Although electronics is an industry on its own, it really must be used to supplement all other industries, updating our older industry, making it more productive, making it more competitive, and really bringing it up to world standards. Today electronics has permeated just about every field – industry, education, of course, defence, information handling. There is no place where you do not have electronics, India is still lagging far behind. I was just told that on an average you have to dial twelve times before you can get through. So, there are these problems and we have to get rid of these problems.

Government Policy

You have mentioned, Sir, about certain problems with Government policy, especially taxation and duties. We have been looking at these for the past couple of years. We came out with a completely new package for the electronics industry some months ago, and I think you will like the package that we shall present you in the next Session of the Parliament. But I should like to point out that many of the concessions that we gave, many of the reductions in controls, have not been passed on to the consumers in the way they should have been. The industry has not been as dynamic as it should have been. Well, we shall give you another chance. If it does not work, we shall have to think of prodding a little harder, not by force but by some other means. I feel, for example, that protection should be of only one sort, preferably only fiscal protection and not licence protection, which means that you will have to be more efficient. You will have to compete. You have mentioned import duties go together with import protection, and there again we have preferably to have only one.

Need for More Institutes

To get electronics really moving in India, we have to go down to the other end of the chain. We are mostly talking about manufacturing and selling. We have to go to other end and produce enough people who will be able to deal with the equipment that you are about to produce, which means a turnaround in our education system. We need many more institutes such as the ITI's, but oriented and run in a much more professional manner, oriented towards more modern fields of technology. We need to really develop a mentality in our people of using modern methods.

And somewhere along the line in stressing equality and equal rights, we have gone a little off the track and we have promoted only mediocrity. We have to look at this and once again bring excellence out, lift excellence up and not try to pull excellence down to make everybody equal and mediocre. We shall be looking at this aspect, with regard to the education system, and I hope that this will, over a long term, help industry to develop and expand.

Telecommunication System

One of the complaints was the telecommunication system. We have been looking at this sector and I think that in the coming policies which will be put before you, may be a month from now, you will find that we have tried within our resource constraints to do something for telecommunications. We are already looking at the licensing policy; much of what you have said we have already done. It will take some time to get to you. But, on most of it, action has been taken pre-empting your thoughts.

Now to the banking sector. May be, the less said about it the better. We have not had the time to look at it, because the last couple of months have been extremely rushed. I think in the coming months we shall take a deep look at it and it does need a thorough overhaul. Readily, what is needed is much more electronics in banking.

Clearing Procedural Problems

Electronics in India has been developed by the small scale sector and by the public sector. We have got a very large gap in between. We would like to fill this gap. But while filling this gap we shall try and see that the present industry is protected, not completely but to some extent. We shall in the coming months see that many of the procedural problems that you have raised are cleared. But as we develop new policies, as we move ahead, we shall have to feel our way and get proper feedback from you. Because every step we take will raise new problems, and we would like to get quick feedbacks so that we can take quick action to correct them.

You will find this Government is moving faster than you are moving. The problem will not be with Government constraints or Government restrictions or the time taken by Government but with "can you keep up with what we are doing?"

❐

2

New Opportunities for Indian Industry

The engineering industry is amongst our oldest industries and also the newest, the most modern. Between these two extremes we fit in every type, every technology, every method of working. In a way our engineering industry is representative of all our industry – small enterprises, large industries, public sector, private sector. It goes right acrose the spectrum and when we look at it we can see both the problems that India's industry faces and its achievements during these past 35 years.

Our growth since independence has been good, but not as good as we would have liked it to be. And if we look ahead to the future, we must grow very much faster to be able to catch up with the world. Our industries have matured tremendously. They have widened their base to incorporate a very broad spectrum of products. But technology in the world is growing very fast. And if we are to catch up, we have to move faster than any other country. Otherwise there is no catching up.

Indian industry has its extremes. The good is as good as any industry in the world. It can compete with any industry in the world. The bad, unfortunately, is nowhere near our good. And this is where we must do some work. We must raise the average level of our industry. We have certain industries which can achieve this. We have the

* National Conference on Engineering Exports, New Delhi, 22 March 1985.

capability. We have the competence. We must let it seep down to the bottom. We have everything going for us.

The problem is that we don't use the full potential that is available to us. When I say full potential, I don't mean just in a percentage of output of a particular factory but manpower, human resources, everything that is available. We have to see, how we can utilize everything that we have got going for us. In that I would include many Indians who are not in India today but living abroad, who are not finding adequate employment within our country. We must treat them as an available resource, although temporarily not in circulation within the country. We must create a climate to bring them back and use them, especially in areas where we feel we need immediate results.

Emphasis on Quality

The quality of our products really leaves very much to be desired. One of the problems is that we have been selling to a captive market. We are selling really in an absolutely sellers market. Such a market is not responsive to quality. This has to change. In our recent policy statements, in our budget, we have tried to change this to some degree. But our market of 700 million is so vast that it is not going to change quickly. The industry will have to change faster and will have to make the market change. Ultimately you will be called upon to compete not with each other but with other industries in the world. And we must prepare today for that day.

Most of our technology is not really up-to-date. By the time we buy a technology and start working it, and by the time we start producing, we are already one or two generations behind. We should decide what we really want. In certain areas, it is not necessary that we have the most modern technology and it does not matter if we are one or two generations late. But in other areas, even one generation late is too late. And we cannot afford to be that, especially in the fast growing industries. We must see that we are moving at least as fast as anybody else. And here we must really plan ahead not to take what other people have developed but look ahead to see what they will develop 10 or 15 years from now, and work towards that target so that after a given period, we are together with them, and not left behind. In the system that we have been following, we see what other countries have got and we try either to buy that technology or develop that technology. Naturally we are left behind. We want to change this.

We shall on the part of the Government, choose a few areas which we feel are important for the Government. I should like you also to choose areas which are important for your industries and to concentrate on those areas to bring us on par with or ahead of anybody in, let us say, five or ten or fifteen years depending on what challenge we have in front of us. We shall be bringing out a programme on behalf of the Government, hopefully during this Session of the Parliament; and we shall put this before you. We should like you to respond to it and to help our industry, both public and private, to move ahead.

One other problem which will come up and which we must address ourselves to immediately, is employment. There are many areas where we just cannot continue with labour intensive industry. It will just not be feasible after a few years. And we must plan for that day today, which means re-educating our labour, which means re-educating them to a different type of work. And we must prepare now, so that this change over is smooth, and labour is not jobless. In fact, if it is handled well, we can have a much larger employment but in different areas and have a much more efficient industry. We must produce a programme which will meet this problem.

Importance of Exports

For our industry to grow and expand, we must get

many things from abroad, and we must pay for them with our exports. Import substitution has been one of the key factors in our development process. With import substitution, we have been able to develop our own technology and to be equal to any other country's technology in certain fields. But sometimes this has gone astray. It has been brought to my notice that on occasions parts that may cost a few dollars and are not of strategic importance are costing us thousands of dollars because we are substituting them with local manufacturers. We must decide what we really want. In certain strategic fields there can be no compromise. We have to develop our own technology, our own products, but there are other fields where we need not try to develop everything from A to Z in our country all at the same time. We can make a programme over a period of 10,20 or 30 years, and say that in these years we can develop so much, in the next 10 years so much more, and at a reasonable cost we should be able to import the other products. But this must we paid for by exports, which means much more competitive markets, much higher qualities, better delivery schedules, and upgrading of technology as soon as possible. You must respond to this. You must be able to increase our export earnings so that we shall be able to have this freedom to be able to import a few items which might make our products much cheaper. Much more competitive and much more efficient. Our R&D must be developed in such a manner that it really ends up with the finished product. Too much of it is getting left behind in the laboratories today. The technology aspect is not being reflected enough while we are pushing very hard on the science-projects. This again is a problem that we are looking into, but we would also like you to try and incorporate newer developments into your products and not take advantage of the market that you have been waiting in India.

The government, as you have seen, has taken very concrete steps to give India's industry a push. With the

Budget, the various industrial policy announcements, we are now going to concentrate on the infrastructure to see that you get what you really need. We need a response from you, not just the private sector, but even more so the public sector. We are not fighting with each other – Government and industry or public sector and private sector. This is a joint venture to take our country forward. And we must look at it as such. And then we shall be able to cooperate to get the maximum from what we have, from our resources, from what is available in the country. And we shall be able to move at a fast pace.

Sickness Must End

The last point I should like to raise is sickness. This is something which is dragging our industries down. We are not going to put up with sickness. And this will be very clear to you in the coming weeks. We shall make it very expensive to go sick and you must also respond by seeing that industry does not go sick or does not go towards sickness. Certain industries must die. We cannot pretend that all industries which are going on for the last 300 years must carry on into the 22nd century. Excluding that category – we must accept this fact that some industries have to be allowed to die- we must make it penal for somebody who makes an industry sick which has no reason to go sick. When I said penal I don't mean only the managements, I also mean the financial institutions which are backing them and anybody else who is involved in that.

Management, really, is the core of the whole issue. I have seen that even the worst labour relations have changed dramatically when the management has taken a positive step, when the management has been, not necessarily soft, but positive in redressing the genuine grievances of labour, when it has been able to think ahead of the unions and identify the problems of labour. There are some anomalies in our labour laws. There are problems. We shall be looking at these. But the responsibility must lie with management. And it should be a question of pride in one's management that one does not let an industry go sick, that one does not let have strikes and unrest in one's industry.

The tasks ahead are tremendously challenging. India is ready to move. From the Government we have given it a push, now it is your turn to give it another push.

❒

3

New Outlook for Developing India

I am delighted to be here amongst you and to have heard the presentations that you have made. They have been interesting, informative, and I am sure that they will be very useful when we go back and see the plans that we have to make in technology, see how we can use what you have shown us.

From the time that we got independence, we have looked at technology as a means of developing India, of bringing out the best in our people, and we have been fairly successful in the last 37 years. We have, with your help, had a "green revolution" which has transformed our economy. We could well have been today in a similar position to Africa, but because of the "green revolution", because of science, we have been able to send 100,000 tonnes of wheat to Africa. This is the way that we would like to use science in India. But today India is more developed, and our people have an appetite and a need for newer technology, information technology, other methods of really producing more efficiently anything that we are trying to do. We are looking to your country to help us in developing these areas.

We would, of course, like that the development is done together with us like you have said, Indians have progressed in many fields and are working at the forefront

* Address at the U.S. National Academy of Sciences, Washington, 12 June, 1985.

of technology in your country and in other countries. We could attract them back, we could set up systems to work together, to develop technologies that are specifically suitable to our conditions, suitable to our problems, because invariably, technologies which fit into a slot in a developed country do not find a similar slot in developing countries. There is some problem in trying to integrate them. We do look forward to co-operating with the United States in these areas; some of the subjects that have come up today are of interest to us, but so are many, more. And we look forward to co-operating and may be seeing some of you in India. Thank you.

Question: *Mr. Gandhi, Dr. Ross described the exponential improvements in photonics and in electronics that are going on. You also indicated the productivity of software continues increasing rather slowly over the past decades. Now, my question is, judging the, looking at the strong educational system in India and the intellectual capacity of the country, would you consider software as an area in which India perhaps could develop unique or distinctive skills?*

Prime Minister: This is an area, we think, we could be especially good. The Indian mind somehow adapts well to producing software! And, we have already got some units going which are producing software and are doing fairly well. We would like to look into this and cooperate in software production.

Question: *I have been to India several times and have had many Indian students in my laboratory, and, as you know, many of them, many Indians, do very well in areas of basic science. What I see is that the wonderful basic science inventions that have come from India have not yet had the practical applications that bring to reality the types of things Dr. Ross has talked about. What plans do you have to translate this wonderful intellectual wealth you have into practice?*

Prime Minister: Yes, this has been one of our major problems-- not being able to convert our development into usable technology in a short enough time span. We are looking at how we can get over this. One thing we are going to do is to decide on a few areas where we can concentrate, and not concentrate across the board and try to do everything that the world has already done. We have already identified about 20 areas where we would like to give a thrust, but we would like to whittle this down to about may be half a dozen or ten, and describe them as "mission areas", and concentrate hard on those specific areas. This will be a mix of science, or pure development of science and of converting that into actual usage. We should be ready, we are almost ready in fact, but I have had about a month when I have not been in India. So as soon as we get back, we will be able to sort this out and get going.

Question: *Mr. Prime Minister, what do you think the realistic chances are of getting a fair number of your expatriates to come back to India to work with you on these problems?*

Prime Minister: A lot of them want to come back, some of them have already come back; a few are working with Goverment, and I am optimistic. What we have to do is to create the need for that type of persons in India, and that will of course depend on the areas that we choose, the direction we want to direct our science and technological development. But I am confident that they will come back. And, I don't really see Indians working abroad in high technology as a "brain drain". I would rather look at it as sending our people to you to gain experience in training, and having a bank available outside India to draw on, when required.

❐

4

Institute Awards for Agricultural Productivity

Let me first congratulate all the winners of the awards for 1984. Productivity is of basic essence to any developing country. We have developed our industries during the past 38 years of independence. We have made tremendous strides in many areas. But our industries still do not have the dynamism that is required of industry in the 'eighties—productivity not just in the sense of producing more, but efficiency of materials, efficiency of energy and efficiency of time. It must also reflect on the quality of the product that is being produced. I trust that most of these factors are taken into account when the productivity awards are given.

Our capital-output ratio unfortunately has not improved in the manner we think it should have improved. We still spend too much money but do not get enough productivity. We have to have a major look at this to see how we can get more out of what we put in, how the basic efficiency of our industries can be improved. Perhaps this is the root of our problems with productivity. In the Seventh Plan we have laid down a number of priorities—food, employment, etc. But perhaps the one factor which we have stressed, which cuts across all sectors is that of productivity and productivity in government offices, in every field. We hope that the thrust

* National Productivity Awards for 1984, New Delhi, 1 November 1985.

that we are trying to give will bring about a major improvement in productivity, as productivity really is critical to anything that we are trying to do.

For better productivity, the beginning is better training of all people, whether on the shop-floor or in management. Our shop-floor techniques or technology leave a lot to be desired. We still talk about point of quality control, and point of rejection. Surely, the training of a worker should be such that no worker produces work that requires to be rejected. This is something which must be built into individuals. The training process in industry must bring it out in them. The same feeling should be there in management as well-striving for better quality, for better production, a striving for a better product and a pride in the product that one produces. We have not been able to do this in India. May be, certain Government policies have been responsible for this. May be, certain new technologies are to be brought in. Ultimately, it is very much a state of mind of the whole industry. And a major change has to be brought about in this state of mind. Productivity consciousness or awareness is something that we must build. Perhaps much of the present attitude has developed out of a captive market, a market that does not reject poor products, that does not reject inferior quality.

Consumer awareness, consumer consciousness must be built up in India. It is ultimately the consumer that decides what type of product a factory makes. And when I talk of the consumer. I do not just mean the average person on the street who decides on tooth pastes and tooth brushes. I include the Government which buys heavy industrial items from public sector companies. There is not enough rejection on the part of the consumer. That is why inferior products are sold. We must bring this about. We should start by the Government rejecting an inferior product, even from public sector companies, and not accepting them. The management of those companies must be held responsible.

Protected markets are another factor. We have already indicated that this protection must gradually be removed; protection not necessarily from abroad, but even from within. We must develop much more competitiveness in our industry, amongst various units, amongst different manufacturers of similar products. This shift together with a change in consumer awareness, will, I am sure, bring about a dramatic change in the quality and productivity of our industries, in their competitiveness. Ultimately the competitiveness is in how our industry can serve the country better, how it is going to help India in facing the challenges of tomorrow. Without such competitiveness it is going to bind India and hold India back from a dramatic advance into the future.

Productivity must become a way of life in industry, a change in the way of thinking, a different culture, a different work ethic on the shop-floor. This is a challenge that industry must face. We have seen how industries are in other countries which at a particular stage in their development were facing very similar problems. Some countries which some years ago were known for shoddy goods, for cheap goods, are suddenly producing very advanced goods of very high quality and very superior finish and they have done it in a matter of years. There is no reason why Indian industry cannot do the same thing. Perhaps the key lies in the education that we give to our people, not just to the factory employee or manager, but the average person who has to interact with industrial production.

We have started to change the educational system. We are hopeful that it will bring about a change in awareness, a change in the demand for goods. I should like to quote Panditji. When he spoke at the National Productivity Council meeting in 1960, he said;

"Universal education is the base of a productive economy." Then he went on to say that application of modern techniques by mediaeval minds is not possible. Perhaps we still have to change that mind. We have laid great stress on education, and I hope that we shall be able to achieve that.

We have made tremendous strides in these past years in industrialization. Education has played a role but in certain areas education has not played the role that it should have. Education today is not developing skills which makes a person employable. Our educational system doesn't build initiative in individuals. It makes them wait for government or for somebody to do something for them. They are not willing to grab the challenge and go out and do things. This is something that our educational system must build. We have also, by somehow reducing everything to the lowest common denomination, removed quality consciousness completely from our educational system. This must come back. Ultimately, poor education gives us poor consumers, who give us poor producers. We have to change all three.

There is one other factor which does hamper productivity and efficiency, that is, the vested interest that industry and certain managements build into not improving their product, not improving their methods of production or improving their qualities. This we have to fight. We have to remove vested interests anywhere that damage our progress. And more specially in industry. Vested interests can be in management. They can also be in labour. We must keep in mind that factories and industries are not an end to get jobs. We must remember that the first requirement of a factory is to produce some goods or get some output from it. The jobs are only an incidental benefit from that factory and labour must understand this. It is then that our industry will start becoming efficient. And that, will, in fact, lead to many more jobs. We have too often tried to make industries much too labour-intensive. The result has been that the product has cost us too much. It has not been saleable and, in fact, we have lost a much larger number of jobs lower down the street from that product. There are numerous examples that I could give. Each one has cost the country in productivity, in progress. It has cost, may be lacks of jobs which would have been created if that primary product has been that much cheaper and that much more easily obtainable. We must change this attitude.

As I said, bad education can lead to unemployment, unemployableness. Similarly, inappropriate education can lead to a lower productivity and a bad shop-floor ethos. Education is not just something confined to schools and colleges. Education is something that must continue right through. If one is in industry, it must continue in the development of new processes and prevention of stagnation. Of course, it applies not just to the shop-floor but also the management. Ultimately it is the awareness and modernness of the management which filters down to the shop-floor. A good management sees that its workers on the shop-floor are at their highest efficiency. This must include adequate interaction between the workers and management, adequate input from the workers in the shop-floor.

This cannot be achieved just by government action, by government edicts. It must be done across industry by an involvement of the whole industry in the process of modernizing, in the process of being able to challenge industries from other countries, on their own terms. Unless we are able to do that, India cannot come out of the developing stage. Today we are within striking distance of doing this. Our industry must rise to the occasion and in the coming years become equal to industry from any other part of the world.

We have taken certain measures at the beginning of this year—liberalization of taxes and prices in agriculture, in the stock market, and in the capital market. I am very glad to say that we are getting a very positive feedback on all fronts. I hope that industry will respond equally in the matter of efficiency, productivity, and quality. The net result of what we have started doing will begin showing in our industrial production, in our being able to face the challenge of industry from other countries.

Lastly, I should like to say that although we have productivity awards in industry, over 60 per cent of our economy is agriculture and I should wish that you would include agricultural productivity awards from next year onwards. We have seen that India has always responded positively when it has a challenge before it. Today we are facing the challenge and I know that you will respond positively.

❐

5

Technology for a Better World Environment

It is appropriate that the theme for this conference is "Technology for a Better World Environment." For thousands of years, India has developed more in the spiritual direction than in the material direction. India traditionally has believed Man and Nature to be one and inseparable. This has given us an awareness of Nature, a feeling of Nature.

With the technological revolution coming into India, there has been some tension between the two directions. We have developed our technology. We have developed our industries and we have found ourselves more and more separated from our traditional spiritual depth and strength. This has caused some problems in our social structure. Today, we once more look towards building both aspects equally.

Protecting the environment is very much part of this effort. India has special problems because of the sheer size of our population. The pressure that population puts on the environment is perhaps more in India than in any other country. This is compounded by the development process, and by poverty. Because of poverty people have to rely more on what is available to them and accessible to them. They have less capacity to go in

* Second World Congress on Engineering and Environment, New Delhi, 7 November 1985.

for high technology to preserve Nature. But we are bringing about right from our school stage an awareness of protecting the environment, an awareness of the dangers of damaging our environment. Ultimately it is the people's awareness that will help us protect the environment. No amount of legislation will bring about the type of protection that is required in a country like India. Such seminars help the process of awareness. And I hope that we shall have many more such seminars at all levels, not just in Delhi but in all parts of the country to build this awareness.

In a developing country one has to balance, the costs and benefits of exploiting resources and protecting the environment, whether it is in terms of destruction of certain areas to put up industry or to put up mines or other development projects; whether it is in terms of pollution of rivers, of air or various areas. We must bear in mind that ultimately there is no short cut. If we do not pay a price today we will invariably pay a much heavier price tomorrow. We must build this into our awareness.

We have enacted many laws which do not allow certain types of industries to come up in certain areas, and we are trying to give a policy direction so that protected areas will get industries that do not pollute and are clean. We have incorporated this consideration into the very process of clearance of projects. No project can even start unless it has full environmental clearance. We have also gone a step further and ensured that if a particular forest has to be cut to accommodate a project, an equivalent area is replaced at some other location preferably near the same area. Our forest cover in India is already much too low.

Water pollution is one of our major problems. We have tackled our first major project-that of cleaning up the Ganga. This is a project which is close to the heart of every Indian and it will not only bring about a new spiritual feeling but, much more than that, it will also give clean water to thousands of villages and millions of people living in the gangetic base. Sometimes the problem is fairly simple. It is just a question of better administrative control to get things going. Many of the towns along the Ganges do not have sewage protection plants. Some have. One, I know, was closed because electricity bills had not been paid. Sometimes the problem is difficult specially with industrial pollution. Although the concentration levels are low, the toxic levels are high. This is where engineering design must come in.

We have to build in adequate anti-pollution measures at the very first stage of setting up industry. We must adequately identify the particular toxins and remove them before we get the plant going. We have had a very bad experience in Bhopal with air pollution - with a chemical plant getting out of control. Again, it is not just a question of safety measures but a much deeper question of also taking adequate protection measures in case something goes wrong- really having a full fail-safe structure. We have seen that this does not take place in many chemical plants.

Industry while chasing profit, does not pay adequate attention to the dangers of particular chemicals. We know that high toxic chemicals are still carried in drums, in tankers across the country. We have stopped it in our country. But we know that this happens even in developed countries. Industry is not taking the responsibility of protecting the environment from its side effects. This responsibility must be squarely fixed on industry. It is by bringing about an awareness of the dangers of failure or slip that the people will accept the extra cost of protection.

The extra cost, when it is spread out over all the consumers and over the full time span of a particular process, is very easy to bear, but when that cost comes at a particular time, as it did in Bhopal. It becomes a much harder problem, not only in terms of relief measures for the Governments that are involved but also in terms of compensation for the industry that is involved. And, a little foresight in planning, proper safety measures will prevent such accidents and will prevent such high costs. The priorities on pollution must be an integral part of all new technologies that we are developing. The emphasis must be in shifting to low pollution industries and also to industries that use less natural resources and cause less damage to our environment.

We have found in India that by protecting specific areas we are able to protect the environment. By protecting a particular animal like the tiger but we have protected the whole environment in that area. Through such integrated projects, integrated in regard to protection and integrated in the matter of location and grading of industries, having proper laws to control the damaging effects of industries, we have started out on actually improving the environment, in spite of the pressure of development and the pressure of the population.

This is only a first step. This awareness must be brought about to a much greater degree in our country. We are doing this. It is equally important to bring about this awareness in other countries, more specially in the developing countries where there is a feeling that environment protection costs a tremendous amount. But the cost that we have to pay by changes of climate, by natural calamities caused by environmental damage, the costs that we have to pay if we do not protect our environment today will be much greater tomorrow. This awareness right across the globe is what we must work for today.

❑

6

Science, Technology and National Development

You have quoted Panditji from the Scientific Policy Resolution. It is really for that we have met today. We are not here merely for the development of science, or the development of technology. The concept is much broader. What we are talking about is the development of India. That does not mean just industrial development. Somehow the word 'development' has been reduced in meaning to straight forward economic development. But surely that is not really what Panditji was talking about or what we are really meaning today.

Development must mean the development of society. Science and technology have a key role in that development. Panditji talked about developing a scientific temper. The question I should like to ask is: Have we developed that scientific temper or have we developed certain laboratories with certain highly trained scientists? They are two completely different things. It is only if we first develop that temper that we shall develop the scientists who will grow out of that temper. And we must target not only at the top esoteric places but also at the bottom, and build from there.

Even the purely economic side of development needs science and technology. Panditji talked of science and

* Conference on Science and Technology in India - Retrospect and Prospect, New Delhi, 13 November 1985.

technology at a time when nobody believed that India could really do very much in that direction. There was tremendous scepticism. You must remember what sort of argument and discussions went on those days about whether we should have a purely rural Khadi industry or a proper modern industry. The fact is that if India is to get out of its poverty, to become a developed country, it can only do so by developing science and technology. This involves a fight against the vested interests which want to see the status quo remain. At that time it was one set of vested interests. Today it is a vested interest in imported technology, it is vested interest in a market share that somebody might have got, it is a vested interest in blocking other people from coming into the mainstream. If you are to cut through it all, it has to be with science. Scientists and technologists must develop an atmosphere which is able to do that.

Past policies have done very well, as Prof. M.G.K. Menon has said. I do not think any one can dispute what is in the Scientific Policy Resolution. It has stood us well. It has been able to bring about substantial development in many areas. But it has also had problems. You have mentioned space, atomic energy, some biogenetic areas, some other fields, yes, we have done well. But has our science done well as a whole? Has it changed the culture of our people? Does the average man have even a basic idea of science and technology? Will science and technology be confined to the select few or can we go down to the people? And it is not much use if it is only at the top, we have to bring it down to the bottom. Doesn't the electrician have to understand how to wire a house? Doesn't a plumber have to know how to fix pipes? This is all technology. It is all part of the culture.

You have talked of demand. Where is this demand for new technology coming from? It is going to come when there is an understanding amongst the average people of the inadequacy of outdated and the dangers of badly implemented technology. I shall give you an example: the electrician in our house does not think twice, he opens out the plug, he leaves all the wires open and off he goes. Somebody has not taught him just the basics. So while we look at the top we have also to look at the bottom.

The problem in the development of our science and technology has been very much managerial, as you have said. This is an area that we would like to straighten out, clean up and speed up as much as possible. But of course you have to tell us what we should do. And I have found that our bureaucracy is very good in the areas in which they have been trained. But once you get out of that area into specialized areas then you get terribly bogged down. Science and technology is one such area and we have to see how we can speed things up and rationalize them.

We have a very substantial scientific and technological base. We have to look ahead to see how India, which is at a turning point, will develop. We are a developing country. But there are many fields where we are well ahead of other developing countries. In them we cannot really be counted as a developing country. The question is how soon can we spread that to more areas.?

One basic problem has always slowed us down - the bugbear of import substitution. It was very important 30 or 35 years ago, when we were in certain types of difficulties. But today the situation has changed very much. We have a certain elasticity in our imports. We should not be forced to substitute everything. The cost of substitution has to be a factor that must be counted. If a minor component, which might cost almost nothing to import, cost us a very substantial amount to produce. I don't think it is worth going through that exercise; and I have been given examples, by, I think, Prof. Yashpal about components costing a dollar which we have substituted by over a thousand rupees. If it is a strategic component for a military hardware or something, yes we might have to just do something like that. But, for normal everyday use, I don't think we need to go in for that.

Another and more serious problem which import substitution has caused is that it has always limited our thinking to the technology that we are trying to replace. If you were to replace and substitute some imported components it is a component which has already been developed, it is a component which is not really in frontline. Otherwise they might not have sold it to us. And we are now working to replace that. By the time we replace it, that component is totally outdated. And what have we really done? We have given very poor targets to our scientists and technologists. This has to change.

We have got to tell them, "No, you do not have to replace a component. You have to replace the whole thing, with something new, something as advanced as is available at the time that you come out with it. That is when our science and technology will really start pushing to the frontiers and start equating with the science and technology in other countries.

We have to look at our needs. Let me separate the two first. As you have said, there is a very basic need for fundamental research. This is not something which should be accountable in terms of how much have we gained and has it paid us back. Fundamental research cannot be accountable in that manner. That does not mean that there should be no accountability; there must be some accountability even for fundamental research. You must set your own targets, you must set your own deadlines and proceed in a certain direction. You might want to change direction after a while. We do not want to carry on a particular research for fifty years once we have realized that nothing is going to happen in it. So these sort of checkpoints must be established, even in fundamental research. And a certain amount of accountability, but not an accountability in terms of cash input, equal to positive gain from that; might not be there, but accountability in scientific productivity must be there.

In industry we have a very wide base. But what is this wide base? Is it really our industry or is it something that we have bought out and not even been able to understand ourselves? I don't think we have even improved how to make a plain paper clip. We carry on the same thing, and in fact, what actually happens is that materials deteriorate and what started off as an acceptable product ends up as an unacceptable product. Our industry is today functioning almost entirely on imported technology. May be bought out, may be copied. But how much of our industries are actually functioning on Indian developed technologies? A very small fraction.

This is what we have got to change. And this will change when there is a basic thrust not just for developing a particular product or trying to improve a product or to substitute materials in a product. We must go down to the manufacturing process or the production process.. Are we looking at that side, are we trying to understand it, are we trying to get our own processes? Very seldom. Is our R&D looking at productivity, is it looking at efficiency? Is it looking at quality? Are we doing research to see how we can replace or substitute raw-materials? Are we looking at economy in the use of materials, energy conservation, energy recovery? Are we doing R&D on each specific process to see whether we can save energy on that? I don't think we are doing enough. Have we done enough work on improving quality, building in an excellence? All this is a part of culture. Unfortunately culture somehow has come to mean dance and music. Culture is not merely dance and music. Culture is how we live, how we think, how we behave. And unless that scientific temper comes in to our culture today, we are going to be in very poor shape going into the next century.

Quality, bringing in excellence, is not a question of putting more quality controls; it must start with the user or consumer. That is where the demand for quality must come. That is when the pressure will come in to produce quality. As long as the customer or user accepts whatever is given to him, there is no way we will get quality. In that I am including government. Government is a major user of almost everything we produce. And government must bring a quality.

There is a lot to be said for the tender system to see that we get the best deal. But there is a lot to be said for the tender system in destroying quality, in destroying any sense of excellence of doing things a little better. So basic Government thinking has got to change. Simple things like a public sector captive factory supplying to Government, can they get away with giving in rubbish? Can they get away with delays which cost us year? Why does this happen? Because, the technology is not good enough. When I talk of technology, I don't mean hard equipment. I am including the workers, because he is very much part of that process. If the worker does not have a scientific temper, he is not going to be able to produce quality, he is not going to be able to produce work on schedules. How much are we going to pay for all this? And are we accounting for this in some way? This is the saving that we can make by building in a proper scientific temper into our culture, by building in a demand for quality. We need feedback from the field to see how components are failing. What are the problems that the users are having? That will then give the direction for research to be done. I don't think there is enough feedback coming in that sense.

Coming to more specific projects or targets, the productivity is not good enough. More accountability has got to come in. As I said certain areas of fundamental research must be accountable only in that they achieve something scientifically, not necessarily as a return of capital; but other research must include the cost factor. If we are going to look at improving our technology in a particular field, the cost of that improvement is important. The time taken for that improvement is important. If by the time we develop a particular process or develop a new or a better component, that very component is outdated and replaced by something completely new, the whole exercise is a waste of time. I think we must be more careful how we hand out particular research projects. It must come under one command. If it is one lab, everything should be under one lab. Research in a particular aspect should not be spread out, with too many people getting responsibility at different levels at different places. The responsibility must be pinpointed at one place wherever, it is, whether it is lab-wise or agency-wise. This is for you to work out depending on the size of the project and the complications involved.

Also we must have some idea of checking progress. At what point are we going to cut off and say, "All right, we have made no headway in this, let us, scrap this, and let us look for something else." May be you don't want to scrap it, may be you want a different direction. These sorts of checkpoints must be built in, and there must be a final cut off point. If you feel things have gone on and you have not achieved anything just cut it off and go to something else. Unless we are able to do this, our technology will never catch up.

Perhaps managing science, as you said, is a problem and we really need to think more about how we are going to handle the management of science. Too often, the Press seems to think management means getting somebody from the private sector who can manage everything. But it is not as simple as that; it is something that we have got to develop, we have got to think. Management means everything from the vision to the thinking to the actual implementation. It is not just getting a production line going.

We have come out with the idea of having missions. But somehow the mission of getting the Missions ready is not ready. Now, my concept of Missions was a limited number of fields with very specific targets. Limited number, because if there are too many then it is not a mission, it is what we are doing today anyway. If we have 70-80 items that we are going to try and do, we will not be able to concentrate on any of them and we will get the same sort of diffused thrust that we have got today. The idea and concept of a Mission was that we choose, say half a dozen, or a maximum of ten areas where we can really do well. Ten areas where in five years or ten years we will be the leaders in technology or in science in those particular areas. We try to target those areas in directions that will give us a direct fall out.

Family planning may be an area. I am not specifying how we would have a thrust in family planning. Agriculture, energy, other infrastructural items, may be aspects of removing poverty. But they must be missions which go all the way from A to Z. This will involve more than just the scientific community. The science part could develop it. The technology part we would try to implement it and fit it into real life on the ground. But you will need an administration to actually get it to crores of people. So a Mission like this has to have a much wider aspect than just the scientific thrust.

We must also have Missions which terminate with a scientific result or a technological result. We still have not got the list of Missions. That is why we are stuck. If we are going to decide on ten Missions, and you give us a list of ten, it is going to be very difficult, specially if those ten are limited to one particular field. We have to look right across the board and say O.K. We are going to have one in agriculture, two on energy, two on population. You know, we have to divide that up somehow. And we can't do that unless the full picture is in front of us. So, we need that full picture before we can take a decision on which are the areas that we are going to have a thrust.

The concept is that we would give much more freedom, remove all the strings in these areas, give proper funding to see that we can make real progress as we did in space, as we did in atomic energy, as we did in a number of areas. But wherever we have made this progress, it appears to be because a specific target had been given, a group of people had been chosen and told "O.K. Now you go ahead and do it", without too much interference in what they are doing on a day-to-day basis. The idea of Missions is to do this. If we try to take up 60 or 70 items, I don't think we shall be able to achieve that end. We should start with a small number. Once they get going, next year, may be we can look on another 10, the year after we could look at 20. But that initial thrust must come with a limited number.

One of our problems in India has been with our scientists' salaries, their facilities, their perks, perhaps even more important, with the recognition they get, with the special standing they get. And these are areas that we must somehow come face to face with and sort out. Social recognition is perhaps one of the most difficult areas to tackle. Our friends in the Press, for example, concentrate much, too on politicians, and no other field seems to exist in India. Whether you are a top scientist, whether you are a top dancer, whether you are a top musician, you are top in anything, it doesn't count. But if you are the worst politician, you get the headlines. This has to change in the Press, and perhaps as part of our culture we have got to broad-base more areas, we have got to produce more focal points for people to try to strive for and achieve. Perhaps that will also build in an incentive for a scientific culture.

Some of the problems are of our own making. Mobility, for example. Scientists must have mobility. In our system they get stuck in a particular place. Even within a department. I believe, it is difficult to shift them around, if the particular research changes, or a subject changes. So, we have to look at that. Perhaps we also have to look at age, with due respect to older scientists who are here when I talk to scientists in the USA, in England and other places one thing comes out, that even those who are with me, are today finding that we are just not in touch with the new that is coming out. If basic research has to be done, it is the chap who is just coming out of University, perhaps even below 25, who is able to really cope up with that. We must work in a similar way. I am not saying that all the older scientists must be made jobless or thrown out. But that opportunity must be given to fresh minds as they come out with all the new ideas from university, from college. This we are not able to do in our system. We have to develop somehow to allow this to happen.

Lastly, I would just like to reiterate that ultimately what will help us to develop a real base for science and technology is an involvement of the average person with science and technology, whether it is a question of appliances that he is using at home, whether it is in the field where a farmer is using technology. Unless this scientific temper, as Panditji said, really seeps down to our society, we will never be able to get the inputs for science that are within our capability which are available to us, but are just not being allowed to develop. I hope I shall take some time out over the next two days to talk with you informally instead of talking to you.

We must have more such meetings. Let me wish you all the best in your deliberations. I hope that something really positive does come out of this, that we can use, that we can work on, and that will really help science in India.

❐

7

Atomic Energy for India

First of all I would like to extend to you my best wishes for Diwali. Having done this, I would like to congratulate you on the excellent work done by the Atomic Energy Department. We have made a lot of progress in many fields but the performance of the Atomic Energy Department has been outstanding indeed. I offer my congratulations to you and to all the officers and staff of your Department. It was Dr. Homi Bhabha who had launched our atomic energy programme many years ago. We must be thankful to him for his vision as also to Panditji and Indiraji for their farsightedness.

The Atomic Energy Department has demonstrated not only to India but to the entire world that India can make progress in science. You were able to accomplish whatever targets we had set for you. After my arrival here first of all I dedicated the Dhruva Reactor to the nation. Next month I shall be visiting Kalapakkam where our second reactor is to be commissioned. I congratulate you on both these achievements. These two reactors are the landmarks in your progress and India's progress.

You have set an example for the other fields of science and technology. This will inspire us to work more vigorously, more efficiently and compete with other countries of the world. We must take this spirit to people in every part of our country. We must show the same

* Dedicating the Dhruva Reactor to the Nation, Bombay, 11 November 1985.

capacity for hard work, so that we achieve similar success everywhere.

Today our endeavour is to advance India in every way. We have to look at the difficulties ahead. We have also to look back and find out the mistakes committed. Over the years we have achieved great success in our programmes to eradicate poverty. Our success during last five years, in our Sixth Plan, has surpassed our earlier records in the field. In the year 1979-80 no less than 52.4 per cent of the population was below the line of poverty. According to the latest figures available for the last four years this percentage has gone down to 37- a reduction of 15 per cent. This at the same time has created some concomitant problems. This has revealed the weakness of our basic infrastructure. We have to pay attention to both the sides; on the one hand we must not in any way slacken our efforts to remove poverty, while on the other we must strengthen the necessary infrastructure wherever it is weak or non-existent.

The infrastructure basically, means electricity, energy communication and transport. We must ensure that these facilities are made available in the quickest possible time. You have to play an important role in this regard. Electricity is one thing which is in acute shortage. Our plants are able to utilize only about 40 to 50 per cent of their installed capacity for want of sufficient electricity. Due to this shortage our farmers are not able to operate their pumps, and get the maximum yield. Sometimes when they get power supply, the voltage is inadequate. At times they get power supply is erratic. We must set all this right. In the present Plan* we have allocated maximum funds for power. In this regard you too can contribute a lot. As you have rightly pointed out, we can hope in future only through atomic energy which is going to be our chief source of power.

* Seventh Five-Year Plan, 1984-89.

What is the situation today? If we set up thermal power plants for all the electricity we need today, all our trains, and our entire freight-carrying capacity would have to be pressed into service for carrying coal and all other transport would come to a halt. Therefore, on balance, nuclear energy can be of the greatest benefit to us. You have shown us the way by your research work and by setting up new reactors. It is in this way that the energy requirements of the country can be met. We have to consider how best we can do this.

You must diversify your research, make foolproof plans which will result in increased efficiency and meet the highest safety requirements. Our nuclear programme has to its credit a very good safety record. I congratulate you on this. But it is very important that you work with even great vigour. Although you have done commendable work, still there are certain shortcomings in the atomic energy programme. In some cases the work is not finished on time, in some other cases we are lagging behind. This should not be so. We have to go ahead with full vigour. India today is in a position to compete with other countries of the world, and you, especially, are in a position where you can help India to do so. I know that whenever the people of India have had to face such challenges, they have risen like one man and overcame them. Earlier too you have faced such challenges. You have enabled India to stand on its own in the matter of nuclear energy. Now you have to make India even stronger so that it can be in the forefront in this sphere.

I know you will bend your energies to accomplish this task. I congratulate you once again.

❒

8

Energy Generation for Economic Development

It gives me great pleasure today to dedicate the expansion project to the nation. As you have already been told, the Refinery has been working very well since its inception. It has an impressive record. With its expansion its capacity is almost doubled. Various additions have been made at crude distillation unit, fluid catalytic tracking unit— both on time and within the same financial allocations. The maintenance standards, I believe, are very high.

Let me first congratulate the management and the labour on their achievement. I am also told that the labour relations ever since its inception have been extremely good. Again, congratulations to the management and the labour for cooperating. Good labour relations really means, you have an imaginative and sensitive management which is able to feel the pulse of the labour and the labour, the unions, are able to work dedicatedly for the factory, for the unit and for the country.

My congratulations to both of you.

Nawal Kishoreji has just talked about your further development. I must say that I am very sympathetic but we have one problem and which is the usual problem—

* Dedicating to the nation the expanded project of Madras Refineries Ltd., Madras, 16 December 1985.

that is finances. So within that constraint, I shall do what I can to help you in getting this done.

Energy is the key to the growth and development of any nation. In India, much of what we have invested is not giving us adequate returns because we are not able to generate or give enough energy. Whether it is agriculture or industry, a very large capacity is left un-utilized because of lack of energy and that is why in the Seventh Plan we have given the highest priority to energy. Our first attempt is to get our installed capacities working well close to 100 per cent before we start investing more in new capacities. This must be a major thrust and we have asked the Planning Commission to plan so that by 1990 there will be no shortage of energy. And after they gave us the figure we boosted it by ten per cent just to make the margin on that. I hope that the Planning Commission has not miscalculated too much on that.

Thanks to Bombay High and our other Gas Finds, we have been able to save a very large amount of foreign exchange on imports of oil. But we still are having one of the largest foreign exchange problems with the import of oil. And this work must continue at a much higher pace, much faster pace.

Today, we have in the Seventh Plan 1984-89, allocated Rs.12,500 crores for exploration and for development. This compares very favorably with the Rs.8,500 crores that we have allocated in the Sixth Plan. It is a 50 per cent increase on that. And when we have such high allocations, we must see that we get adequate returns on this. Of course, there is a very big risk factor involved in any such exploration but there must be a positive return on that investment.

We have to learn the geology of our own areas which may be slightly different from other areas. We must develop this expertise, and it must be good so that returns on this investment are commensurate with the actual investments that we have done.

Your Refinery has worked well whether it is labour whether it is efficiency in saving energy and perhaps that is one of the most important areas that India must concentrate on today.

Our energy conservation measures have not been good enough. We have basically two sections to target for. At the micro-level we have the various alternate energy systems, designs and research going on. But for quite some time it appears that they will remain as a very minor source of energy. In the meantime our major energy sources will be fossilized fuels whether crude or coal, may be nuclear. And what we must look at is the conservation of energy, more efficient use of energy whether it is in transport or in industry. There are tremendous savings to be made. We have not done enough towards this end.

We want technology for better combustion, better heat exchanges and basically for more fuel efficiency. At MRL you are optimizing your preheat exchanges at your high efficiency furnaces. This must percolate to every section of our industry.

You have shown what can be done with good labour relations. And, perhaps this is one of the most challenging areas for our industry today. Not just labour relations but the work ethos on the shop-floor, the work output and the quality input of each worker, his dedication to the work he is doing. From the side of the employer it should be improvement in working conditions, educating the workers so that they are able to do better jobs, qualifying them better for higher jobs and helping them to have a genuine progression in work which will mesh in with modernization and improvements of technology in the units themselves.

You have introduced computer controlled system with real time feedback, I believe, updating after every two seconds. We must in a similar way update our workers so that they are able to use such systems not just at one point but right down the line in every industry. Quality control must not be something which is left to a few inspectors to be done at specific points. Quality control is the pride of a worker in the job that he is doing. And if every workers has that pride, ultimately there should be no need for quality control checks; every worker at every single point will be his own personal quality control check. If we can induce such an ethos in our workers, we will really be taking our country towards the next century, towards the next millennium.

Production, quality, quantity and efficiency of production can only come up if the workers are enthused and educated in the correct manner. This is really the task for management and for the labour unions. You have shown a good direction. I hope you will do more and this mood will spread to other industries.

Another vital factor for us is the indegenisation of processes and of doing adequate R & D on our own, converting that R & D into useful technology.

Oil is a major thrust. I hope that you will accept these challenges in this sector. With your past record I know that MRL has a bright future and we look forward to even better performance from MRL.

❒

9

Peaceful Uses of Atomic Energy

It gives me great pleasure to be here today to dedicate this Centre at Kalpakkam to the memory of my mother Smt. Indira Gandhi. She was truly dedicated to developing Indian science and technology, developing not to just have the backup to imported or import technology but to develop it right to the forefront, to the frontiers of knowledge and in a number of spheres, she has been successful in taking Indian technology and science to those limits.

I must congratulate our scientists who have been able to achieve this. By splitting the atom, we have released boundless energy. It must be our task to see that this energy is utilized positively for the development of mankind, for the furtherance of our civilization and we must be careful that this tremendous force and energy is not misused for the destruction of human kind.

India is committed to the peaceful use of atomic energy. Our conditions are such that we must exploit all our energy resources to the maximum to back up our development efforts. Our history and heritage of tolerance, of non-violence, more recently of non-alignment makes us, allows us, to use this energy positively for generating energy and we have seen that it allows us to use self-restraint and self-control and not use this energy for negative purposes.

* Speech while dedicating the fast breeder reactor to the nation at Madras Atomic Power Project, Madras, 16 December 1985.

India is committed to the peaceful uses of atomic energy and to working for complete nuclear disarmament in the world. The mass reactors, the transfeeder test reactors and other reactors are all committed to peaceful uses, to research and to the generation of energy. Indiraji's five point programme was the kernel of the Delhi Declaration calling for complete disarmament.

Our abhorrence for nuclear weapons for war is total. Our research centres show our keenness to be self-reliant, our thrust for indegenisation. We have shown that where we have had a target, where we have had a thrust, we have been able to achieve great heights in science and technology.

The mass reactors are of indigenous design, of indigenous construction; they are being commissioned by Indian engineers and their operation will be completely indigenous. The pioneering research and development was also by our scientists, the rigidity which they have stuck to specifications and produced a unit comparable with any in the world, shows that with a drive our scientists are capable of reaching the highest heights.

Looking to the future we need to look with a big vision and with a practicality. Homi Bhabha had a vision many years ago, a vision of fast breeder reactor. His vision of a fast breeder was long before people were talking about fast breeders and long before people were actually getting down to working at it. But it was that vision which has served us well today. It is in a similar way that we must look towards the future.

It is in the same way that we must look at our target today, not just to target to achieve what is available in the world elsewhere, not just target for what might come in the immediate future but we must look beyond, we must take a leap ahead so that we catch up with the most advanced technologies in the next generation. Just as Homi Bhabha had a vision of a fast breeder while listening to the sounds of a creaking bullock cart, we must today look ahead, not just to today but ahead to the third millennium. But a vision which cannot be applied to day-to-day life, a vision without a practical use, is not the type of vision that we are looking for— Homi Bhabha's vision has given us Kalpakkam, given us energy, from thorium–a basic material which we have in abundance.

This system of programme must be brought into every section, every sector of our economy, our industry, our agriculture and our basic research and development. Such programmes must also be used as vehicles for development of the scientific temper, as Panditji used to describe it amongst our people, to produce a team work to produce an enthusiasm in our people so that every section rises to the level of our best. The leap from colonialism to modern technological nation will require such a thrust in every section of our society.

The atomic energy sector has been a pacesetter for India's research & development activities and industries, it must be so in the future also. The front line for technological development for maintaining high quality standards, for cost efficiency, for more R & D and perhaps, most important for the application of all this research and development to practical uses, for the practical benefit for the millions of people in India.

The Atomic Energy Commission record has been good. It has passed on its R&D to industry— public sector, joint sector and private sector— for development, for its indigenous fabrication and I must congratulate all the scientists and technologists who have made this possible.

Nuclear energy gives us clean, potentially cheap and economically phased power. Environmentally, we have had a very good record and again this speaks for the high standards that our scientists and technologists have maintained. Our target of ten per cent of our energy generation by the turn of the century is unfortunately still too low, others are already around 14 per cent. We hope the restrictions on our fuel supply will be overcome and now we will be able to accelerate this programme and use more nuclear energy for power generation.

I hope that the symposium on fast breeders will contribute towards this. Nuclear energy must supplement our thermal and hydel resources. Our science and indegenisations, our usage of Indian technology has given us great dividend but there were certain anomalies. Sometimes our management systems are still a little outdated, our work ethic whether in public sector or private sector are still outdated. The ethos on the shop-floor is not one which belongs to the twentieth century. Highly sophisticated modern technology, modern plants need much more training at the lowest level. They need much more training to broaden the base of a technological environment among the people. This is a real challenge for our industry today. We have come a long way from wrap to map but sometimes I get the feeling that one foot is still got left behind: Dependability, slow rectification of faults, inefficient management system, inventory management, standardization and delay. Sometimes, when I read the files, I am reminded of a little notice that used to hang on a lot of Government offices, quoting my grandfather, Panditji; if I remember the words correctly, "I am not interested in excuses for delay, I am interested in the work being done." We, too, are not interested in excuses. We are looking for results.

At Kalpakkam our scientists have produced a new monument to India. Panditji used to say that these are the temples of modern India. At Kalpakkam you are situated right next door to one of our oldest temples. Kalpakkam represents a symbol of progress, of self-reliance, of a commitment to development. At Kalpakkam you harness energy from the atom. In Mahabalipuram, not far from here a temple was constructed to harness another energy, the spiritual energy. Many of the problems that the world faces today are because of a growing gap between the harnessing of these two types of energy. The question before us today is whether man will be able to develop his spiritual strength at the rate at which he is developing his scientific and technical knowledge. Will he be able to develop himself adequately to be able to control the tremendous knowledge that he is generating on the scientific and technical side? Perhaps, the biggest task for our scriptures *Mrityorma amritangamaya.* Lead us from death to immortality."

❐

10

Technical Manpower for India

It is indeed a great pleasure to be amongst you today when you complete 25 years of true service to the nation.

Every developing country needs technical manpower if it is to develop and move out of the developing category into the developed one. The biggest problem faced by all developing countries is this lack of trained manpower. There is a lack in the technological field, in the scientific field, in the management and administration. And the IITs have filled this gap to a very great extent-not just with a large number of people but also with the high quality of individuals that they have turned out. I must congratulate the IITs and the young men and women who have gone through these institutions.

But you are a very privileged group - privileged in terms of the assistance given to enable you to achieve this quality and standard, which compare with institutions outside the country. This privilege must help to strengthen India. India's economy. India`s science and technology. It is only when we are really strong within ourselves that we are independent and can stand firm and fast on the principle that uphold India. This is the task before you. We have won political independence, but the freedom fighters for our full economic independence must come out of such institutions.

* Silver Jubilee Convocation Address, Indian Institute of Technology, New Delhi, 19 December 1985.

Mention has been made of brain-drain. This is one of our major problems, but I see it slightly differently. When one talks of brain-drain, one assumes that the phase of learning ends as you get your degree; that you have a developed brain, and now you are leaving the country; so it is brain-drain. But I don't agree with that at all. Learning continues right through life. It does not stop at any stage. If a few people go out, they are going out to increase that learning. What we must see is that ultimately when further knowledge has been gained, further experience has been gained, these brains come back to contribute to our country again. If somebody does not come back at all, yes, that is brain-drain. But if somebody goes out when he is 23 or 25 or 30. I don't consider that brain-drain, provided we can get him back at a later date to use his further experience, his further knowledge, for the benefit of our country.

We must produce the atmosphere, the infrastructure, for it in industry, in our research establishments, in our academic institutions. And we are attempting to do this. But in any developing country this does take time. We in India are privileged that we are able to produce more such people. We are ahead on the human development side. We have produced more able people than we can use. It is a much better situation than having fewer people that are needed. The optimum would be if we could balance the two. But it takes a little while to do that.

The Chairman of the Board (Dr. H.N. Sethna) has raised a very valid point about relationship with industry. The relationship has to be not just in research but also in getting to the shop floor. Perhaps our biggest impediment to fast growth is the lack of a proper work ethic in industry. Our education system was inherited from a colonial era when the jobs were basically clerical white collar jobs. A white collar mentality is ingrained in every one who goes through our education system. He or she is unwilling to use their hands on machines, on the shop floor in doing things. This has to be changed.

The relationship with industry must be much deeper. Our industry has been mollycoddled for too long with protectionism and many types of assistance. The system cannot just be switched around. It will take a bit of time but we have to do some basic thinking now. Our industrial development has come through the first phase of basic and heavy industries, the phase that should have come 200 years ago. At that stage unfortunately we entered a period when our own genius were suppressed. So we are late.

We have to make up these 200 years. It cannot be made up by always being followers. If we are only striving to do something that the others have already done, we shall always remain one step or two steps, behind. We have to jump these steps. That is the only way. We have set up the basis for that. The foundations have been laid. It is for this generation to see that we make these leaps and are abreast of the most advanced nations - not in every field but certainly in fields that are critical to us.

This is really the challenge that you will be facing and that must overcome. Our industry has been protected, as I pointed out. We are going through a phase of allowing them to import technology. Unfortunately our industry has done almost no development of technology. We import technology, we use it, and 20 years later we are still using the same technology. We have done no homework of our own. We have done no development of our own, not even in the small sector. Of course I am talking in general terms. There are certain thrust areas where our science and technology have done tremendous work. In the nuclear field, for example; in space, in certain biotechnology areas. But by and large our industry has relied too much on importing technology. And because of the protection, they have not bothered to develop technology.

This must be changed and we are attempting to change it from the government side. But the pressure must also come from within industry, from within our technological and scientific communities. It is only when our industry will be able to generate its own development that we can say that we are on the road to industrial development. We cannot resort every 20 years or 30 years to an injection of technology. This is what you have to do when you go out into the real world.

Perhaps the biggest challenge that we face today in science and technology is not in regard to the peaks that we produce. We are happy that many have gone to the top of their fields. We have people who are equal to any in the world. But this has not filtered down enough, has not spread enough, amongst our people. We want not merely pillars of knowledge but pyramids of knowledge. This change has to be brought about.

Panditji spoke many years ago about developing a scientific temper. This has not yet spread among the masses. A scientific temper does not mean just using high technology but seeing to it that things work properly. I was reminded of it when you graduates today were tripping over the carpet and the wire. That is what I mean by the scientific temper. This mind must go into putting things right. As we go into the next phase of industrializations and technological development, this is going to be a very real and serious challenge for us. We are producing people in IITs and certain other key institutes who are really top brains. But with electronics coming in, the sophistication is going up. We are using very sophisticated control for very simple gadgets five or ten years ago. We are getting micro-processors into areas which we could not have dreamt of earlier. These are getting cheaper and cheaper. They are going to proliferate. Soon we are going to have them all over, not just in consumer areas, but also in industrial areas and various others. Who will service these gadgets? They are not going to come from these institutes. You are at a much higher level. Even today cars are using one computer, may be two computers, one for fuel management, one for other things. Is our car mechanic able to service the cars which are being produced today?

These are the questions that we must face. This peak that we have produced must broaden out into a pyramid, so that the technological attitude, the technological temper, goes down to our masses.

I should like to congratulate the Delhi IIT on its Silver Jubilee, and the girls and boys on their graduation. The challenges that are ahead of you are indeed tremendous. We look towards you to give a lead in these areas. There is one area which I must mention. Our scientific and technological institutions somehow do not allow young minds to come out to the fore. There is an administrative or may be a bureaucratic block and somehow this has to be overcome if we are to truly progress.

I have been talking to Indians who are non-resident. Our own scientists, and scientists from other countries. One thing is very clear - that at the rate at which science and technology is advancing, delay of even one or two generations of graduation may be too much of a gap to be able to be in touch with the latest technology. I was talking with some Indians who handle very highly sophisticated technology in advanced communications in the US, and they were saying that once a man is over 35, he is just not in touch with the frontline technology and he has to be moved out of basic Research and Design and to some other fields so that new minds can come i.e. I don't say that we will be so drastic here. But the thinking has to be in this direction. We have to bring dynamism and movement in our more senior institutions.

Let me thank you once again for giving this opportunity to be with you today. We look forward to the next 25 years of the IITs.

❐

11

Development of Pharmaceutical Industry

Your profession is an extremely demanding profession. Much too often in India not adequate attention is paid to the importance of the pharmacists who play such a key role in dispensing the medicines, the drugs, that are required for the treatment of any illness.

The pharmaceutical profession has a very good record in India and with the substantial increase in health care, with a new awareness spreading to more remote rural areas, there is a much greater need for more pharmacists, for more dedicated pharmacists, perhaps the pharmacists going into areas which are not so easily accessible and that involve a certain amount of hardship.

During the Sixth Plan, our drug production has more than doubled. It has reduced the import requirements and has made us to a large extent self-sufficient. Being self-sufficient in drugs is and will be one of the key factors in truly remaining independent and standing on our own feet. We have seen attempts to give up developing countries' drugs at very high rates by certain manufacturers, While there is a certain cost for research, I do not think it is fair that it should be passed on only to those who do not have the capability to develop their own drugs. What we must do is to develop that capability so that we can counter with our own research, with our own

* Indian Pharmaceutical Congress, New Delhi, 26 December 1985.

production and with our own development of pharmaceutical industry. The industry has shown a very good shared development between the public sector and the private sector, perhaps better coordination than has taken place in many other areas.

Today, we are proud of the drug industry, our pharmaceutical industry, but at the same time, there is no place for complacency. Developments are taking place very rapidly and if we are not alert, if we are not quick we are liable to get left very far behind.

Perhaps, the biggest question that affects our drug industry is that of spurious drugs, that is, poor quality drugs produced by non-licenced or clandestine manufacturers and this must be tackled seriously not just by Government but also by the industry that is involved in the manufacture of the proper licenced drugs. Government will always be one step behind because our task will be to try and catch some one and then stop it. But you will be able to come out with procedures, may be, with the types of packaging, may be, with other methods, which could prevent imitations from being brought out at all. In this area we should cooperate and see what we can do together to prevent this terrible practice that has started.

Within the industry, there is a question of quality, of purity and stability of the product. The laws, regulations, are not enough to really guarantee these factors. Effective regulations must come from within the community, must come from within your own pharmacist community. There must be a sense of social responsibility, a certain work ethic or work ethos developed in the units which give a certain amount of dedication on the part of each worker to produce a better product. There must be a professional tribe not just at the top level but permeating down to the lowest level in the industry because only then this quality that we are looking for will really come out. Perhaps, the key must lie in the management which must enthuse the whole system to develop along these lines.

The pharmacist has, as you have said, the responsibility to dispense, the explain the side-effects, to explain how best the drugs can be taken. But there is also another responsibility, that of preventing the spread of harmful, spurious adulterated, substandard or imitation drugs. He must also see that drugs that are narcotic or habit forming are not accessible without a proper prescription and that they are accessible only to the proper people. This is one of the areas that we are a little worried about, that of drug-abuse, and we are taking certain steps on the part of Government to try and prevent this. But what is really required is a social awareness and one of the key areas has to be the pharmacists to see that drugs do not spread specially amongst the younger generation.

Getting back to the spurious and imitation or adulterated drugs, we have laws; perhaps they could be implemented better. We will try and look into that. But what we are really looking for is to seek out the basic root causes that allow such manufacturers to stay in the game. We must collate all the information that we can gather, that you can gather. We must have the system of cooperation between the administration, between the pharmacists and with other social voluntary organizations which could help fight this. There must be no stone left unturned to stamp out spurious or adulterated drugs.

Technology, as you have said, is moving very fast and specially in your industry. We have seen major advances in molecular biology, bio-technology and there are tremendous exciting challenges that lie ahead in pharmacy. As you have yourself said, in India there is not an adequate trust for developing this base and we must build so that we develop enough people, we generate the manpower that is required for a lively thriving pharmaceutical industry. It must not be just a question of importing a technology and then producing a drug on the technology. We must develop our own technology. In some areas we could start from scrap, in other areas we could import a certain technology, but from there we must develop through our own R & D and we must make our own base for a strong industry. We must see that there are adequate links between the R & D scientific establishments, the actual production units, the consumer and the doctor.

The challenge is not just in developing the drugs but in also ensuring the safety of the drugs and an acceptability of the drugs. This can only come about if there is this sort of cooperation right from the lab to the patient. We hope that through your Congress, through the Health Ministry, such cooperation will be forthcoming and we will be able to make some movement along that line.

Our drug industry still rely too much on allopathic research. There are many other fields which have not been researched; I don't say that they are right, at the same time, we cannot say that they are wrong. What is needed is to research these areas, to try to find answers to questions which are not being answered through the allopathic system. There is some research but this is not enough. In India we have many systems which still work, which are cheaper, which are more acceptable to the average Indian in the rural areas and the villages. But these systems need to be developed on more scientific lines so that they can be more precise and specific diseases get specific cures which are not too nebulous but can be prescribed by somebody trained properly in the system.

We have, in the past, imported technology at various levels to develop our drugs, and we have developed from them. But if we are to get at the frontline of the developing pharmaceutical industry, this can never happen by importing technology. Because, by importing technology, we will always be importing a technology which the others are willing to give us, in other words, the second level technology, and when we start with second level technology and we continue at that second level we can never get to that first level of technology. For that there has to be some leapfrogging, some jumping over the technology and today is the time when India is really ready to do this. From a technological and scientific point of view the challenge really is yours, to see how, may be in specific areas to start with which are more relevant to us, may be in those areas where we would like a certain drug to be tailored to our physiology, to Indians and their way of life. Perhaps, you can look at these areas and see where you would like a certain thrust and where you feel that we could achieve enough advancement to get on to the frontline of the industry.

One area which is very important today is that of safety. Safety on the one hand, of trying to ensure that dangerous drugs or powerful drugs are not accessible to small children by having adequate safeguards on the containers in which these drugs are sold. The second is the question of safety in the production units in case of accidents. We have seen during the past years, year and a half a number of accidents in the chemical industry which have caused tremendous distress to the people living in that area, to the whole country. The drug industry has a good safety record today, but what we must do is to look deeper into the safety aspects, into the precautions that we are taking to prevent accidents and the safety of the workers who are working in the factories. The trust of developing our own technologies, our own R & D must not forget the safety factor, must not skip on the dangerous aspect of an accident.

You have mentioned the National Institute for Pharmaceutical Education and Research. As you know, when you go to a doctor for an illness, he first diagnoses it then he gives his prescription and then there is the formulation of drugs, and then the drug has to be taken and then you get a cure. Well, I hope that the Ministry will try and expedite this process. There is a need for such an Institution. But the Ministry has to see that there are no side-effects. We hope that they will be quick in dealing with this.

You have also mentioned an involvement of pharmacists in the drug administration. You are right but there is a need for such involvement of professionals in the system and we have already said that preference must be given to such professionals. I believe, one or two States have already adopted this. We will pursue along this line but sometimes there is a shortage of professionals coming forward, so we must have such a position where vacancies are not left unfilled and people do come and fill those vacancies but as you say if we can get enough pharmacists to come forward and be involved in the administration. I think we should try and do that. And we will look into that further.

Lastly, the pharmacist is perhaps the key man between the doctor and the patient and the responsibility in seeing that the compliance of the prescription, in explaining the prescription, in bringing home the medical aspects, bringing home what the dangers of a particular drug are, must be borne by the pharmacists. The precautions that may be required for a particular drug, the interaction of that drug with other drugs which a patient might feel is not well, but may be a drug that he might be taking for some other disease as a routine, may be some pain killers, may be some other normal medicine that a person takes without going to a doctor. So, such interaction of drugs must be explained, the dosage, the complications, incompatibilities; these must all come from the pharmacists and they will come if there is a feeling in the community of service, of dedication. This, you must build. The bridge that the pharmacist is, between the industry, the doctor and the patient on the other hand, must not just be a connecting link, but it must be much stronger than that and perhaps it can even act in the reverse direction in informing on what feedback the pharmacist might get of a particular drug.

It gives me great pleasure to inaugurate your thirty-seventh conference today and I do hope that the pharmaceutical industry in India will develop and carry the responsibility and burden that it needs to and must today.

❒

12

Excellence in Science and Technology

The Indian scientific tradition dates back to ancient times. There was a period when India was sought out as a centre of learning, a centre of science and technology. Indian scientists made an appreciable contribution for the development of science in those early days. Without going into the long list of specific details, let me quote from a seventh century Syrian Bishop, Severe Sebokht. Referring to Indian scientists, he says, there are subtle discoveries in astronomy, discoveries that are more famous than those of the Greeks and the Babylonians. Their valuable methods of calculations and their computing surpasses description." That perhaps describes what Indian science was like a couple, of thousand years ago.

Unfortunately we went through a period of subjugation which saw the destruction of this scientific and technological tradition. It saw India reduced from a much sought after destination for knowledge and riches to an underdeveloped and developing country.

Today the challenge that our scientists and technologists face is greater than the challenge that our scientists face a couple of thousands of years ago. The challenge now is not just to catch up with the equal, what

* 73rd Session of the Indian Science Congress Association, New Delhi, 8 January 1986.

is going on in the rest of the world. But the challenge is to surpass and once more give a lead that we used to some thousands of years ago. Our scientists must concentrate on what is most meaningful for a country like India. And in today's circumstances that means in the rural areas, the agricultural sector, and the various sectors that support our agriculture and rural industry. Our scientists have considerable achievements to their credit during these past years. They have put India in a strong, self-reliant position, not just in agriculture but also in certain strategic and sensitive areas where it was difficult for us to import technology, where there have been a real challenge, where the chips have been down, our scientists have risen to the occasion and have shown the world that they are second to none when it comes to capability, competence and achievement.

Thrust Areas

The question today is how are we going to spread this out to other areas. While we have been tremendously successful in certain specific areas, we have been wobbling around and not really achieving anything in many other areas. The question is not just of scientists. The scientists are there, the brains are there. The real question which we are facing in science, in technology, in research and generally across the board is that of management. How are we going to handle our scientific management? This perhaps is the root of getting more output from our scientists.

Pandit Nehru, addressing the Indian Science Congress in 1963, has said, "Our laboratories have done good work and yet I have a feeling that all is not quite well with these labs." Perhaps I could repeat that today. Questions of seniority, questions of a bureaucracy coming into scientific management, or mediocrity, creeping in at the higher administrative level and many other such questions have to be answered. They cannot be answered by us, they must be answered by you scientists. The only real way to get your best scientists operational in their fields is to refuse to accept mediocrity at any level. And this is the real challenge that our scientists must tackle on their own.

We have seen by experience, as I have just mentioned, that where we have set out a particular task or challenge, our scientists and technocrats have responded and delivered. Perhaps it was seeing a goal in front of them, or just the fact of having either to deliver or to have wind up a particular scheme or the threat of a close down of a particular research which worked. But the fact is that it has worked and we have now tried to follow this in other areas as well.

We have already identified certain thrust areas where we will concentrate in such a manner as we have done with our space research, our food production, our nuclear research, and some other areas. We would like now to broaden that thrust into areas which are critical to us; energy; oilseeds, and certain high technology areas where we need the technology which we are not able to get from other countries. What is required is not just for Government to sponsor scientific research. Government sponsorship will perforce be limited to certain areas and also in quantum to certain limits. We have traditionally spent too little on scientific research. We have to increase this, But we must get a proportionate increase also from industry, from various other sectors.

We have also to try and see that our research is once more, brought into the centres of learning. Our universities are not being used for research as they should be. Our industries are not going to our universities and wanting research done, wanting improvements. This, somehow, must happen. We have already given instructions to the public sector units that they must go to Universities, they must go to our labs and ask for results. I hope that this will begin happening. Similarly, we have asked our defence industries to try and reach out as many institutions as possible and not to concentrate in their few establishments. Again this will give a new life, a new thrust, to scientific research right across the country.

Must Jump to the Front

Still, what is lacking is a demand to improve what we already have imported. If we get a technology, weather it is a production technology, or a particular technology for defence or any other frontline technology, we must not be satisfied with just getting it and sitting on it for twenty or thirty years and suddenly saying "My God, we have got left behind!" That should only be a stepping stone, a starting point, from which our scientists must take up the challenge and catch up and get ahead of other countries in basic research, in basic understanding.

Today we are in a position from which we can take this lead in many areas. For much, too long we have been playing this game of chasing other people's research. It is not good enough. It is not going to work any longer. It has served its purpose during this phase of our development, but that phase is over. Now we must target for frontline research, to try and do what others have already done. We must learn form what we have done, and we must take that jump and get to the front, to the cutting edge of research, the cutting edge of technology. I know that the capability is there in our scientists, but it requires just that little bit more thrust.

I think we are amongst the top countries in the numbers of papers that our scientists produce. But how many of these are quoted by other scientists? How many are referred to by others? Do we ever hear of these papers some year later they just disappear? This is a question that we must put, and we must see that what we produce is really top-grade frontline stuff. We have the capability. We have demonstrated it, our scientists have demonstrated it. We must bring them out and let them flower in a similar manner in every field. Of course our funds are limited and it will mean certain restrictions, but what is required is that whatever investment we made is utilized, used in the most effective manners that it can be. We are today looking towards developing various technologies, whether it is in energy, whether it is in certain areas of food production, oilseeds, whether it is in certain specific defence areas. What we are looking for is to use the most modern technology for the benefit of the poorest and the most depressed in our country.

"Appropriate" Technology Concept,

There have been theories of appropriate technology, but "appropriate" to some means second-rate, being deliberately kept backward so that we keep playing a game of catch- up. We are fed up of playing the game of catchup. We want now to get on to the frontline. We should not be satisfied with second -rate technologies, second-rate development. We must go to the front.

Our farmers have demonstrated that they are capable of using frontline technologies. That is why we are self-sufficient in food today. And if our farmers, who perhaps could have been considered one of the most backward groups as far as scientific education is concerned are capable of this jump, then almost every section of our society is capable of absorbing technology. We have to see that we create the correct educational environment for them to be able to absorb these.

Scientific research is not just a question of producing a few handpicked scientists who can reach pinnacles of achievement. It must be supported by a very broad base of people who have scientific learning, from which we can draw and reach out to the best people that are available. This we have long been able to do. We have got pillars which reach out to great heights, but they remain pillars. We have to turn them into pyramids.

When Panditji talked about the scientific temper, it was not limited to developing a handful of scientists. It was a scientific temper that had to permeate down to the average Indian, whether he was living in a town or whether he was living in the remotest village. This perhaps is another major challenge that we must face. We have to develop our education system so that this scientific temper permeates down to the average person. It is only when that happens that more people will be drawn into the scientific fields, that more people will get the opportunity and that will enable us to tap the best brains that there area which today are not accessible to us.

Ecological Challenge

You have been discussing and talking about ecological problems. Perhaps this again is one of the biggest challenges that we in India face today, that the world faces today. As science develops, it is no more a question of whether man himself as a human being will be able to advance adequately to cope with this knowledge that he is gaining. Will he be able to handle this knowledge or will science and technology take over and lead us down the path which ends in some sort of holocaust either a traumatic nuclear holocaust or an environmental collapse? And the challenge is in linking the development of the human beings with the development of science and technology.

In India, traditionally we have concentrated on the development of the soul and the mind, the spiritual development of the human beings. Today the challenge that we are faced with is of combining this traditional Indian heritage with modern material development. It would not be satisfactory for us to achieve only material technological development. We have to match it with the development of the human beings, with the inner spiritual development of every individual in India. We are trying to marry the two to get the best from both. We feel that without this linkage we would not be getting true development of the human beings in India.

With our traditions, we should be able to find some options which have been rather elusive. Our task in India is to end poverty. The challenge to our scientists is: How can modern, scientific and technological knowledge be brought to bear on the task of removing poverty? How we can bring our rural, more backward areas not just a step behind the other countries but equal to the most developed countries? That challenge has been in front of our scientists, in specific fields. They have shown that they can do it. I look forward to our scientists accepting that challenge and bringing India ahead of the most developed countries in certain fields and gradually in all the fields.

❒

13

Forest Conservation and Social Development

There can be no development without adequate ecological protection of the environment. The development of our forests will help our development. Development will be hindered by degeneration of the forests. The question that we face today is not just how fast we can grow but whether we will not be jeopardizing our future by further reducing our forest cover.

The national forest policy is aimed at conserving forests, resurrecting our ecosystem, and restoring the geophysical balance along with economic development. This is critical to any country. But to India, in its present state, it is even more than critical. It is vital for our survival. It is estimated that one-third of forest cover is a minimum that any country should have. We have various estimates of the actual situation today. Shri Ansari (Minister, Environment and Forests) mentioned 22.7 per cent, with only 10.9 per cent as good cover. When we look at the NRAC estimates they are somewhere around 15 per cent. I do not want to go into which number is right and which is wrong, where the forest ends, where the shrub-lands come, or whether the aerial photographs are of the right season or the wrong season. But I think it is fairly well understood that much of the forest land that is shown as forest land in our books, in fact, does not

* 21st Meeting of the Central Board of Forestry, New Delhi, 22 January 1986.

have forest on it. Many times, people have come to me and said: "Why are you stopping construction on that land? There is no forest on that land? But that land with no forest on it is part of the 22.7 per cent. Forest cover appears to be much closer to 10 to 15 per cent than to even 22 per cent let alone an optimal figure of close to 33 per cent. This puts us squarely in a very dangerous position. The question today is not just of conserving our forests. It must be of increasing the cover under forest. Afforestation must be one of our primary aims.

Conservation must be a first step, because if we do not preserve what we have got, it is pointless trying to plant new areas. It is also cheaper, it is better, it is faster than afforestation. To conserve a forest, we must right at the beginning look at the forests.

I should like to say that I have spent substantial time in forest areas, have talked to foresters alone or in groups and have a very high respect for foresters. I have some idea of the type of pressures that they come under, the type of conditions they have to operate in, the type of facilities that we give them. Perhaps the starting point, when we look at our foresters, must be the training and education that we have given them. Much of our training and education dates back to the British time when the primary aim of a forester was not to conserve and to protect, but to exploit and use the forest. And unless this basic training is changed right at the beginning we are going to find it very difficult at a later stage to suddenly start convincing the forester that he is going down the wrong route.

So, this must be the starting-point. I hope that we have already done that during the past months in our colleges and training institutions. The forester, as you have said, must bridge the links between a forest and the people who live in the forest, around the forest, and close to the forest. Again, it is not a question of just shutting the boundaries and saying: 'You cannot enter this forest, you cannot use the wood, you cannot use various other forest produce.' That cannot work and that would not work. This exercise must be a joint exercise done by the Government, the Forest Department and the people who live in and around the forest. I have seen on my tours that it does work where the political and the administrative systems have involved the local people. They have understood the problem and ultimately the threat from deforestation is faced by the people who live there. The forester may be transferred, the Minister may be somewhere else, but the local people have to face the reality of deforestation.

When I was touring Barmer in Rajasthan, I visited a village Ranigaon, where a project had been undertaken to stop sand dunes from shifting and it had worked. It had worked because the local people had not allowed their cattle and goats to graze in that area. The Forest Department had not put any huge barbed wire fences or physical blocks. It had worked without all that, for the people were convinced that this was in their interest.

From there we went to another place in Jaisalmer. There was similar project of consolidation of the dunes. There I had a huge delegation of villagers who came to see me and complained very loudly about not being allowed to graze their cattle in the area. So it is not just a question of what rules we pass or what laws we make, but it must be a question of involving the people in that area, explaining to them the consequences, the dangers.

Of course, in Barmer it is much easier because the desert is coming in and eating up their village. So it is absolutely visible to the people that sand dunes move. They see it from day to day or week to week. But in other areas the task of explaining becomes much harder. But without that we cannot be successful in this task.

The needs of the people from a forest must be met. It is again not good enough to say that you will not cut a piece of wood which is left (and I do not know what the specification is in different States, somewhere it is 10 centimeters, somewhere it is 3 inches, somewhere it is different) but we can only say that if we are in a position to give him an alternative source. Is our forest depot close enough for him to go and buy a bally (log) to put on his roof or do we have some substitute material available which he can use?

If we do not give that to him, the alternative he faces is very very tough for him– he cannot have a roof over his head, nor can he eat. But he cannot starve. So, these consequences must be taken into consideration right at the earliest stages of any conservation or development scheme.

As I said, the critical factor must be the involvement of the people. A bureaucratic approach cannot work, specially where we are dealing with people, with the social system. The people or village will be affected by your actions, and they must be involved in what you do.

Another area which need consideration is the relationship with other departments, and how you can secure help from other departments to reduce the pressure on the forests. We could try and supply fuel in area close to forests more efficiently. Perhaps some of the forest produce could be replaced with the help of research or development in a particular direction. It will need the involvement of many different ministries to see that no blocks are put to the population in and around a forest which is dependent on it for livelihood. Once you start doing that, the people will not obey your laws and your rules. It will lead to confrontation.

The Forest Conservation Act is a legal framework. Much has been said about the involvement of the Centre, the amount of funding by the Centre and how much we can help you. We should not try and separate the Centre and the States on any issue, but much more so on issues that are critical to our very survival as a nation. We shall try and help you wherever we can. I believe on most projects we are already giving 50 per cent, which is a good amount, and we shall work hopefully together to conserve and build up our forests.

The State Governments have certain difficulties which the Centre might not have. Basically, they are the ones who have to implement wherever has to be done. They come face to face with the people when a particular law is passed or when a particular action is to be taken. That is why it is better that they have elbow-room and they are able to face this pressure better at the lower level. There have been problems mainly in regards to the time taken to clear certain projects where forest land is involved. We have streamlined this during the past months and I believe that now the time taken at the Centre will be very very little provided all the questions are answered when that note comes to us.

We would like you also to cooperate and not mislead us where we give some elbow-room. Take the instance of roads. I believe we allow one kilometer of road to be made without permission and we have been told of roads which are 50-60 kilometers long- all built in one kilometer pieces, sometimes separated by one meter or one yard between them, which can later, of course, be quite easily rectified. When such instances happen the automatic reaction is that the Centre should clamp down and say: 'What is this nonsense?" There must be understanding between the State and the Centre. Both of us are setting out to do something which is critical for the country. But sometimes it is difficult to explain to the people who get affected by it. And if there is a conflict between the State Government, the Central Government or the administration, then the work will not be done.

We must also see what needs to be done to protect forests. Perhaps the Wasteland Development Board might first look at the areas around forests to build up a certain buffer area which could give more protection to the forest, which would provide fuel and fodder and protect the forest. Other scheme can be undertaken. The Petroleum Ministry is looking at schemes for gas distribution to lessen the demand for firewood. Like this, if you get ideas, you may transmit them to us. We shall definitely try to see how we can reduce the pressure on you.

Tribals come under a lot of pressure whenever any Forest Act is made or whenever a forest conservation measures takes place. We start accusing the tribals of doing all sorts of things in the forests, forgetting that they have lived in those forests for hundreds and thousands of years. And, somehow forests have survived everything that the tribals might have done to them. Perhaps the problem is not what the tribals do but what we ourselves do in their name. Perhaps some of the trouble is due to a changing social system. The answer does not lie in harsh measures. The answer can only be in the form of explanation, understanding, working together with the tribals to see how the forest can be protected. Wherever I have talked with the tribals I have found that their interest in protecting forests have been more than my own.

I look forward to a new thrust from all the States in conserving our forests and in the matter of afforestation. You should not succumb to the easy methods of raising revenue that some States seem to follow. Conservation is not something that we can force on people. It is something which we must build into our thinking right from the early stages of education. It is only then that our children will feel, from deep inside, that it is their duty to conserve and protect what they have inherited and hand it down to the coming generations. I hope that from this meeting we shall be able to give a new, dynamic thrust to this particular programme.

❐

14

New Thrust Areas in Agriculture

It gives me great pleasure to be with you today. Agriculture is the most important part of our economy and of our development process. The role that the IARI has played in India's agricultural development is known not only in India but right across the globe. As we look towards the next century, when we think of how India is to develop, when we think of new technologies, new sciences for India, our attention must remain centered on the agricultural sector. This will be so for many years. We have to see how we can develop our agriculture, to break the hold of poverty, to bring our people out of the mire that hundreds of years of colonialism has thrust us into. Panditji had said, *"Everything can wait but not agriculture."* That has not changed. Indiraji had described agriculture as our *Adi mantra.* It shows the kind of importance that has been given to agriculture in the past.

Today, when we look back, we see the tremendous progress that our agriculture has made. But when we look ahead, the challenges are no less daunting. For our economic development, we have to see that agriculture develops. And to develop agriculture we have to look at many other areas. There has been an old argument about a dichotomy between agriculture and industry. That, in

* Silver Jubilee Convocation, Indian Agricultural Research Institute, New Delhi, 6 February 1986.

fact, does not exist. If we look at our economy we see that most of our industrial development, when traced back , ends up as a support for agriculture.

When we talk of high technology today we are talking about bioengineering, we are talking of better power for agriculture, better implements, better tools. We are talking of better forecast of the rains, the monsoons. All this requires a very high level of technology. When we talk of the monsoon, we need the biggest computers to be able to predict rains and do research on the monsoon. So, if we start with the field and the farmer and then work backwards to see what is needed to support that farmer, we cover almost every section of our industrial development.

It is when these developments are coordinated that true progress will take place. The breakthrough will come when the technology is brought together with proper extension work, so that the benefits can go from the lab right down to the farmer's field.

We have achieved a Green Revolution mostly in wheat in the North-Western parts of India. Today, our wheat production has gone up almost sevenfold. Our food reserves are very large. A country which was dependent on wheat imports is not only self-sufficient but has more than enough. We have to replicate this in other parts of the country and with other crops.

This is the real challenge that faces all of us today. We have to see that the balance is maintained regionwise and cropwise. We have to start looking not just at wheat but also at how we can give a balanced diet, better nutrition to our people. If we look at the economy, we need a major breakthrough in rice, oilseeds and pulses. We have to see how marginal land can be transformed for fuel and fodders so that our forests do not come under pressure and wastelands are utilized. Our concentration and attention must go towards cash crops as well. As our productivity on the food front increases, hopefully less and less land will be required to produce more and more food crops and our attention must go to the cash crops to see that our imports are cut.

Looking back at the Green Revolution, we must give much of the credit for this to the IARI. The IARI must now look towards how to achieve the same in other areas. Perhaps the first area to concentrate on should be rice - high yielding, better qualities of rice with better productivity. Our productivity of rice is still very low - under two tones per hectare - while other countries have already gone over five. These are the sorts of challenges that you have to face. You have to see how better technologies can be brought in - technologies not just in the search for better seeds, but better methods in fertilizer use, better utilization of the resources. Are we using too much fertilizer? Can we do better? Are we using too much water? Can we economize and get better productivity from less water? These are the types of questions that you must address your minds to.

The areas where we would like concentration are the semi-arid areas - the zones where productivity is very low, where poverty is still a very major problem. If our agricultural institutions can give a thrust that will break poverty in these areas, that will increase purchasing power which will then snowball and develop the entire region.

We have produced a lot of wheat but unfortunately our population seems to be increasing almost equally rapidly. So, this challenge must not finish here. As I said, the challenge should not be just to increase the area under which the wheat is sown. The real challenge is to increase the productivity and lower the cost of production. We are falling into a very dangerous trap. We are subsidizing food to a very great degree and if we go back to see exactly how much subsidy there is then the amount truly becomes astronomical. If we see how much subsidy there is in irrigation, how much subsidy there is in fertilizers. How much subsidy there is in certain kinds of transport, apart from the other inputs, this is becoming one of our major problems with our Plans. So the thrust has to be on how to reduce the cost of production of all our crops-cash crops and food crops-because the country must become truly competitive.

We have set up bio-technology research centres here in the IARI and in Izzatnagar. These centres will be the key to the next phase of our agricultural development. Your research will lead India into a new generation of development. We must see that this research is concentrated on the objective. We must not let in drift. We must see that certain targets, and certain time-limits for particular developments, are established and checks undertaken along the line. The research must be result-oriented. And the result must come within a time-frame that is relevant. We have to go to our eastern regions to see that our resources are used in the best possible way, whether it is irrigation, water management, soil management or agricultural implements. Basically, we must develop a scientific ethos in the farmers. This will involve a lot of people going into the rural areas, a lot of practical work, a lot of hardship.

But without hardship nothing can ever be achieved. No nation can be built if the people are not willing to sweat and not willing to put up with difficulties. If we are to build India, we must sacrifice something on our part. This means hard work in the lab. But perhaps more important, it means going out and passing on our knowledge to the farmers, not just in the areas where development has taken place (because that is much easier) but in those areas where development has been slower, where agricultural productivity has not increased.

Our biggest problem today in the agricultural sector is oilseeds. We are setting up a thrust-mission for oilseeds production. When we talk of a mission, we mean an exercise starting from the labs, starting from the engineering of the seeds, and finishing with the finished products of vegetable oil which could be delivered to the consumer. We would like to put one person in-charge of such a mission with full funding, with no restrictions on him whether bureaucratic or otherwise. The only limit will be certain achievements which must come within a certain time-frame. This will cut across a number of ministries where we find a lot of hassles and we find our projects getting stalled because the interaction is not smooth enough. We have already decided on this particular mission, and a number of other mission.

This is an area where you will find that tremendous energy has to be put in and we are looking forward to input from all of you. We have made tremendous progress with wheat, some with rice and pulses. But unfortunately, we are falling behind. Output has stagnated. This is affecting the nutritional intake of our people, specially the poorer people in the arid and semi-arid areas. We need a thrust to develop better productivity in these areas as well, standardized procedures, stable remunerative and the best irrigation that we can do.

Perhaps the one key factor for better agricultural productivity is land reforms. This is an area where a lot has been talked about, a lot of work has been done in some areas, but by and large it has fallen by the wayside. We are committed to tackle this problem and see that land reforms do take place and take place effectively. We are now studying what has happened in the past and soon we will be coming out with a programme which we will implement, hopefully, fast.

One other difficult area is that of the environment. When we talk of better productivity in the fields, it is related very much to what is happening with the whole environment. It is not just a question of the amount of forest we have which determines the amount of moisture that is available, but also the type of pollutants that are thrown into the atmosphere, into water, into land, which affect the health of the crop, not to speak of the health of the people. We need a major thrust and we will be coming out soon with certain laws which, we hope, will make it easier to preserve the ecological and environmental balance.

The challenge in front of you is formidable. Agriculture is the vanguard of our economy, and it must be the basic thrust area for our development, and research is the core of agriculture. The challenge that you face is tremendous. But just as you rose to the challenge when India was going through difficulties in the sixties. I am confident that you will rise to this challenge today and deliver a new agriculture for India, more productive, more efficient, bringing more prosperity to every farmer.

❐

15

Quality of Scientific Management

Shanti Swarup Bhatnagar was one of our most distinguished scientists in basic and applied chemistry. He established a chain of national laboratories and stood for developing a scientific temper in India. He always strove for excellence and perfection for the best intellect, scientific integrity and social relevance of science. It is that spirit that is needed today.

We have a good infrastructure of scientific institutions. Funding is not too much of a problem. Our achievements, whether in the agricultural sciences, atomic energy or space, are very highly commendable. But it is still odd that with so much better facilities than those available to Bose, Raman, Sahni or Bhabha, we are not able to produce that level of work. There can be no shortcoming in our scientists. We have proved that in India, and our scientists have proved that when they go out of India. We have to get to the key of this problem if our science is to compete with the science in the most advanced nations, which is must it India is to go the way we want her to go.

We can achieve world leadership in key areas by refocusing our strategies on areas that we feel are more relevant or necessary to us, or areas that we want to go

* While giving away the Shanti Swarup Bhatnagar prizes for Science and Technology, New Delhi, 27 February 1986.

ahead in, and, may be, reduce our efforts in those areas which we find of less significance. Of course, we would like to give the same thrust and push in all areas, but being a developing country with constrains, we cannot go out in every field that is interesting, or even needed. To this end, we have developed a new strategy which, we hope, will give you new energy for your work. We are dividing them into missions and thrust areas. Basically, the idea is to identify specific areas where we want really top-grade work. They may be for a social objective-drinking water, oilseeds, illiteracy. They may be in highly technical areas— fusion, lasers. We may want to do some work in blue-sky areas of fundamental research.

But what is important is the quality of scientific management that we are able to give. Although we have produced the best scientists, our successes in scientific management have been a bit sporadic; if the individuals could, we have done well, otherwise we have just drifted, much to the frustration of the brilliant scientists who had to suffer the consequences. We must produce the correct environment, better institutional management. We must also see that the best intellects are brought into the field and not allowed to drift away. When I talk of the best intellects, we must look further. Today, the range from which we are able to draw our scientists is very narrow. There are the good institutions or nothing. And the result is that we can only draw from those people who are able to fight their way into those institutions- I do not mean fight physically but intellectually.

If the base could be broader, the scientific temper could permeate deeper, we would draw from a much larger number of people. And I am sure that many people who are being missed today would be brought in and the country could benefit from them.

During these past months, we have been looking at science and our scientists, to try to see how we can improve their functioning. We have also tried to get some more scientific thinking into the other Departments by putting scientists into more areas where we feel there is a need for scientific thinking.

Ultimately, everything comes to the quality of work, the excellence towards which you drive yourself. Nobody else can drive you to that sort of excellence that is required in the type of work that you are doing. It is only when this kind of self-thrust for excellence, for perfection, is inculcated in many more of our people, that we will get the scientific temper that Panditji talked about. But I still believe we have not got it in the country in the way that we should have. There should be thinking at all levels; it is not there. It only comes in after a very substantial amount of education. We have to try and change that scene.

Lastly, may I congratulate you. You are the brilliant people of our country, the future leaders, who must scale even higher to reach peaks of excellence not just that we feel are good in India, but that would be comparable with any in the world.

❐

16

Competitive Industrialization in India

Indian Business and industry has come of age after 38 years of independence. If we think back to what we ourselves had at the time of independence, the number of industries, the types of industries, the number of people involved at every level, whether at the top or on the shop-floor, and then compare that with where we have come today, we can see the tremendous achievement that the country has made. We have during these years proved our self-reliance in many fields-- in manufacturing, in exports to pay for our imports, in developing our own indigenous skills, scientific, technological managerial. We have during these years developed an entrepreneurial base, widened and deepened it. Over, a million small scale industries have come up and if we go into the service areas to see how technology has been absorbed by mechanics, technician, artisans, we see how much the country, the industry in the country, has achieved during these years. One phase of our industrialization is most definitely over. We must now look ahead, and try to see where we would like our industry, our country, to go. What are the targets that we must set for ourselves?

During these past years, we have been more or less content with absorbing technology that has been developed in other countries, getting it over, using it,

* Inaugural address to the All India Businessmen's Convention, New Delhi, 12 March 1986.

and educating our people how they can develop by using this technology, either on the shop-floor or on the farm. But I feel the time has come when this basic attitude must change. If India is not to lag behind other countries then our basic thinking has to change. We should not be thinking of what we can import and then learn from that, but we should identify certain areas where we will forge ahead, equal to any other country in the world. We can do this and have done this in a number of fields. There is no reason why it cannot be done in many more fields. It needs a will, it needs a determination and it needs certain involvement of all the people who are doing it. Whether in government or out of government we must work together to achieve this end.

In the past, our industrialization has been on the policies that the Government put forward but basically the target has been to increase the number of jobs, to increase employment, to train our people in very basic talents. We have to achieve a substantial amount there. Today the question of our competitiveness is coming in. Are we being able to cope with the market pressures around the world? We have a very pushy soft market at home. Almost anything that is made is very easily sold. There are no pressures as such and the system that has evolved whether by the industry or by certain policies put forward by the Government has resulted in this easy market.

We have also, for various reasons, ended up with a very high-cost economy, very high cost of inputs-- whether it is energy or transport or materials. We are slowly pricing ourselves out of world markets and it will only be a matter of time before we price ourselves out of our own market. We already see that when we have to import large capital equipment, we find that Indian companies are not able to compete, not because they are not good, but because the system is such that the cost efficiency that should be there is not there. We find it cheaper to import than to buy our own. This is a very peculiar state of affairs, and it must be changed. Of course, it cannot be changed overnight. It would cause tremendous trauma to everyone who is involved in it, but very definite steps must be taken so that we many win back from this high-cost economy to a much more competitive economy-- an economy that can produce an industry that can compete with industry anywhere else in the world. It will require a lot of changes in our thinking, and it will require a lot of time between us, sitting together and deciding how this can be done.

I have talked to the Industry Minister and he has assured me that he will meet businessmen and industrialists regularly. The time, of course, is for him to fix with you, but I would suggest something like once a quarter and discuss the directions that various policies are taking. Are they going the way we want them to or is there something wrong, some tailoring is required, more directions need to be given. I have also suggested to him, that we should have a monthly meeting at Joint Secretary level or at an administrative level where the ambiguity can be sorted out and problems are not allowed to come to a head and are solved before they become much too large. To produce this change in our industry, we will need the full genius of our people. We have seen how Indian industrialists, scientists, technologists are able to cope when they go abroad. It is very difficult to keep them down. They invariably rise to the top and do extremely well. But somehow that dash seems to be lacking at home. Now, we must produce that here. If it is a question of altering some of the policies, we already are in that process, and we would like to continue that.

So far, industry has been treated very much as a place to create jobs. It is a place to create jobs, but we must not get bogged down because if we just try to create jobs then we will actually have fewer jobs than we could have if the same industry was running much more efficiently.

This point has to be brought home to our people fast. Industries must be such that jobs multiply and increase not where jobs get reserved and blocked for just a particular group of people and they do not, in fact, increase adequately compared to the industries that are going in. Perhaps, what we must remember most of all, whether it is Government handling public money, or the industrialists handling public money, is that we have the responsibility to invest that money in the best possible way. That goes as much for the Government as it goes for the private sector. If we do not invest it properly, if it is used inefficiently, if it is wasted, then we are cheating the people to whom the money belongs, that is, the people of India. So, if there is an inefficient public sector unit which is sucking up vast amounts of finances, it is really robbing the average or the poorest person in the country of what is his due. This point must come home to the industry. It is only then that we will really be able to make all our units fully efficient and give the returns that our people deserve for their investment in the industry.

Industry today has to catch up with industry all over the world. In everything that we have done today, except perhaps in a very few limited sectors, we have limited ourselves or satisfied ourselves with buying a certain technology, never attempting to develop that technology and catch up with the people who sold that technology; not have we gone ahead of the people who sold that technology to us. Most probably, it has not even been attempted. This basic attitude must change. We can identify which sectors we want to handle. But unless we change the attitude, India cannot be where you and I want India to be. If this attitude remains in our people, we will always remain number two, and we do not want to remain number two, whether it is industry or anything else. We have the capability of going ahead equally well like any other country in the world, and we must do that today. It will come when each one of us puts in his best and really puts in a certain drive to challenge what has been accepted as a norm in India. It must be the responsibility of the managers, whether in the private sector or in the public sector, to see that this attitude also goes down to the labour, goes down to the shop-floor or the lower management and we are able to develop a new work ethos on the shop-floor, on the factory front, something that will pull us out of this second position that we have satisfied ourselves with. The reason that we have taken certain steps with government policy is to try and bring this about.

Earlier, we had always limited industry to certain production limits-- you cannot make more than this and you cannot make more than that. We are now trying to change that by saying that you cannot make less than this because it is inefficient. You must put up a bigger unit. But of course, things do not happen suddenly. But, there must be a slow transition to this, preferably not too slow. From our side we will try and push you to meet this as fast as possible.

Capacity utilizations has been another area where we have been unnecessarily sticky. We used to penalize industries for being efficient. But we hope that we have been able to change that and we will be able to reward efficiency. But the full impact of these various measures that we have taken will take a number of years to be seen. It will also take some time for industry to adjust itself. Industries got used to investing money in a certain way. Now, if we change our policies, that must change as well. But it will take a little time, we appreciate that. The type of industries that come up with a particular type of economy might not be those that come up when people are spending their money in buying shares. So, there will be a shift in certain units, and what we must be alive to is to see that this shift takes place very smoothly, and no sudden change causes a large number of units to close down or become sick.

Sickness is another very sensitive area. Actually I had covered that area of sickness when I said that when we look after investment of public money we must invest it properly and not waste it. This means that we must look at sick units in a very practical way. If it is not possible to bring them up and make them viable, then we should accept the challenge of closing them down giving alternative employment or finding some methods of not throwing a large number of people on to the streets which will cause various problems-- personal problems to the individual and problems of administration in other industries. But this is not something that we can put off for very long.

During this Budget, the Finance Minister has made it very clear that he is running out of areas to collect money and ultimately we are going to be left with basically just two areas-- improving the efficiency of the Government and making the public sector efficient. During the past three or four months, we had a tremendous amount of rationalization in the Government. Many offices which had been running for twenty years have been closed down. A large number of posts have been shut down. Nobody has been thrown out or sacked because they will be redeployed. But bases and positions which were totally unnecessary have been shut down. This is an exercise that we will be continuing. We have got a team which is just looking into the Ministries, trying to spot areas or Departments which are totally redundant and need shutting down.

The other area where we have to get some finances from is the public sector. We must make it more efficient. There is no alternative to that. It will require hard decisions and we are ready to take those hard decisions. We have already taken a few and we will be carrying on with that.

The third, of course, is private industries and the joint

sector where resource generation must take place. But whenever we look at industry, whether it is private or public. I think it is important that the taxation system should be such that the basic inputs are not loaded very heavily, and the taxes are visible at the end. So we actually know what we are doing when we look at a particular product, which we are not in a position to say today.

If today, I ask what is the percentage of tax on a particular piece of equipment, it is very difficult for anybody to tell me because the number of places you have to go back to see where the taxes have been paid are so many that we ourselves do not know how to balance products in a particular way. We might want to tax certain consumer products. We might not have to tax certain agricultural inputs, but the system today is that we do not even know. For example, if I ask the Agriculture or Food Ministry what one kilo* of wheat costs us today in terms of subsidies and how much tax has gone into producing that, there is no way that they can tell me that. This is a very sad state of affairs because it makes it very difficult for us to make basic decisions on what to do with a kilo of wheat if we have got it spare. For example, if we want to export it and the export price is Rs. 2.80 or something a Kilo, we should know whether we are paying Rs. 5 a Kilo to produce and that we are going to export to some other country. Unfortunately this information is just not available because the taxation system, the subsidy system is such that it just cannot be got together.

It is much more complicated in the agricultural sector because you have things like irrigation which is totally unquantified, you have power which is not paid for in certain States, and things like that, so it is very difficult to say what we are really producing and for how much. In Industry it is a little easier, but still it would be much easier if we had a taxation system which presented the total picture at the end. The Finance Minister has tried

* Kilo gram

to bring in just such a system but I believe there are a lot of problems coming up with this. We will try and sit across the table and sort out the problems that are coming up. Such problems have come up in other countries also when VAT had been introduced. I remember I was in England when this happened and there was a tremendous furor from industry, from business, from everyone, but once it came in, the bugs were removed and it started operating smoothly. It is a better system than the system that we have had and we would like to sit with you and try and sort out these problems so that the functioning is smooth.

The biggest challenge that we are going to face is that of exports really earning enough money to import items that we are forced to import. Here your competitiveness, your efficiency, will really be on the lines, so to say, and if we are not able to compete then it will put us in a very awkward position. There is no reason why we cannot compete. Other countries, smaller countries, even some big countries have developed their industries to a level where they can compete with the best. Again, we should identify areas, and concentrate on those perhaps jointly, and develop those areas so that we are as competent and efficient as any other country in the world.

We have the capability, and we must do it. We have always kept the public sector at the peak of our industrializations thrust. I know there have been tremendous complaints of how inefficient and how bad the public sector is and how many subsidies it swallows up. I have just said so myself. But the public sector has been used by us not just to produce. This is a point which we must remember. It has been used to go into very backward and remote areas to open up those areas, to train the people there, to cope with difficulties that other industries in more convenient areas do not have to cope, and when I say 'backward areas' I do not mean the zones which are ten kilometers or 15 kilometers from a major metro and are categorized as backward areas, but actually going to areas where there is difficulty with even roads, with power, with rails, with everything. So, when you force somebody to go into areas like that you are really forcing him to go and train the people in that area, to bring in a sort of an industrial ethos into that area and we pay a price for that-- the price is in the efficiency of the unit that we send there. But, I feel that there can be no compromise on this, and we have to carry this on till we are in a position where all our people have adequate access to industries and to training.

Much of our Budget, and especially this year you will have noticed, has been allocated for the antipoverty programmes. Anti-poverty programmes are not programmes which are separated from industrial development and you must not see them as such. Our industrial development depends entirely on the market that we can create to absorb the goods that are manufactured and one area has to be in widening that part which means opening up the rural areas, increasing the buying power in the rural areas. So, when we look at our total budget or plan, from a purely industrial and development viewpoint, there is a very definite logic in having programmes which on the face of it look unproductive, but it is only if we can lift these people up to levels where they have a certain buying power that they will be able to help in the total industrialization of the country.

During this year, we have improved the efficiency in various Government sectors. For example, coal despatches are up around twenty per cent. The freight being carried by the railways is almost one third more than it was in the previous year. Power generation is up, the hydel power and the thermal power balance has been improved. But a lot still has to be done, and our major weaknesses in the coming years are going to be in the power, communication and transport sectors. We have in this Plan given a very large outlay to power and the

Planning Commission has guaranteed that by 1990 we will not be short of power. I am not too sure, but they gave me a figure. I increased that by one third but still I do not know whether the suppressed/surplus demand will be so much that when power is actually available, the demand will be very much more than anything that we would have anticipated. But we are looking again to see how we can improve investment in these three sectors. We feel that they are very crucial to our industry.

The other area that we have decided to tackle is to try and hold the prices of basic inputs. Of course, we cannot guarantee anything but the attempt will be to absorb the increasing costs by making the units more efficient. Now, if we can keep the rate of efficiency up to the average inflation rate, I think we will more or less manage. In one or two areas, we are fairly sure that we can do well over the next four or five years, but in other there is a bit of a question mark. But there will be no effort spared on our part. And that includes taking very hard decisions if required to close down or to rationalise units.

Another area which FICCI has attacked, which private sector and public sector must tackle together, is that of energy efficiency or energy conservation. Other countries have saved tremendous amounts. But we continue wasting energy. Here we will be again back to the taxation policy. Perhaps we are taxing our capital goods and our inputs too much so that energy really is a very small input into what you are doing, so you do not worry too much if you waste or burn a little bit extra. But while we try and turn back around, you must make a very definite effort to reduce the consumption of energy and regenerate, reuse, whatever is available. There are numerous methods available today. I was told by the Dutch that in some factories they are saving as much as sixty per cent of what they were using originally. R & D really goes back to what I started with, that of bringing India up from second runners to amongst the first runners. We must invest in our own business. Unless our business and industry looks within itself for development instead or always looking out and abroad for development, we will never be able to do what they are doing in other countries. If we have a challenge today, we immediately look abroad to see how the Japanese did it, or how the Americans have done it or how the Europeans have done it. We seldom actually try to attack the problem ourselves. Of course, on small things, it can be very expensive, but with that cost we must weigh the gain in a particular attitude or mentality towards our own products. We also do not spend enough time or energy in refining our products and making them really comfortable or easy to use or fail-proof. Again there is no market pressure to demand that. But if we are to export and if we are to compete with other markets, this must come in. I am not just talking of VCRs and television sets but also of heavy machines and everything really.

We also seldom look at our products from the users' point of view. If we make a car, it is seldom that we ourselves or the designer of that car actually drives that car. So, it is seldom that he realises that a switch which should be here is in fact somewhere else. He does not relate it with the driver who drives the car, and I see that in everything, whether I go to defence industry, it is the same. The man who makes the tank does not talk with the man who drives the tank or who fires the gun. We have a work system where we do not like to talk with people who are sort of below our level; and there is no way we can make our product efficiently if we do not go down there and see how that product is going to be used by the person who is going to use that product. This interaction also must come in. And the same thing applies on the shop-floor; in processes, in methods there must be much more interaction between various levels of management.

Lastly, let this convention be a convention for stock

taking to see and assess what we have achieved in the past thirty-eight years, what certain directions that we have given during the past year have achieved, where we have gone wrong and how that can be corrected, whether it is in the long term policy, whether it is in what we did in the past year.

What we need is an Indian approach to Indian problems. We should not be looking for a Japanese or an American or a German solution to Indian problems. Let me at the end say that what we would like to give is to have a constructive dialogue on how to develop Indian industry and today we would like every energy that is available in India, in every sector, to be channelised positively in one direction, that of taking India ahead, of bringing it in line with the best in the world and after that aiming for beyond that.

❒

17

Science, Technology and Society

Shri Om Prakash Bhasin saw a picture of Indian science which is very relevant to us today for giving a thrust to our development. His donation that has made these prizes possible will encourage our scientists in India to work in those fields which are relevant to our people today.

Let me first congratulate all the award-winner on their achievements. Their work will contribute to our development process. There seems to be a big gap today between what people perceive as development and the technology that is required to achieve it. There appears to be an inherent feeling of not wanting technology but somehow wanting development. To me this seems to be totally contradictory. Development of any kind is basically using better technology to give a better life to the people. Somehow this has not got home to our people, particularly in the villages. When they talk of development they talk of the end result of technology without releasing that there is a certain amount of technology involved in achieving that. We have to get this home to our people and make them understand that the technology that is required is not necessarily the most sophisticated technology. It has to be appropriate to the environment but it must be the best possible that can be used in any field in that environment.

* Address at the presentation of the Om Prakash Bhasin Awards for Science and Technology, New Delhi, 17 March 1986.

The biggest need is in the area of poverty alleviation. Application of new technology must start with agriculture and go on to other areas of rural production and related subjects, emphasizing self-employment. Today, you have been given awards in a number of spheres. All of them directly reflect on the lives of the poorest, the most depressed persons in our country. Even when we talk of satellite communication, or our space programme, the benefit really is targeted there.

When we talk of big computers we must understand that the aim is not just juggling with numbers but to see how we can help the farmer with his understanding of monsoons. So it is the relationship and the connection that are more important than just the mere advance of technology. Agriculture has to be our primary thrust. It involves the largest number of people and it is a very basic need for our survival. We have had the Green Revolution in northwest India. Wheat production has gone up almost sevenfold, thanks to it. This must now spread eastward where it has not yet taken place. Our targets for food production in the next fifteen years are such that production must rise almost fifty per cent.

Agricultural development is perhaps the most effective way of removing poverty. It we can spread the Green Revolution to more areas, to more States, it will help in removing poverty and bringing our people up. The Green Revolution was not brought about just by distributing seeds and popularizing new methods. A tremendous amount of technology was involved not just in one or two fields but right across the board from bio-technology, energy, irrigation, to teaching the farmer how to use all these methods, which is also technology.

Such efforts are required in other fields as well. We must spread from wheat to other crops. One of our major thrust areas will be in oilseeds, in edible oils. We hope that this will be as dramatic as the Green Revolution was in the sixties. One aspect of being a developing country is that we do not use high enough levels of technology. The other seems to be that we are unaware of the wastage of materials. We do not use the inputs economically whether it is power, water for irrigation or other materials. We squander them. We are reluctant to use better methods. The irony is that, being a developing country, we can least afford such wastage.

We have recently started a new Department of Bio-technology. This is because we feel that this is an area where India can reach tremendous heights, where we can be amongst the leaders. Bio-technology is used for agriculture, for health, for industry. The new advances on cellular and molecular biology must be used for finding practical solutions to many of our problems.

An area where we have tremendous shortfalls is that of energy. We have not concentrated enough on it. The result is that much of our production is well below par whether it is our industries or agriculture. We just do not realize the built-in potential. The investments that are already made are not utilized fully because adequate energy supplies are just not available at all, or they are not available at the right time. Sufficient reliability is not built in. In the Seventh Plan the single largest investment that we will be making will be on energy. But still it is not enough when we look towards the Eighth Plan (1990-95). Very major work will be required in the energy sector. In the matter of energy utilization, we are squandering large amounts. Other countries, who can afford to use much more energy, have begun to be very conservative in their use of energy-- whether it is in the transmission, actual delivery of the energy, or developing new methods for producing that energy. A tremendous amount of work has to be done by us-- in traditional methods, non-conventional methods, and renewable sources. At the same time we must also see how we can make the best use of our traditional sources of oil, coal, and new areas of nuclear and fusion energies.

Another area where we have not been really effective is that of communication. Although in certain fields of military communication we have done very well, on the civilian side a lot is lacking. We have taken a number of technologies but they somehow have not suited our system and have not worked well. This is an area where we cannot afford to lag behind at all. It is an area where indigenous technology must be brought up to design equipment that is suited to our environment, to our usage, to our people. It is only then that we will really be able to produce equipment which works in India with Indians using it. It also perhaps would be more suitable equipment for other developing countries where similar problems are faced.

Electronics in telecommunication also gives very large opportunities for employment, specially for women.

Health again, reflects directly on our population problem. Every effort must be made to give confidence to our people that the child that is born is going to survive. That will really be the first step in a positive reduction of our population. All effort has to be made to provide the best available technology for children, women and older people.

Communicable diseases must be tackled on a war-footing. Nutrition is still an area where we have not achieved what we should have achieved in spite of self-sufficiency in food.

In Space, we have made great achievements. It is one of the areas where we are truly among the leaders in the world. These must now be translated for the best utilization of our people. This is one area where we can very proudly say that the advantages of utilization have been recognized by our people. Demands and pressures are increasing tremendously on the hardware that is available and the efforts that we can make, which only means we have to make much more efforts, whether it is in satellites for communication, for remote-sensing, telecommunication, broadcasting or developing our own launching systems. The challenges before our scientists are tremendous.

We have made tremendous strides in science but still sometimes one gets a feeling that we could have achieved much more if the thrusts had not been so dispersed and we had really concentrated on areas that are most urgent. We have done so in certain areas and we have shown results equal to any. We must now concentrate on more areas which are necessary for our development process. Of course, that does not mean that we do not do any esoteric blue-sky research That also is a necessity. But the prime thrust has to be in areas where the research is for a particular end-use and benefits society or has an impact on our daily lives.

Agriculture must be one of the main thrust areas. Our concentration must be on getting from the lab to the farm or to the factory as quickly as possible, as effectively as possible. Results must be such that they are visible in the daily life of our people.

❐

18

Science and Technology for the Common Man

The foundation of our scientific and technological developments were laid many years ago by Panditji and a major thrust was given to our science and technology by Indiraji. It is on this base that we are able today to use our science and technology to help the poorest people in our country. Indian scientists have shown that they are up to the best in the world when it comes to developing technology and when it comes to taking our nation forward.

Development - its Meaning and Significant

2.1 Perhaps it is worth spending a moment on just thinking what we mean by development because everybody talks "development", "development must take place", "we are very backward", What is development? What is the difference between a backward and developed area, a non-developed country and a developed country.

2.2 I would beg to state that there is only one difference and that it is the difference in technology that they use in their day-to-day lives. If a country uses better technology. It is a developed country. If it uses worse or older technology, it is a backward country and an underdeveloped country. Within our country, the same

* Speech in the Lok Sabha on 10 April 1986.

thing holds true. What is the difference between the most backward village in India and Delhi or Bombay or one of the major metropolis? It is the level and quantity of technology that is used in our daily lives, right from the very basics to the extravagance, the extras, that you get. But the difference is in the science and technology that you apply to your life and if we are to alter the standard of living in the rural areas, if you do take that as a definition, then by definition it means, putting in more S&T into the rural areas, better technology for their improved living. Where is this going to come from and how will we target it?

Technology for the Common Man

3.1 Much has been said of appropriate technology or suitable technology. Lots of words have been used. But ultimately what we have to see is that the best possible technology that can be used for a particular task in the circumstances in which it is being used, must be available if rapid development is to take place. In some areas, it could mean a better bullock-cart, but in other areas we see that the farmers are not really interested in a better bullock-cart, they want a tractor. So, we have to see what they are willing to use and what they are capable of using and try and bring that in for them.

3.2 Our priority is basically removal of poverty in the rural areas, and the fundamental part of that has to be the development of our agriculture and downstream products from agriculture. We have seen that, with the most advanced technologies, the most advanced scientific developments being applied to agriculture and related industries, we have achieved a green revolution in the north-western States. This did not come about by ignoring science and technology. It came about by using science and technology at the right point and by using appropriate technology. It came about by using the most advanced and sophisticated technology, biotechnology, genetic technology, use of fertilizer and electricity. And that is what has changed that picture of our rural areas. Basically, what we mean by technology is to try and see how it can help us to produce more by using the same effort, increase productivity with better tools, with better equipment. And this is the task that our scientists have before them today.

3.3 Our scientists have many achievements behind them. They have made us self-reliant in very basic areas. Whether it is in food, whether it is in certain strategic areas of defence, in space, in nuclear sciences, they have shown that, where there is a challenge, they are up to that challenge and they have the capacity to lift India up when they are given that chance and when they are given full backing. They have responded admirably to this challenge. Whether we look at Space, the Satellites that we have put up, the launching system that we have developed, there have been tremendous spin-offs for everyone.

3.4 Today I go to the most backward area. There are many difficulties. But the main demand that comes is that for T.V. for a low power T.V. transmitter or a Relay Station. This is what technology is doing to the lives for our people. It is giving them a better quality of life. Whether it is a question of broadcasting or telecommunication for better administration, for better productivity or a better assessment of markets for the farmer, whether it is better weather information to help the farmer sow his seeds or help the farmer protect his crops, it is all technology working for the poorest people in our country.

High Technology for the Common Man

4.1 Another example I would like to give because many times when we talk of advanced technology our mind immediately goes to large industries, to fancy offices and to very sophisticated laboratories. But what goes sometimes into the most mundane objects which help the poorest people. A case in point is the India Mark-II Hand Pump. It looks a very simple device but today we are exporting it in thousands to different corners of the world. Inside it is perhaps one of the most advanced technology mechanisms and materials that are used. That is why it survives. So this is the type of development that we need - high technology applied in a simple manner to everyday objects that are needed in our rural areas.

4.2 Another example is that of root nodule bacteria developed by our scientists which can be tailored to specific crops, or specific regions, climates and environments. It puts approximately 40 KG of nitrogen every year into the soil and into the plant without any extra expense or very very cheaply. Again it is very advanced high technology used at a very basic level and this is what is going to change the life of the average person in India. The tissue culture whether it is for better crops, better trees, faster growing trees, whether it is for vaccines, immunization, etc.; again it is very high technology but applied to everyone in the country. Disaster satellites. Can one today imagine what it was like going along the East Coast of Andhra five years or ten years ago when there was no disaster warning system and the damage that was done. Today it is behind us. We do not even think about it. But again it is the most advanced technology giving protection to the poorest people on that belt.

4.3 I can go on with a very long list whether it is electronic testing of soil, whether it is testing of quantity of humidity in the soil, whether it is testing grain for quality to help the farmer get the correct price, but perhaps the most striking is our programme to clean the Ganga. There can be no question about the purity of the Ganga, but it still requires the most modern science and technology to identify what sort of pollutants are going into the Ganga and it requires the most modern technology to remove those pollutants and once more clean the water.

Technology for a Better Life

5.4 So it is a question of putting the best technology that we have for use of our average person not for the elite. The elite will get it anyway. But our thrust must be for the rural areas. Here we come up against resistance. Resistance because there is a feeling that technology will bring about unemployment. If we think back of the time of the Industrial Revolution, the same resistance was felt then when it was said that machine coming in would bring about tremendous unemployment. But it did not happen. Employment shifted but increased. Wealth generation increased. The average person who was poor got wealthy. He lives a better life. Today the reason for parts of our country being still very backward is that the Industrial Revolution has not yet arrived there. Mechanization has not arrived there. We must today not only bring that mechanizations but we must help them take a jump ahead and bring them into the world as it is today instead of trying to bring them into yesterday. And anyone who thinks otherwise has a vested interest in keeping those areas backward, in keeping our people backward and dependent on an ideology, on a theory, on a political system and we must do everything possible to bring about this change so that our people are not left backward and they have the most modern tools and machine available for their own better living.

Scientific Temper

6.1 One of the key factors has to be that of developing a scientific temper like Panditji had said so often. Without that scientific temper, it cannot be possible and a scientific temper is not necessarily only for the scientists, the scientific temper must come into the average Indian if he is to start developing. It can be brought about by the media, it can be brought about by education and we must do everything that we can to bring this about. Once we have a scientific temper, basically it will remove the fear of the unknown which keeps people back, which keeps people from moving ahead and using the tools that are available to them. The scientific temper will help develop an inquisitive spirit where people will ask questions, where people will ask why does milk turn sour, why cannot it be kept in some way so that in the villages they do not need refrigeration. Why their plough does not plough better under certain circumstances. It is when we start thinking in this manner that a scientific temper will develop and we ourselves will start improving the tools that we have got and that we live with. Today you go to a village. You go to a backward area, you see that there has been no improvement. In my area. I see some have bullock carts which still have not got steel tyres on the wheels. They start with the wheel that is that big, slowly it wears down, and after sometimes they change the wheel and go back to a big wheel again. They have not even thought that they can put something on the wheel to prevent its wear. So, it is this type of thinking which must be brought into the rural areas and that could be the basis of our scientific temper.

6.2 Our scientists, like I have said, have developed a tremendous capability. They have developed reputation which is not limited by our boundaries, but goes right across the world and they have developed this reputation working in parallel, with perhaps the best brain in the world. The brain of our scientists are second to none. We have developed a very large infrastructure of scientists we have developed very sound linkages among various fields. But still all is not as well as it should be as we have not got the maximum out of our investment and we have been thinking about this. We have analyzed where we have done extremely well; for example, our space programme is second to none. In atomic energy, we have risen to great heights. In biotechnology, in certain fields in defence we are equal to the best in the world. So obviously, there are areas where it has worked extremely well; at the same time there are other areas where we have done miserably. So, we have done something right, obviously something wrong, and we must try and identify what was right and correct and try and use that in other areas where we want similar development. Like some members have pointed out, it cannot be possible for a country like India to develop across the board in every single field. We just do not have the resources or the capability to do that, but we must choose those areas which we feel are vital and we must give a very strong push in those areas to that in a certain number of years we are as advanced as anybody else.

Import of Technology and Technology Missions

7.1 One of the problems of a developing country is that it is much easier to buy technology which is available in the market than to start reinventing the same technology, rediscovering what others have already discovered. But, of course, if you take that route, then you will always be left with second rate technology, because that is what others are going to give you. Now when a country comes to the development stage, that India is in today, we must rethink on this. Are we going to settle for second-rate technology for ever? Or, is there going to be a stage when we will say: "No, we want to shift over to frontline technology"? We cannot do that in every field. It is not possible. But we must identify certain areas where we will give this trust. We have identified a number of such areas starting with those that affect the life of the average person in the villages, in the more backward or depressed areas. We are identifying these as Mission, because we thought that the success of some of these programmes, that I mentioned earlier, was because one person was in command, he had full authority to run that exercise, he had full funding, he had the backing of all the institutions that be needed.

When we talk of the Mission, we intend to draw it up in that same broad concept.

7.2 We have decided on a number of Missions already. Five have already been established. Drinking water - it might sound simple that we will just be digging holes in the ground and pulling out water, but out of the all these five missions, the maximum amount of scientific development and technological development will go into drinking water and the highest technology out of any of these missions will be used to give drinking water specially in those areas where there is a tremendous shortage of drinking water. Another mission will be that of oil seeds and another of vaccination for children, vaccination for the health of our children and eradication of illiteracy. Again, we will need a very high technology to transmit the message. What education? Education is communicating a message to the younger generation, to the children. We must use the best methods that are available to be able to do this. Telecommunication will be another mission.

New Approach to Research

8.1 We are dividing these thrust areas into basically three areas. The first and perhaps the most important and the most difficult will be the Missions, because they will stretch from the laboratory. Oil seeds for example will mean development of the oil seeds in a genetic laboratory, transferring that into the extension work of actually getting it to the farmer, explaining to the farmer how he is going to use it, turning his produce into oil, marketing the oil and getting it to the consumer, and keeping the costs down right across that exercise. So these are extremely complicated exercises which will cut across many Ministries, many State governments and if these are to succeed, we would need really good men at the top, who would be able to really cut through all this red tape and deliver the results that are required if this country has to survive.

8.2 On the other hand, we will have, what we are going to call, the thrust areas which will be slightly more specific. We might identify a particular line of development which we need for strategic use, may be nitrogen devices, may be lasers, may be something like that. And again, we will give everything that is required for development. The third area will be what scientists refer to as *'blue-sky research'* which means basic or fundamental research. Here of course, we cannot ask for results in the same way that we ask for in the other two areas. But the basic thrust will be on some sort of accountability in all these three areas, accountability in terms of scientific development in a certain time, accountability for the funds that have been spent in terms of scientific development. And we will have certain cut off points. We will decide that at this point we will not go further along this road and we will take a different track. Perhaps, we will decide that is enough, that we cannot go further at all and we shut that area down. But unless we do that, we cannot get results for the money and investment that we are putting in.

8.3 Our attempt will also be to try and shift the management of our other scientific projects on to a similar type of management. But because they will much more general, the attention that we will pay and the financing that they will get will not be of the same level as in the missions and thrust areas and basic research that we will be pushing forward.

Brain- Drain

9.1 Another point which has been talked about many times is that of the brain-drain or as I prefer to call it, "the brain-bank". We are looking at this from the starting point and that is the education policy. When the Minister for Human Resources Development will put this in front of the House during this Session, we will see that an attempt has been made to look at the teaching of science, because we have to start building scientific temper on a much broader base of our scientific pyramid. Today, we have achieved great heights, but the base is very narrow. We have very few people who go straight to the top. The average person does not have a scientific thinking of any sort. We must broaden that base, because when that base really becomes a broad-based pyramid, then we will really be able to draw upon the best that is available in the rural areas. And to do this, we must build in into our education system.

9.2 At the same time, If we are to stop this brain-drain of too many scientists and technologists leaving the country, we have to tailor the subjects that we are teaching to the needs for our development. If we teach everyone very esoteric subjects which do not relate to the development in India, of course they will leave the country, they will go away and they will look for jobs elsewhere. So, we need in the exercise of the New Education Policy to first try and assess what will be our need of agricultural scientists, what will be our need of technologists, of engineers, of other specialized training and then try to fit that back into the Education Policy. When that tailoring is done, and it is not something that we even attempt to say we will do in the next 4 or 5 years, it is only a very modest beginning that we can make now; but unless this sort of training is done effectively, we will not be able to use the best resources in terms of brain power in our country, for our development purposes.

9.3 Again, training does not end, qualification does not end by getting a degree from an I.I.T. Or from a University. It is a continuing process and if a scientist or a technologist is to be useful to us, he can be useful to us at every level of training, at every level of experience. We might want to use the young men who are 25 years old, and who have just got a degree. At the same time, we might prefer to send some of them out. Let them work in very advanced fields with top scientists in the world, and we might want to bring them back five years or ten years later.

9.4 So, this sort of exercise has to be a continuing process, an updating exercise; it has to relate to our development process. It must relate to our education process as well. Our attempt will be to try and do this. We have taken a number of steps to attract such people back to the country; and there has been a movement back. We will continue this. However, achievements in the past are there for everyone to see, right across the world. Certain areas, like I said earlier, Space, Agriculture, Defence and in the Nuclear fields, we have done extremely well, and have shown that India is equal to the best.

9.5 We have shown that when India accepts a challenge, when our scientists, when our technologists accept a challenge, they need that challenge and they deliver the goods. Today, we must give them the backing that they need to achieve similar results in many other fields. Once more we would like to show that India can do it, and will do it.

9.6 Where science and technology is concerned, we must keep in mind that nothing but the best will do for the country; and we must work towards that end. With everybody's support. I believe we will be able to do it.

❑

19

Targetting Beyond Self-Reliance

I should first like to thank the scientists who gave the presentations, gave us some idea of what the CSIR laboratories have achieved and are doing today. CSIR with forty laboratories, many of which have already celebrated their silver jubilee, and over 5000 scientists, is one of our premier organizations. I do not think we look at it as an organization just for scientific and industrial research. We see it as a basic tool in our developmental process. If we are going to restructure and reorient our society, it will only be possible if we have substantial achievements in areas of frontline technology.

Development and science are related. Underdevelopment by definition is the lack of being able to use modern science and technology for the benefit of our people, to increase their productivity, to increase their comforts, to improve their life span. If we are going to break this barrier it must come from our scientific institutions and from our scientists, technologists and industrialists.

The CSIR has done tremendous work in creating a base for development. Unfortunately or fortunately, the speed at which development is taking place all over the

* Conference of the Directors of the National Laboratories of the Council of Scientific and Industrial Research, New Delhi, 28 May 1986.

world is very very high. If we are to catch up with the most advanced countries, we must go faster than they are going today. Otherwise there is no catching up. We cannot go faster if we do not think ahead of them. If we are thinking ahead to the next century or the next millennium, whichever way you want to look at it, we must not think just of what is in the minds of other people today. And then let us work on that, let us be in the very frontline. There are areas that we can choose, and decide that in two, three, four, five areas, we are going to be the front runners in 'x' number of years. We can think of fifty years if we like, but let us lay down a positive goal that in these fields in so many years India will be the best. We will not be the best unless we are thinking well beyond what anybody else is thinking today.

Innovation is the one word which will represent what you must try and do. By merely trying to see what others have done we are not going to benefit. To have a ceramic engine is good, yes, we should do it and save fuel. But we are really going into an area which somebody else has already done. The Japanese are doing it. We also have to do this. I am not trying to deride that. But let us not stop our thinking at the point where the Japanese have already reached. We should have thought of these ceramic engines before the Japanese thought of them. That is the type of thinking we have got to do all we are going to get ahead, not by imitating what others have already done. That has to be part of the exercise, but it cannot be the complete or whole exercise. If we are going to concentrate, then we have to concentrate on a few areas. We cannot take up a few thousand projects and pretend that we are going to achieve everything. We may not achieve anything by diluting our efforts. We must decide what we want to concentrate on. We can give you a general political decision and tell you we want something in the rural areas - may be, in processing foods which will help the farmers, in oilseeds, in drinking water. We might like to point out certain areas which are strategic for defence, and other areas, such as energy. But from that point on, it is you who must take them up and see that your efforts are not too diffused or diluted. Otherwise there will not be adequate achievements and the achievements that will come about too late. Even if we have the most brilliant ideas, which is well ahead of what anybody else has and it takes us too long to develop it, then again it does not help. So we have got to get the right idea and we have got to be quick enough to turn that into a usable product for our people - it must go beyond the industry, beyond the market place and reach the people. After you sell, it has got to work. You will have to really look at the ultimate user.

You will have to redeploy your resources and re-examine your priorities. Most of all, you will need a very accurate monitoring system of what you are actually doing, at what rate you are achieving the targets, and at what point you want to take a decision, whether to continue along the same track or change direction, and go on to a totally new area, or just cancel the project.

This really means that what we are looking for is much better scientific administration. Scientific administration must be a subject on its own. It cannot be borrowed from our general bureaucratic system because it is not going to work. At the same time the answer is not to find the best scientist we have got and put him in charge as an administrator because then we lose a scientist. Perhaps we do not even gain in administration. IT is a very specialized task. We have not developed people in this area and we must see how we can develop this. Again this is an area where you could debate and see what are the qualities that are needed, what sort of training and direction are required to produce this cadre of people who would really support our scientists and our laboratories. It is only when we are able to work in this manner that we will be striving for world leadership in a number of fields. When I talk o our scientists I know that they have the capabilities, they certainly have the brains. We have got to give them the infrastructure. Then we have to push them hard enough so that they really get ahead of what others are doing. We have got a number of thrust areas. We have got some societal missions. We have got certain areas where there will be concentration, better coordinations, some of which you have shown me in your presentations. We hope that this will give a new boost to scientific activity and achieve better results than we actually get from these areas.

The three Missions on potable water, oilseeds and wastelands are very critical for our economy. They must be handled with the utmost priority and efficiency. The water mission will require a tremendous amount of technical and scientific input. When we look at areas that will benefit our society, one of the most important aspects is the cost of the finished products. If it is going to cost too much, then perhaps it is just not good enough. This will be more specially important when you come to water, oilseeds and perhaps most of all when we look at the environment and the wastelands. I will not go into the details of what all you are doing in these areas.

The mention of wastelands takes me to the environment. You have started some work on ecology. But it is still much too limited. We are today faced with a situation where our environment is in very serious danger of such grave damage that it might never be able to be restored to a satisfactory condition. We have to protect the environment in whatever way we can. This is not just a question for the biologists or the biological engineering people who work on how to improve seeds, and how to get more trees growing. It is also the responsibility in every part of industry to see that you do not pollute or produce such chemicals in the atmosphere in an area which is dangerous to the environment in that particular area. Whenever you are doing research on a new process, on a new product, you must bear in mind that no environmental damage should result from the process that you are designing or the product that you are designing. We have taken some precaution by passing an Act which makes it a criminal liability for anyone to do it. The rules will be out soon and perhaps that will put a little more pressure for compliance. We will need a lot of zeal and vigour, a personal involvement from everyone from the top scientists to the junior most worker in your labs. If your leadership is good, we will get the results. If there is something lacking, we shall find our Missions floundering and getting caught up in their own web. We should not allow that to happen.

There are other projects, some of which you have just talked about, such as fertility control, drugs, vector control and salt-iodization. In the physical and earth sciences you have just shown the areas you are working in -materials, electronics, instrumentation, geophysics, oceanography, chemical plants, petrochemicals and leather; then the biosciences - toxicology, parasitic diseases etc. In some areas we are in the frontline for example, in molecular characterization of chloroplast, in myochondrial DNAs. So, there are some very good areas. In engineering sciences, again we are doing some notable work for example in mine safety, environment, control of effluents, aeronautics, slurry transport, tribology conditioning and monitoring plant equipment. The emphasis must be on the quality of the work that we do. It is not adequate to just produce what others have produced. We must widen our perspectives, we must take up multi–disciplinary joint projects and improve coordination. But what we are really looking for is to produce the best and to remove any signs or mediocrity, whether in the labs or whatever you produce. There is always a vested interest to see that mediocrity is not removed. By inclination, most people would like to see that mediocrity remains. So it is there. But it will be our failing if we are not able to remove mediocrity.

The CSIR laboratories have done tremendously well in providing a base for science and technology throughout the country. It is very easy for us now to say that some of the research was not really necessary. But when we think back to what India was like in the early fifties and then see what has actually been achieved, then we see the tremendous contribution that the CSIR labs have made to the country, and it is no mean achievement. But again, it is not enough.

Today the challenges are many more and unless we reach out well beyond what others are reaching for, we shall not be doing justice to our own scientists, to our people in the country. I know that you have it in you to do this. We would like to see you do this.

❑

20

Operation Clean Ganga

You just witnessed water from various rivers of the country mingling with the Ganga water. Thus are energies generated in all parts of the country unified. Thus is the country made strong. I recall an ancient hymn:

गंगे च यमुनेचैव
गोदावरी सरस्वती
नर्मदे सिन्धु कावेरी
जलऽस्मिन सन्निधिं कुरू ।

Ganga, Yamuna, Godavari, Saraswati, Narmada, Sindhu and Cauvery— May the holy waters of these rivers bless us.

The Ganga is a part of our ancient history. It is a symbol of India's spirituality. When we behold the Ganga, the history of the past five thousand years takes form before our eyes. For these five thousand years India has retained its unified identity. There are very few countries in the world which show this continuity with their history. India is one of those very few. However hard may have been the times, however harsh the difficulties we may have had to face, we have never lost our essential Indianness, our spiritual moorings. And this is true not of any one part of India but of the entire country. It is this spirit that keeps the country strong and united in the face of any aggression, any pressure. How did this come about? Our

* **Clean Ganga Operation, Varanasi, 14 June 1986.**

religiousity is perhaps the most important ingredient of our spirituality. However diverse our creeds, we respect them all, follow them all and encourage them all. This is not a new development. It is a tradition that has continued through the centuries and that has made us strong. The secret of India's strength is thus *Sarvadharma Samabhava*-- equal respect for all religions. If we want to see India strong we must cling to this principle. The other source of our strength is this: whichever cultures came to India, whichever peoples crossed the borders into this land, we made them our own. We kept our hearts and minds open. ,We remained ever willing to hear and understand other point of view. All faiths, all cultures were respected and were always made strong in India. This Indianness has been the source of our strength and it will continue to bring us strength.

India's civilizations of over five thousand years has developed a very deep spirituality in our people, a spirituality which is not bound by rituals and religious rites, but a spirituality which transcends all normal barriers. India, throughout its history has absorbed diverse cultures and civilizations to develop its own glorious civilization. Today, on the banks of the Ganga fed by the mighty snows of the Himalayas and stretching down 2,500 kms. to the Bay of Bengal in the Indian Ocean, we see the area of India which sustains one-third of its population and half its irrigated land. The Ganga is a symbol of our prosperity, our culture, our heritage, our civilization, our philosophy. Many of our religions are linked to the Ganga and perhaps most of all it is the holder of our spirituality and our tradition. Panditji had said: "The Ganga especially is the river of India, beloved of her people, round which are interwined her racial memories, her hopes and fears, her victories and her defeats. She has been a symbol of India's age-long culture and civilization, ever-changing, ever -flowing, yet ever the same Ganga."

The Ganga binds us together. It imbues a unity amongst our people. It makes us one civilization, one nation. The Ganga is a symbol of our tradition of tolerance of synthesis, of poise, it is a challenge to the dark forces that undermine our unity and integrity that try to subvert our ethical and traditional values. These forces of violence and separatism, casteism, of petty self-seeking loyalties, parochialisms, and linguistic and other fanaticism are the forces which threaten to tear India apart. Today, we should pledge, from here on the banks of the Ganga, to fight and uphold the unity and integrity of India, not to be cowed down by terrorism, to preserve our traditional values, our civilization.

We are the inheritors of five thousand years of wisdom, of a relentless freedom struggle against the mightiest of imperial powers, we must not allow this tradition to be subverted by divisions among our people, by divisive forces within us. Our nation stands strong when we are secular— a secular India where every faith, all peoples, all cultures and languages are made stronger, an India where we all develop to the benefit of each and every person in the country, to the benefit of the nation. There is no place for narrow compartments or narrow loyalties. We have to strengthen today the forces that bind India. We have revitalized the National Integration Council and given highest priority to the integrity of the nation, to strengthen our country.

Today, here at Varanasi, we are setting out on a vigorous programme of cleaning the Ganga. No one has ever questioned the purity of the Ganga. But it has been observed of late that we have been letting the purifying waters of the Ganga become polluted. The indiscriminate felling of trees, the destruction of the forests has increased the frequency and intensity of floods, carrying into the Ganga ever increasing amount of filth and silt. The bed of the river has consequently been rising and river transport by boats and barges has been rendered difficult. Then there is the pollution caused by the sullage, the effluents from factories and carcasses of animals, which uninterruptedly find their way into the river. We are now going to stop all this. We are going to see that the water of the river regains its pristine purity. There are many large cities situated on the banks of the Ganga: Kanpur, Allahabad, Patna, Calcutta. There are besides thirty other cities with population exceeding one lakh. Every year some 900 million liters of sullage is discharged from these cities into the Ganga. It will be our endeavour in the next four or five years to see that the discharge of this sullage into the river is stopped and where it cannot be stopped it is allowed to go into the river only after suitable treatment. Doing this will certainly improve the lives of the people living in the vicinity of the river. But the Government alone cannot achieve this. The Government will certainly make sure that the discharge of pollutants into the river is checked. We will bring into operation laws which will ensure that only water free from impurities goes into the Ganga and make an effort to recycle the waste from cities, generate power from it. But the 'Ganga Action Plan' is essentially not a Government plan. It is not intended to be carried out through the P.W.D. and other government agencies. It is intended for people as a whole. People must come forward to clean the river and to see that draining of pollutants into the river is stopped. We have taken the first step. We have cleaned the Ganga in the Rishikesh-Haridwar stretch. You will have noted during the last Kumbh Mela the change in the colour of the water. It is our earnest hope that the water of the river will show a similar change in the vicinity of Varanasi and Calcutta in the coming few years.

It will be our endeavour to get afforestation under way in areas where there has been large-scale felling and in other where the land has been lying fallow so that floods are prevented and silt is not carried into the river. Reclamation of wasteland through social forestry will, I am sure, go a long way towards achieving this end. Along with this, it is also of paramount importance that sullage from cities and other pollutants are prevented from entering the Ganga. Towards this end we have enacted strict deterrent legislation, because if we wish to save India we must save our environment. When the environment is damaged, a bit of India dies. This process has been going on and the task before us is to bring back the dead part to life. I trust that the people of the entire country will enthusiastically, participate, in the programme and it will be transformed into a people's movement. I trust that the beginning made here today at Varanasi, will in time grow into a mighty programme encompassing the whole of India, every river valley, so that not only the Ganga but all the rivers of India will once again regain the purity of waters that characterized them thousands of years ago.

Varanasi lies on the Ganga and is inextricably bound up with the history of India, with the ancient wisdom of India and the philosophies of India. For thousands of years our seers and savants have sat on the *ghats* here asking and answering questions about life, about the outer space, about the cosmos. It was on the banks of the Ganga here that Tulsidas composed the *Ramacharitamanas,* it was from here that Ravidas sent out his message, and it was a few kilometers from here, at Sarnath that the Buddha for the first time preached his gospel. It was here that the Jain Tirthankar Parsvanath attained *mahaparinirvana.* Guru Nanak travelled all the way here to meet Sant Kabir and Baba Farid. Guru Tegh Badhadur practised his penance here for seven long months. Guru Gobind Singh lived here at the Bibi Bagh gurudwara and Bhai Gurudas wrote many hymns for the *Guru Granth Sahib* here. The gold plating on the temple of Vishwanath was donation, from Maharaja Ranjit Singh, Mirza Ghalib in his 'Chiraghe Dair' says of Varanasi.

तं आला बनारस चश्मे बद्दूर
बहिश्ते रघुर्रमो फिरदोसे मामूर ।

May God, the Most High save the city
of Banaras from the evil eye.
Because it is a pleasant heaven and an
abundant paradise in itself.

Many churches too came up in Varanasi in the course of time. Mother Teresa has started an institution here. The Theosophical Society and various other societies are also represented here. Among the buildings here we find the Vishwanath temple, gurudwara Guru Bagh, the mosque of Alamgir and the temple of Bharat Mata. Whether we consider the temples and the mosques or the secular institutions such as schools, colleges and universities, we see that people of diverse faiths, speaking diverse languages, have been coming here from all parts of India to acquire knowledge and to seek spiritual solace.

The contribution of Varanasi in our struggle for freedom has also been considerable. Newab Wazir Ali Khan resorted to civil disobedience here, first in 1799 and then again in 1810. In 1905 it was the venue of the Congress Session. In the early years of the national movement Varanasi stood at the vanguard. We are trying to carry the spirit of Varanasi, its message of knowledge, tolerance, *Sarvadharma Samabhava,* equal respect for all religions and its patriotism to every part of India. We trust that we shall be able to achieve this purpose through the Ganga Action Plan.

It is our endeavour to enlist the co-operation of the various voluntary organisations in the country for this effort. We must see that the Ganga does not remain an empty symbol but becomes a means for furthering the unity and strength of India and enriching our national life and our future.

As we begin the programme of cleaning the Ganga

here we hope a sewage plant will be set up so that the sewage does not flow into the Ganga. It will then provide us manure as well as power. Let us further hope that the construction of the bridge which has been hanging fire ever since Indiraji laid its foundation stone many years ago will be expedited. Soon after we assumed office we had taken the work in hand. The loan from the World Bank has been sanctioned. Tenders are being invited and the work will start very soon.

In the end, I would like to say that just as we mingled the waters from various rivers from all over the country with the Ganga water, we must see that energies from all parts of India are welded together to make India strong and united.

❐

21

Create Scientific Awareness

This Conference of experts from the world working in the frontiers of science being held in Delhi brings home to us the need of science and technology in our development process. Many of us feel that without scientific and technological developments, India, and for that matter any developing country, cannot progress. Others question this and feel that for a country like India, with only one-third of our population literate, with approximately one-third of it below the poverty line, science and technology are a sort of esoteric waste of time; they are not really necessary for our country. Perhaps the answer lies in the relationship of that research in the science and technology that we develop with the daily lives of our people, with rural India, with our war on poverty and to bring back to our people what they have forgotten, and that is that India at one time was a centre of learning, was a centre of wisdom and technology that India got colonized; it was the better European technology, better utilizations of energy, the industrial revolution which bypassed us, that allowed others to put us down and it is only if we are able to once more develop our own technologies, once more get back to the forefront of learning that we will really be able to be strong and independent.

If we want, as Prof. M.G.K. Menon has said quoting Gandhiji, to remove every tear from every eye, it can only

* Address after inaugurating the laboratory building of the National Institute of Immunology, New Delhi, 6 October 1986.

be done with science and technology. There can be no better example that this Institute that we are inaugurating today.

Immunizations has change the life all over the world. In India, more specially in the last few years we have been able to eradicate a number of diseases and with your help we look forward to eradicate many more. Ultimately, it all leads to a better life for our people. We could not possibly have achieved this without technology.

When we talk of technology, it is not just a question of getting a computer here or a very highly sophisticated piece of equipment there, it is how that equipment is used for the benefit of an average individual in his everyday life and the instrument need not be such that it is utilized by an average Indian; there are many examples; immunization is one. You work at the frontiers of science in an establishment such as this of universities, but your work goes out to hundreds of millions of people who need not have ever come close to the level of technology that you would be using. We have seen a similar interaction of science and rural India in the Green Revolution where very highly sophisticated work on seeds is used by farmers in their daily work. Again very high technology was used by perhaps illiterate people. Similarly, we had a white revolution in dairying again it is using the best modern technology but in such a manner that illiterate people are able to benefit from it, and this is what we must do.

The feeling that technology is bad and a developing country must not use technology is a totally negative thinking. It result in people who are willing to work, have the experience and have the knowledge leave India and go and work elsewhere. If we are to utilize the brains that are available in India, we must create an environment in which they can work. An environment which promotes mediocrity cannot be an environment in which excellence can flourish. We must change this mood which benefits non-achievers to a mood which really benefits the achievers and then we will really be able to move much faster. It is only then that Indians, many in very high positions in the forefront of technology and research, will want to come back and help in our work, in institutions such as this, for the development of India, for our progress.

We have to see that such institutions move on and do not continue to rely on foreign inputs but at the same time I would like to say that it is also not adequate to try and cut off all foreign links and only look within. We have to have a healthy interaction but we must develop strength enough in ourselves to be able to stand on our own feet. Imported technology should be used as a stepping stone to get to our goals and targets, not to be relied upon at every stage of our development.

Again it is not enough just to be working at the frontiers of science and technology, we must develop the capability of changing that into a useful product to be used by our people. Traditionally, we have not been very good at that in India; but we are trying to change that. We have set up a number of technology missions which start with the frontiers of science and hopefully will end up in the homes of our people, in their daily lives. If India is to win the struggle against poverty, it is only with the most modern and best methods that we stand a chance.

We look forward to you and many other scientists like you to help us in this giant step that the country has to take.

❒

22

Inculcate Scientific Temper

We celebrate today Panditji's 97th birthday, having an exhibition on Science and land for a holiday home for children.

The science exhibition which I had the pleasure of seeing this morning is terribly exciting and I would right at the beginning like to congratulate all those who have been involved in putting it up, those behind the scene, and specially all those children who helped us in going around the exhibition and explain all the little bits and pieces, even though we did not give them enough time to do it thoroughly.

Panditji's main thrust when he looked to the future of India and the world, was on science and on children, as the two strengths which could take our country to face the challenges of the future. We have from that early beginning developed our sciences to a very high degree. Today, in certain fields India is right there at the forefront with the leading nations and we are proud that we have achieved this. We know that we could not have achieved this without the foundation that Panditji had laid almost forty years ago. Panditji had talked of a scientific temper and interest in science, in logical thinking, in reasoning, and no bigotry or superstition.

* Address while inaugurating the Exhibition on New Biology, New Delhi, 14 November 1986.

We still have to reach this scientific temper down to the grassroots in our country, and that is why we have taken up this major challenge with a New Education Policy. We hope we will be able to reach out to every corner of the country, to build this scientific temper, to prepare our youth for the challenges that face them ahead.

Traditionally we have set our learning too much by rote. We accept too readily what our teachers tell us and, of course, we all know that in reality everything that we are taught is likely to change very substantially as knowledge increases in the coming years. When I was in school almost everything that you see in this exhibition was not known and we were taught a completely different set of rules. Of course, our teachers at that time told us that was the Bible and that was absolutely the ultimate knowledge and there was nothing beyond that, but of course we know that there is no such thing. I have no doubt that 20 years or 30 years from now when they have an exhibition here, what we see today will be totally outdated and the new knowledge will replace completely what we hold today as the ultimate knowledge. But this attitude has not come into our teaching process. An inquisitive mind is not built. Perhaps, the teachers lack confidence, perhaps they lack training, perhaps, they lack quality and standards. Well, it is for us to build this into the system so that the children do grow up challenging, questioning, asking, so that their mind broadens into new horizons and does not remain restricted as our education system in the country makes it today.

The scientific thrust in India has been the cutting edge in our industrial revolution. Sometimes we do not see too much of this, when we look at our average market place, but if we look at the more specialized areas, perhaps the seeds that the farmers use, some of our defence equipment, certain other specialized fields like nuclear engineering, like our space programme, we see very clearly how this scientific thrust has helped develop our industries, and now for the first time we are seeing it broaden and reach out to other industry. We look towards expanding this and really energizing the system starting with a scientific thrust and then with a technological push.

The exhibition that you will see today is the essence of what we are all about, and it is research in these fields that is going to be very important for any country, more specially for a country like India which is facing tremendous challenges in almost every field challenging diseases, in the environment, in growing food. Many of the answers lay in these areas, and I have no doubt that our scientists who are already among the top in these fields will rise higher and will deliver for the country what we need for our future. We have seen the Green Revolution, which has come about from just such technology. We look towards tissue culture and other frontline areas to develop our agriculture, our forestry, and to protect our environment. We look towards it for our dairy farming, our food, our medicines. We hope that this exhibition will raise that curiosity in our children so that they may go towards these areas and be ready for the challenges when they come in the next few decades.

Technology sometimes is said to be anti-poor. I see it absolutely as the reverse. Only those countries which have technology have been able to face the challenge of poverty. I would even say, by definition, poverty means using inferior technology in your daily life; being affluent only means using better technology and if we are to remove poverty, we must give better technology in the daily life of the average people in India, not the one which seeks to transfer computers into villages, but the technology properly used, like the examples I have given, in medicine, in agriculture, in forestry, in dairying.

These are frontline technologies but used by our farmers, by our ordinary folk. They do not need university degrees to use such technology, but is only when we make it available to them that we will be able to remove their poverty and to lift them up.

I trust that this exhibition will create that inquisitive spirit and kindle that fire which will drive our younger generation to greater heights.

❒

23

Resources and Human Well-Being: Inputs from Science and Technology

Let me start by wishing you a very happy New Year, and also by congratulating all those who have won awards. It is very heartening to see so many women among the awardees. My special congratulations to them.

The tradition of the Prime Minister addressing the Science Congress was set in motion by Panditji many years ago. Not just because he felt science was important and required government patronage, but because he felt, as we feel today, that India's development was linked entirely to the development of science in our country. The two cannot be separated. If India is to develop, it would have to catch up with the rest of the world. There is only one way this can be done and that way is through the development of science and technology and helping our scientists and technologists to do so.

In addressing you today, I would like to reaffirm that faith which the people of India have in our scientists and the root of development through science.

Bangalore is a very appropriate town to hold the Science Congress. The history of science in Bangalore goes back to a very long time. It is the home of Dr. Visvesvaraya, Prof. C.V. Raman. Dr. Vainu Bappu. Today

* Plenary Session, 74th Session of the Indian Science Congress Association, Bangalore, 3 January 1987.

it boasts of many centres of scientific excellence and technological achievements. This annual conference brings together many scientists, institutions, agencies and disciplines. And that in itself makes it an important forum for communication, for comparing notes, for cross-fertilization of ideas.

Addressing the Science Congress in January 1948, Prof. C.V. Raman said, "There is only one solution for India's economic problems and that is science, more science, and still more science". Yet today we spend less than one per cent of our GNP on science. There is a real constraint on the resources available for scientific development. Industry invests almost nothing in real R & D. We have to alter this. It is perhaps a little late for this plan, but we must set the ball rolling now for the Eighth Plan, 1990-95. So that the proportion is altered positively and our science really gets the thrust that it needs.

In the meantime, we have to deploy our brain power in the most selective way. It is not enough just to pursue excellence. We must at the same time look at the vast mediocrity that has collected in our system. We have to weed it out. We have to select the bad and the worse, and get rid of them both. We have to see that the quality of our science is second to none. This cannot be by Government fiat or Government action alone. This must come through a scientific consensus. It must come from the community. The vested interests must be broken by the community itself. Government cannot be successful in tackling such problems.

India has had a long tradition of scientific, achievements. We have perhaps the highest number of Nobel Laureates in any developing country. Our leading institutions - Indian Institute of Science in Bangalore is a very good example - are at the frontline of research in India and perhaps in the world. We must thrust for more innovation and less imitation. Let us face it. We must get on the right to the frontline. The tradition of Srinivasa Ramanujan whose centenary we have been celebrating this year, of probing, of daring, is what we must aim for. We must link India's needs and the need for the world in science.

Science is a worldwide discipline, not confined by political boundaries or by any narrow walls. It cuts across all such boundaries. What is needed is a better interaction, better cross-fertilization of ideas, or disciplines. It is easier perhaps for our scientists, because India has had a long tradition of assimilation and synthesis. Our five thousand years have developed a civilization that has been ready to adopt from everywhere and to reject what is not good enough. We have shown this in our tradition and in our culture, in our heritage, as it is developed. We must now adopt the same path for our scientific developments as well.

Whatever the origins, however alien an idea may be, we must not reject it on the simple ground that it is not our own. We should be open-minded. This quality has to be imbibed to achieve strength and continuity of science in India perhaps even its real survival. This is what has given our civilization the strength and this is what will give Indian Science its strength. Despite political turbulence, despite economic disruptions, foreign invasions and colonization, India's civilization has survived because of the strength. Our science will flourish to the extent it is self confident and open-minded, keep abreast of what is happening in the rest of the world, recognizes excellence, and exchanges ideas and concepts, technologies and techniques.

The pyramid, to be stable, must have a sound and broad base. The talent at the top must be supported by thousands below.

Panditji had talked of a scientific temper. The scientific temper consists not just of understanding science, but of cultivating through the reasons, or fighting superstition and rule. It is only through such a scientific temper that we can overcome the challenges that our country is facing today. The vast, untapped potential that is available cannot be exploited because of lack of science in our education. Panditji believed that it is ignorance which led to injustice, intolerance and narrow mindedness. And that knowledge, wisdom as a scientific temper would give us the right values of tolerance and secularism.

The scientific temper can be looked at in two aspects. First, ordered thought, logical thinking, going from an established fact to the provable conclusion, subject to intuitive insight, rigorous inductive deduction, the testing of intellectual integrity, the readiness to relinquish a view when proved untenable, however long held and well favoured. The second aspect is equally important; a questing, probing, restless mind which take nothing for granted, challenges any assumption and any convention, a mind that refuses to acquiesce in anything shoddy, that demands the best, that insists on bettering even the best.

Alas, the society at large in India, sometimes even within the scientific community, is lacking in many of these aspects. India's development has been in many ways different from and the reverse of that of the West. In the West, the superstition, bigotry and stagnation of the Dark Ages were followed by centuries of painful awakening, in fits and starts with many setbacks. The first beginning, known as the Renaissance, slowly seeped through art, philosophy and science from Copernicus to James Watt, from the Renaissance to the Industrial Revolution, taking approximately 250 years. It took 150 years to spread from England to the Continent, across the Atlantic to the West, and over the Urals to the East.

In India, the Western experience of four centuries has been telescoped into four decades. We have not gone from a scientific temper to industrialization, but we have industrialization leading to a scientific temper. Therefore, there is too much a race which leads to imitation and too little innovation. We need to break out of the rut. We need bold, revolutionary, assertive and aggressive thinking. We must demand improvement, we must reject what is inadequate, we must try to secure the best.

In education, our school system does not instil the inquiring spirit in the minds of our children. A questioning mind is not developed. We are taught by rote. We are taught that the teacher is always right and correct. We are taught never to question the teacher. Precisely the opposite of what a scientific mind must demand. Our schools are lacking in equipment and aid, our IITs, although they are among the best in the world, are still not used for the development process as they should be used. They remain isolated pockets not entirely related to the problems of the country.

In quantity, we say we have the third largest pool of manpower. But it is grossly bloated by modernity and this must be cut out if our science and our scientists are to compete. Last year we brought out a New Education Policy, which we feel will bring down many of these barriers. It will need the cooperation of the scientific community. It will need fresh guidelines, which must come in now in the initial implementation, to see that the right temper is developed. It will require much greater involvement of the scientific community in the education system. We cannot afford that community to be isolated and un-involved and then expect a scientific temper and the lot of bright minds developing in the country.

Science teaching in our school is poor. The chasm between scientific institutions, which are perhaps equal to those anywhere in the world, and our scientific facilities in the universities is again vast. Progress is not possible if excellence is the exception and mediocrity the norm. We have to concentrate on those areas where excellence is developing.

Our Universities are human resources base for centres of excellence. They are the agencies for translating research into action. We look to our New Education Policy to preserve, nurture and foster excellence. We are looking for a massive quality of upgradation in our schools and in our Universities. We hope that this will lead to a massive increase in the qualitative levels of the scientific output from these institutions. The quality of Indian science must equal the quality of our educational institutions and our management. They must be involved in the creative process. There is too much red-tape, bureaucratic delays and tolerance of irrelevance and mediocrity, which must be removed. The challenge is to make science not an esoteric pursuit, but relevant to the welfare and well-being of people everywhere. I do not mean that science must not strive for blue-sky research and basic fundamental research. But it must at some point link to what is relevant to the people today, because science is a tool of development.

Our overriding priority is the removal of poverty, the war on poverty. Mr. Chief Minister (Shri R.K. Hegde) you have very rightly asked the question why we are so poor while we have such brilliant scientists and such brilliant research. While I shall leave it to you to find an answer to that. I could perhaps just say a few words. One reason, I am sure, is that we from Government do not chase our scientists to give us the answer that we are looking for. Instead we chase the bureaucracy. We must chase the scientists for our answers. We must not get off their backs till they give us the answers.

You mentioned a case in point- water reserves. I know

what it has been like chasing all the State governments, telling them. "Look, here are the maps, for heaven's sake use them" We have got to reverse this. We have to get the Government's coming to the scientific departments and saying. "Look, these are our problems, we want answers. You give us the answers." Well, it is when this basic attitude changes in Government that our scientists will be giving us the results that we are asking for. Today they are giving us the results that they are looking for, which is right. Which must be done. But if we want the answers to our problems, we have got to put the problems to you,. And we have got to bully you and push you and force you into giving us the answer.

We have developed in our planning process a vested interest in keeping things as they are. It might sound contradictory, you want development and you want progress, but at the same time you want things to remain where they were. That is what our educational system has done. It has prevented anyone who has got a good education from using that education effectively. We have channeled that into non-productive areas. The best scientists find it better to go into management than to go into scientific development, into scientific research.

We have got to change these things. We have to change the basic thinking in our society. Development must relate to science and science must relate to development. It is only then that we shall be getting the answers, we shall get the development that we are looking for. Again, there is a very major political question involved. Whenever we talk of using science as tool, immediately we are challenged by a number of political groups within our party and other parties, who have got entrenched in keeping the *status quo,* in keeping things as they are. In the rural areas, in the towns, in our Universities and colleges, sometimes even in our scientific institutions, we must have the will to break this vested interest and weed out mediocrity. When we start talking of science, when we start talking of moving ahead more rapidly, it is the mediocre who are threatened. In keeping the status quo, in keeping mediocrity alive, with whatever label we might call it in our social doctrine or in our political pamphlet, we stifle excellence. We do not allow it to grow.

How is it that Indians, when they go outside India, are able to rise almost immediately to the highest levels in almost any field, not just in science and technology but in every field? But here, it is too stifling, too tough for them to fight the vested interests. This fight has to be a national fight, which we must put up jointly with the help of all our political parties. It is not something which can be made into a party matter. It is only when we are able to tackle this challenge that we shall really start getting result from science and technology relevant to our development programme.

We have tried to give a certain number of thrust in important areas related to our development. We have devised a number of scientific missions. They are missions, because we want to link the scientists in the laboratory with the end result in the field, whether in the village or the town or in a home. Some are ready, some have done well, and some I am told, have not progressed as they should have. I do not want to go through all of them. I am due to get a briefing in the next few days on each of them. I hope that we shall be able, through these missions, to give a proper thrust to scientific development and the relationship between scientific development and economic development. The new areas that these missions will be addressing themselves will be roughly in bio-technology, remote-sensing, weather forecasting, communicable diseases and materials. All these are areas of basic relevance to our development. The needs are immediate. We must see that activity is precise and measured and effective and not bogged down in mediocrity and bureaucracy.

In some areas, the last 40 years since Independence have shown tremendous achievements. In space, we are among the pioneers. In a couple of years, we shall be launching a West German payload. The manner ISRO is developing is equal to any centre in the world. In atomic energy, we are amongst the frontliners. In self-reliance in non-conventional energy we have done useful work. Our agricultural scientists have given us the Green Revolution and really shown that when the chips are down, it is our scientists that give us the answers. We need to look to you, scientists, for answers more often. You have restored the position we held in the past, in the time of Aryabhatta and Bhaskara.

Our economic achievements, although very substantial, have still taken us only to the top of the Junior League. Now we should make it our national objective to get into the Big League and become a front ranker in the Big League. We must match in quality the quantity that we have developed. We must break the chain of high cost inefficiency, poor quality, poor economy of scale, excessive protection, and secondary technology, both indigenous and foreign. We must break into self-reliance, not just to protect inefficiency. We must not shut our eyes to progress anywhere. Self-reliance means indigenous efforts and alertness to outside technological progress. It mean developing imported technology, making the next breakthrough ourselves - closing the technology gap. To monitor changes in that gap and to make optimal use of our assets are the challenge before our scientific community. We have one third of the world's cattle, but only 7 per cent of the milk. It is such challenges that our scientists must face. What is needed is to foster the genius of the most talented and develop a sense of hard work and dedications in the entire scientific community.

Pandit Nehru had said: "It is science alone that can solve the problem of hunger and poverty, of insanitation and illiteracy, or superstition, and vast resources running to waste, of a big country inhabited by starving people". This is the prism which encompasses all our needs and aspirations.

What is needed in our nuclear age is a deep transformaton of the human psyche, to connect thoughts and ideas to contemporary reality. This connection is perhaps the Ahimsa that Gandhiji and Panditji talked of Science validates our ancient wisdom.

❐

24

Make Brand India Products

It gives me great pleasure today to inaugurate this conference, this Congress of Engineers, perhaps the first Congress which cuts across various disciplines of engineers. I feel this is very important today, specially today, because, as each field of engineering advances, the overlap between that and other fields is increasing rapidly and it is very necessary that this cross-fertilization of ideas takes place and there can be nothing better than a Congress like this for such cross-fertilization to take place. Let me congratulate you on this first Congress.

I hope in this Congress, you will step back from your individual disciplines and take a more holistic look at engineering and how engineering can help our industrialization and our development process. The engineer cannot remain just an engineer, he has to be a tool in the development of our society. His role is a societal role. And, as a professional in today's world, this is critical to our development and our progress. Calcutta is a very appropriate venue for your Congress. Calcutta was the best place of the engineering industry in India. This made Calcutta the Industrial Capital of India. Unfortunately things have not developed as they should have and Calcutta and Bengal have fallen behind from that leading

* First Indian Engineering Congress, Calcutta, 10 January 1987.

position. Perhaps we should have a bit of introspection to see why this has happened. I do not intend to go into all the details here, but it could be useful to see why a part of the country, which led in industrialization, today needs a big injection, to even catch up with the rest of the country.

It is not only a question of government policies or labour, it is also a question of the attitudes of the industry itself. Is the industry aggressive enough? Is it looking ahead? Unfortunately industry today is not meeting the challenges like it should. Today, your Congress should address itself to all these challenges right from government policy towards industry, policy towards labour, policy in location, in energy, in communication, right down to what you can do yourself in your industry. Today, from here you should also look into how we can once more make Calcutta and Bengal the leader in our engineering industry. We have committed ourselves to this restructuring, reconstructing of Bengal and we look forward to your cooperation in this venture of building a *Nutan* Bengal. There are certain basic challenges that you face and that we face as a nation. They are not going to be easy to overcome. The renaissance in thinking, is, perhaps, yet to come. The process has been reversed. Perhaps, that is one of the reasons that we are not aggressive enough and innovative enough. And we are always a bit defensive in our engineering, in our technology, but India can no longer remain in that position. That was satisfactory for the first stage of our development, for the first stage of our industrialization. The next stage will not take place if we do not change our basic ways of thinking. We transplanted an engineering industry into a society which reeled under two hundred years of colonization and subjugation. To a very great degree, we have been able to change the society, but as I said earlier, that basic step of changing our way of thinking has not taken place yet, and we must do that now.

The engineering industry has to give the thrust. It gave the thrust initially, bringing about an engineering revolution in the country. It must give a new thrust in innovation and in thinking. It must be the pace-setter like it has been during the initial stages of our development. This gives you a very special responsibility, responsibility of setting standards for the industry, standards of performance, standards of economy, standards of quality. This is another challenge which the industry must meet on its own. It is more difficult in the less competitive environment in which Indian industry operates. Our industry has grown from a very meagre beginning forty years ago to an industry which is extensive and broad-based and has covered just about every angle and every type of production, but we have not broken the barrier on competitive production, on quality production. This is the challenge which you must meet now. The hard fact is that industry cannot grow entirely through protection and through subsidies. A sellers market will mean poor quality goods, will mean high prices.

Panditji said, "The cost is becoming higher and higher and the question today is whether we can afford our own Engineering Industry." I know in certain fields we cannot afford it any more. If an indigenous unit is going to cost us double that of an imported product then the cost is taken from another project, taken from development of the country, pulled out from the pockets of the poor of our country. How long can we afford this? How much longer will the poor of this country put up with industry which is not delivering the goods to them, which is absorbing funds which are rightfully theirs for development? Public sector is the commanding height of our industry today. But every time we subsidies the public sector, we ourselves pay for it. When government pays for it, it is the poor people of India, who pay.

We cannot afford to subsides our industries at the cost of the poor. To my mind, this is not socialism; this is robbing the poor of the country. The private sector does not get such preference. But that does not mean that here efficiency is the rule. It truly shelters behind vast controls and tremendous levels of protection. We cannot continue this for ever. I do not suggest to pull the carpet from under your feet and say tomorrow it is all gone, because, we do not want the industry to collapse. But our industry must deliver competitively for our country, for our people. Only then will it be technologically innovative. Only then will it really help the country in its development process. We have seen too often that the government has to step in and nationalize, or take over sick private sector units. This too, I am told, is socialism. I am told if we waste the money of the poor people, perhaps thousands of people, to save the jobs of perhaps twenty or thirty people, this is considered as socialism. I think we really need to review our thinking.

How long can we pump in forty, fifty crores into industry which perhaps provides jobs to thirty people, fifty people, two hundred people? Would that fifty crores not be better invested in a dynamic industry or perhaps in water supply or in a communication system or a road? I do not suggest that we suddenly switch it off. But a gradual, not too gradual, shift must be made and the people of this country must be made to realize that they cannot be held to ransom by industry and labour that does not perform. This situation can be rectified and it must be rectified.

Our scientists, our engineers, our technologists, invariably rise to the occasion. We have seen it during the sixties when we had tremendous problems with our food. We had to import vast quantities of food and the question before us was whether India could survive as an independent nation or we would get suffocated to death, or be subjugated in one form or another. The challenge was put to our scientists. It was put to our technologists, our extension workers, our farmers, who took that challenge, converted it into engineering goods, into irrigation projects, into power and into production and within a decade and a half we were able to export foodgrains. We must do the same in our industries, more specially in our engineering industry. It is not good enough just to keep importing technology and living with that technology. That phase surely is over. It was the first phase in our industrialization, first phase in our development, when we did not know. We were learning. Now that we have taken the first step, the second step has to be built on that. Every technology that we import must be developed. We must import technology today to export technology tomorrow. If we are not aggressive and we do not go that way, we cannot survive as an independent country. India has shown that it can do it. I have no doubt that the engineering industry will deliver and show the country that when it needs the engineering industry, the engineers will accept the challenge and deliver what the country needs. We have seen the capital goods industry having problems because we opened up imports. We are working on how this can be resolved. Perhaps, the most difficult problem that the industry is facing is that of high cost of imports and this has to be tackled. It will require political will. It will require a lot of fresh thinking on the part of the Planning Commission.

The responsibility of the Institution of Engineers is to stimulate a sense of responsibility in the industry, to encourage new concepts to meet the challenges that lie ahead. Perhaps one of the biggest challenges is going to be to shift our thinking from fiscal or financial targets to physical targets and try to reach those physical targets within the financial constraints that we have. When I say we, I include government, I include the Central Government, the State Governments, all of ourselves, not just Bengal. We divide too easily the work to be done by the funds that are available and say, "cannot be done, more funds are required."

You have, I feel, coined a new word 'technovation'. I looked it up in the dictionary and I could not find it. I hope that this seminar, this Congress will be as innovative in its thinking as you have been in thinking of the terminology which you use on your cover. Innovation cannot be for the sake of novelty alone. It must be linked to better quality, a better product, a more reliable product.

We must, as a country, have our war on poverty, as our prime task and everything else must be linked to that. The engineering industry must gear itself for that battle. We have, on our part, put forward a number of technological missions. We have called them missions because we thought that a new, a totally new, approach was required in these areas, an approach which started in the laboratories and ended in the houses and farms of our people. An approach which not only gave us time bound targets but also gave us the new ways of achieving those targets efficiently on schedule and perhaps at lower costs. Better technology is a better future. When we talk of development we are by definition talking of giving better technology to our people, whatever the level of that better technology may be. A tractor is better than a bullock cart, a water pump is better than a Persian wheel. We do not have to put a computer in the village. That is not development.

Jawaharlal Nehru had said that the aim of scientific progress should be a marriage between ancient Indian thought, based on spriritual approach, and modern scientific endeavour, based on experimentation in search of truth. Nothing could be more right for us than that. Today, you are the inheritors of a great Indian tradition— a tradition spanning back five thousand years.

❐

25

Protect Environment of the Seven Regions

The cause that brings you here is of great concern to us. Your deliberations will be of tremendous importance to the millions of the poorest people who live here in this part of the world. There is no false division between development and the imperative of preserving and enriching our environment. Our experience has shown that the neglect of environment is at the cost of development. We have found that we have not evaluated the cost of the deprived environment while calculating the cost and benefits of particular development projects. We have seen during these past two years that we are giving more and more relief for drought and flood. We have, for example, during the first, one and a half years of the Seventh Plan which is 1985 and half of 1986, given an equal amount to what we gave to the full Sixth Five Year Plan in terms of relief. The floods have been severe, the droughts have been severe. When it rains, the water with the top soil washes out into the sea and it is not available during the rest of the year. Primarily because we have neglected our environment, we have degraded our environment, we are paying a very heavy cost for it now.

We cannot have development today without evaluating the full cost of every project, not just the immediate cost but the long-term cost. We cannot leave

* Third Governing Council Meeting of South Asia Co-operative Environment Programme (SACEP), New Delhi, 12 January 1987.

the long-term part of that cost for future generations to pay. We cannot leave the legacy of deficit in development. We have to account for it during our own generation. The cost of protecting the environment goes up higher as the environment gets more and more degraded. We have seen today the fire-fighting that we are having to do to protect the environment,. It is a very heavy drain on our exchequer. But if it had been during the earlier phases of our development, the cost would have been much less.

The seven regions that are covered by SACEP are amongst the most ravaged and degraded in the world. Our forest cover is among the lowest, there is rampant desertification, rapid denudation, fast soil erosion, and there is a very high rate of growth in air, water, noise and other types of pollution. Our challenge will be to ensure economic development and protect the environment, not to have separate watertight compartments, but evolve one integrated approach to remove backwardness and to move ahead. This integrated approach will require a lot of new thinking in our Planning Commission, in our bureaucracy and political levels. The immediate aspects of protecting the environment become very political. If a forest is to be protected, the immediate result is that fuel wood is not available, timber for construction is not available. Other benefits and fruits from the forests are not available to the poorer sections, to those who live near the forests, those who live in the forests. So, there is a dilemma. This dilemma will have to be faced squarely. It cannot be overcome by stiff legal action. The alternatives must be found. Alternative fuel, alternative construction material, alternatives to the other products that are available through the forests. We have to also look anew at our opening up of forested areas, how we do it, and how we are going to protect those areas which are still heavily forested. We have to give priority in the peripheral areas of forests to things such as fuel, construction material so that forests do not come under pressure. We have to see how we can change our fiscal and taxation policies so that other cheaper materials are more readily available, as an alternative.

What is needed is a holistic view of the human needs of the area, of the poor who are living in and around the forests and the environment that needs protection. Man and nature have lived in harmony for centuries. The balance was not upset. The tribals who lived in forests have not upset the balance in the forests. It is what we call civilization and development that has encroached upon nature and has destroyed her environment. We must develop the right tools of development and for protection of the environment, We must develop the human genius to give us the right answers. The irony is that the technological progress which we have witnessed requires much higher levels of technology to fight the damage that the very technological progress has caused. Engineers who did not think twice about exploiting natural resources must think very carefully about whether that exploitation is to the ultimate benefit of the human beings living in that area. In our part of the world in South Asia, we are very interdependent, perhaps, much more so, when it comes to environment and other spheres of our activities. Degradation in our country-- one part of a country— can have very serious consequences on another country; and it is very necessary that we work together to maintain the ecological balance in South Asia.

We have to look closely at the more endangered areas in our part of the world, the mangrove, the coral islands, the particular ecosystems in each zone. We had a seminar, the first seminar in 1983 but very little action has taken place since then. We need to give a greater thrust to specific actions, time bound actions, regional actions to keep pace with each of our specific national action programmes because time is running out very fast on our environment. In this area, India being the largest, is perhaps the worst affected and that has given us some experience in tackling these problems, in combating the degradation of our forests and our environment. We laid our expertise in front of SACEP and in whatever way we can, we will try to help all our brother countries. Our friends and neighbours have also gained expertise in these areas and we would be happy to cooperate with them in developing our common expertise.

I wish you all the very best in your deliberations to press ahead with deliberate speed. What we need are concrete plans of action that have quick impact on the environment, on the people that are suffering from the consequence of a deprived environment, from the ravaged environment.

❒

26

Excellence in Electronics and Telecommunications

I would like to congratulate your President on his interesting and thought provoking address. Some of the points, he has raised, apply to Government. Many apply to the private sector. We on our part will try and follow them up and see what we can do to help in increasing production. I do hope that industry will also look at the points that have been raised more aggressively, with more innovation and in a more challenging manner than found in most of our industries who always look for handouts and protection. It is not handouts and protection which enables an industry to develop. This applies especially to electronics and telecommunication. They can develop with competition, with a very aggressive attitude on the part of everyone involved. We hope that we shall be able to help you in building such an attitude and atmosphere in the industry.

As I recall, we had a seminar last August, 1986 and at the seminar many new directions were discussed and suggested for detailed workout during the year. Some progress has been made. I believe, in many areas. We should first push harder to ensure that work on those areas is completed, as we open out in new areas.

* 30th Technical Convention, Institute of Electronics and Telecommunication Engineers, New Delhi, 16 January 1987.

Electronics is today an agency for the development of perhaps almost every sector of our growth. Electronics is ushering in a new post-Industrial Revolution. We missed the first one. We cannot miss the second one. Electronics and telecom are the tools for our development today. This convention, I hope will not just give new directions but will look at what happens in between Conventions, not just hope from point to point but cover the ground very thoroughly in those 364 days that pass before the next convention.

Electronics has brought about a revolution in technology. But we have still not been able to bring about a revolution in our thinking. We still think as we did years ago. In India, we are very much tied up in our old, heavy weight and cumbersome systems. But more than that I am referring to a very basic attitude of mind. This, I believe, has not changed very much in other parts of the world either. We are still in a sense not complete master of the technology that we develop. We are always trying to catch up with technological advances. This, surely, is not good enough. We have to have a much faster change in our societies, be revolutionary in our attitudes of mind, to be able to cope with the rapid changes in technology that are coming in. In Government we are trying to bring about these changes, but Government has tremendous inertia and it will need a lot of push and force to make it move. We will not be lacking in this, but we will require the cooperation of everyone involved in the telecom and electronics industry to bring about this change.

One of the most important aspects of the telecom industry or the electronics industry is that we must become self-reliant. It is not enough to keep looking for import concessions and keep asking for protection. Self-reliance will have to be the key. You have raised some very valid points about the volume of production and the price of goods. We shall have to study these to see how we can give you enough volume of production to satisfy the requirement of R&D which is essential. There is today almost no real R&D being done within the country. We must not fall into the trap of mere imitative research. This is what I meant when I said there was no real R&D because with some exceptions, our investment in R&D is in terms of replacing what has already been discovered and invented and manufactured elsewhere by something of our own. This is important, but what is more important is to take that qualitative jump into real frontline thinking. This is still not taking place, the way it should, in India.

We are still looking towards what others are doing. We have seen their discoveries, we read about them. They are not accessible to us because of restrictions. So we channel our R&D to try and work out how they did it. This is good but we should be right up in the front line, thinking ahead of what others are thinking. That is when our industry will really get off its feet. We still have not crossed that barrier.

In some areas, specially in Defence, we are on the borderline of that; we are on the verge of crossing over into really frontline thinking, which will then lead to the truly frontline technologies. But in other areas we are still very far behind. This basic switch in thinking in what is required for dynamism in our industry. We have chased other people's discoveries for forty years and we have built a foundation for our own development. It is time that we change over and try to become world leaders in certain specific areas and then in much broader fields. To become world leaders, we shall have to become a coveted source of supply for others, which mean very high quality standards, very high management levels, very good delivery schedules. Again, we are not up to the mark. Reliability is not good enough. Human engineering is still something that our engineers do not even dream about. It is still banging things in a box, painting it some colour, and throwing it out and hoping that everything will work from there onwards. But a total design package is not done, to the best of my knowledge, in any product that is truly Indian. We cannot become world leaders if we leave this important area out.

Some developing countries have broken a barrier and become world leaders in certain lines of products, mostly consumer products. We have taken a different attitude to our development. We have tried to lay a broader foundation, a stronger foundation, and build more on the industrial and strategic side. This, we still feel, is more important. We still feel our method, our road has been better and will lead ultimately to better gains. But we shall have to move very effectively if we are to reach the targets that we are setting for ourselves. The challenge for us is not to become a world leader in one or two items. That would not be sufficient for a country like India. We must become world leaders across the spectrum. That is the challenge that we must face.

As your President has said, because of small production and inadequate economics of scale, there are high costs, poor quality, and insufficient in-house R&D To stimulate demand, you have sought a reduction in customs duties and in excise duties. I believe these are under consideration. But as I said earlier, for real development in the industry, we have to look for more than just customs duty cuts and excise duty reductions. We have to see that industry too rises to the occasion. There is ample scope for rationalization of production lines, better product mixes, improved technologies, perhaps most of all, better management in our industries. A sheltered market with too much protection has led to shoddy goods and no real development in the industry.

The Industry has been satisfied with importing a particular technology and then living with it for as long as it is possible with no improvement. This must change.

Elsewhere in the world, tumbling costs have meant tremendous increase in demand. Our national per capita income is fairly low. This means that the challenge for reduced prices is even greater for you. If you are to manufacture very high quantities to get the quality that is required, the prices must come down substantially, because only then will the market be available. The market is expanding very fast, but to make it expand faster, you must reach down lower into the market. You must create a market in those areas where very high emoluments are not available to the families.

One area which has not been exploited enough, where a lot of money is available, is the farm sector. There are areas in electronics which are of direct benefit to the farmer. Today he has the financial capacity to pay for them. But what is available is too expensive and it does not reach out to where he is. So we should look at what we can do to reach out to improve our agriculture. What we really need is action on all fronts to ensure quality for the money that we are paying and satisfaction to the consumer whether it is an individual or an organization or government. Satisfaction is perhaps the most important aspect. What the consumer will need, at any given point is a judicious mix of our own technology, with certain amounts of imported technology. But we must look at the imported technology as a stepping stone for our own better technology and development, and not as an end to the production process. For such a fast growing and fast changing industry, we will need a tremendous dynamism within industry, equally within the Government departments. Only then shall we be able to adjust as technology develops.

Sometimes our decision making process are so slow that by the time we decide to do something we have a totally new technology available and then we start rethinking whether we are going right or not. So, our process will have to be speeded up very much. Our demand for the industry to be innovative in technology must be met by a pledge on both sides to give an equal innovativeness in an adaptable policy which develops as technology develops, and as the systems develop. The Government departments like Railways, Defence, Telecom and the State Governments all must be encouraged to establish positive thinking in their various fields.

We are still not linking electronics to all the other fields as it should be linked. Today, electronics and telecom are not something that can be isolated in the telecom industry or the electronics department. They are going into just about every field. From every simple basic equipment to very sophisticated equipment. Government and industry will need to do a lot of new thinking to be able to break the barriers that have departmentalized and compartmentalized all our thinking. We have to change this basic attitude.

One of the ways that we are looking at for bringing about rise in telecom is through the Telecom Mission. The mission is not just targeted to change the communication scenario in the country but to make communication really accessible across the country. From my point of view, what is going to be much more important, is the way the mission is being carried out, because, hopefully, that will bring about a new thinking, a new methodology in Government which will meet the dynamism that is needed for industry today.

We must now start looking beyond the electron to the proton. This is the time that India must switch over. We are ready in terms of manpower, in terms of attitude. But a definite thrust is required. I hope the Government departments will be aggressive in this area and not too cautious and will move in while it is still a new area.

As I said earlier, such conferences are good and necessary, but they are only a beginning. Results are needed on the ground. We must realize the full potential of the telecom and electronics industry. Such professional institutions must be involved in developing talent and in developing attitudes in the country. They must be involved in our decision making process in Government so that we get all the inputs in sufficient time.

I hope that we will be able to follow this up with you. Together we should be able to change our whole development scenario not just in terms of lot of electronics being involved, but in terms of the attitudes that go with running modern machines and coping with modern technology.

❐

27

Telecommunication for Economic Growth

Telecom is one of the key determinants of the growth of an economy of a country today, and perhaps because this has not been fully realized in India that telecom has not got the attention which was its due. Consequently, the growth of telecom has not been keeping pace with the growth of our development and, by not doing so, has hindered our very growth.

One of the problems is what we have always tried to look at other development models of telecom. Our needs are slightly different from the needs of the developed countries, the industrialized countries. But because they have been very quick and good in their development of telecom, we have automatically looked at them for all our answers. Of course, we have not found these answers and the result has been a very unbalanced growth in our telecom system. The areas that need the most communication are more remote, but these are the areas which get the least benefit from the telecom system. The harder it is to administer an area, we make it even harder by making telecom of poorer quality in those areas. I believe, the approximate urban rural bias is something like 90:10, which is much too unbalanced for a balanced growth.

* National Conference on Telecommnications Mission, New Delhi, 3 February 1987.

In our country, the number of PCOs, are much too few. We need to really look at our indigenous problems and having analysed them, go for solution to our own problems instead of trying to match our problems to readymade solutions. It cannot work that way. This is one of the reasons that we have paid so much attention to telecom in the past few years. We have tried to have a holistic approach to the whole problem for quicker access, for faster communication– an approach which will link the urban centres, urban and rural areas and also provide linkages between the rural areas. We must coordinate all the activities that we are doing in the telecom sector, and to do this, we thought the best method is to have a Technology Mission; one umbrella which would look right from the R&D problem, right from the laboratory to the home of the user and try to overcome all the hurdles that we face in that area.

This national conference, I hope, will look at many of the problems that will be faced by the mission, to evolve an integrated strategy, integrating all the elements that are involved - technology, the delivery of technology, the organization that will be required, the manpower that is required, to do it within certain time-bound monitorable targets, with periodic evaluations both in physical terms, in a fixed time frame and with the financial monitors. We hope that this will smoothen out the wrinkles and the hurdles that have developed over time, and will make our target for the year 2000 attainable.

Globally, telecom has been one of the fastest growing industries. In India, we have not either taken benefits from the fruits of telecom - easier, quicker, better communication - or from the development thrust, the industrialization thrust that telecom would have given. Wc have at various stages imported technologies, but like I said, because the technologies never really fitted in and suited the problem, we have not developed those technologies. They have remained stagnant, and although we have gained experience in manufacturing, we really gained very little experience in front- line development and this is the area we must tackle now. The Industrial Revolution led to a gap between the developed and the developing countries. The information revolution today is enlarging that gap. We have during these past 35-40 years closed the gap on the industry side very substantially. If we allow the gap on the information side to widen, it will perhaps take us many hundreds of years to catch up like it has taken us many hundreds of years to catch up on the industrial front. That is why it is all the more important that for communication and information technology, we take leap forward. We don't try and play catch up because as long as we are playing catch up, we will never catch up by definition. We will have to take leap forward, get on to the frontline technology.

Today I have no doubt that our engineers, our technologists, our scientists, have the capability for this leap. It is for us in Government, for the departments, for all the organizations that are involved in this exercise, to make that leap possible and that will mean a lot of new thinking right down the line, a more aggressive thinking, a more objective thinking, not accepting everything that we are given.

We fall too easily into a slot and then carry on along that line. But telecom, as it is one of the leading industries in the world, must give that lead in India. It must be the carrier of a new type of thinking to be brought into the country which means a lot of work right through all the departments, every section that is involved in this, not just at the top level, at the upper levels, but also down the line, training down the line, revitalizing the thinking down the line, raising the level of functioning at every stage. We look towards the telecom industry to bring this about for the whole country. We know that it can be done. We have seen it being done in certain other high technology industries, but they have, because of the type of industry they are, remained limited to their own spheres. Telecom is an industry which reaches out very widely with a very large number of people involved in it. So it can be the carrier for bringing out a new ethos in our industrializations process, in our development process. We have waited too long, watching others, copy others, following others. Let telecom give the thrust, let us break away from this attitude of developing what has already been developed in other countries and patting ourselves on the back and saying. 'We have done a great job'. It was a great job for the first stage of our development. That stage is now over, and we must shift over to a more aggressive, more imaginative thinking. We must not be blocked by what others have already thought about. Our thinking even where we are doing frontline research in the country is still very much looking at what has already been imagined in other countries and then trying to work from that model. We must break that gap. We must be the ones who are doing the original thinking. We must be the ones with the original ideas. Let other follows our ideas. That is when we will have a real breakthrough in our industry. In our technology. And we look for the telecom industry to bring that about in the country.

We have many special problems in the country. The geographical regions, the range of telecom demands, from income groups, from various sections of our society. We cannot deliver these demands unless we start thinking in that original manner, get down to what we really need in the country, and from that, build what will be suitable for the country. And I have not doubt, what will be suitable for India will be suitable for the other developing countries also who must be in a very similar dilemma of having to buy readymade packages which are tailor-made for developed societies and then having to compromise with reference to their own societies, trying to fit them in.

Our challenge at present is the 12 Lakh pending telephone connections. A great effort will be required in the Seventh Plan (1984-89). The waiting list should not go to 15 Lakhs at the end of the Plan, but we hope it come down toward 9, 6, 3 - perhaps zero. But of course, as the service will improve, so the demand will also go up. As development will take place in the country, demand will go up even more. As more people will join the middle class, as more businessmen will come alive to the use of the telephone, the benefits of telecom, 'the demand is going to grow exponentially, and all our forecast. I have not doubt, will be totally wrong if a proper system is not available for the people, which only means that challenges in front of you are that much greater, and there can be no slips, there can be no shortfalls. The Telecom Department, the telecom industries, the various organizations that have been involved in the industry in the past, have shown tremendous dynamism at certain stages. But then at some stage we find they have got totally bogged down in a particular type of thinking, become very insular with no thought - processes crossing their boundaries. This must be broken, we must get back to a dynamic organization, if we are to give the results that the people are demanding today, and will be demanding much more in the future.

I have no doubt if our scientists and technologists are given the freedom that they require, the elbow-room that they require, we can reach the target that we want to reach. I have no doubt that with the knowhow that we have, we can show the developed countries that Indian can come up, can beat them at their own game, compete with them in their own areas. We can show them that the tortoise can overtake the hare. And we look to the Telecom Department to show this not only to the world, but perhaps more so to our own people.

At this national conference you will be deliberating on many issues. But I hope that what comes out of the conference is a consolidated view, not just of the Telecom Department, but of the Electronics Department, the electronics industry, and everyone else involved in it. Because these exercises cannot be done in isolation. They must be done in a coordinated, cohesive manner, and we look forward to that. Give us in the next few years the success which has eluded us in the last few decades. I have no doubt that our telecom scientists, technologists and engineers will do that.

❐

28

India's Space Explorations

The Strength and resilience of any organization is seen not by the measure of successes but how it faces setbacks and problems. ISRO has shown that Indian space scientists can equal the best in the world. ISRO has been at the cutting edge of our science and technological development and I would like to congratulate all our scientists for that.

Today you have suffered a setback. But when you are in the process of learning and gaining knowledge, setbacks are part of that process. Our mistakes sometimes teach us much more than our successes. I have no doubt that the scientists, technologists, workers of ISRO will now rise to the occasion and move ahead learning from this setback.

The world has seen a number of setbacks in every area of high technology and we have seen each organization learning from that and then forging ahead again. I look forward to ISRO forging ahead, setting up new standards for Indian space research. Indian science and technology has developed tremendously in the last couple of years. ISRO has been at the cutting edge of this development, not only within itself, but, perhaps even more so, as a catalyst for such development in other industries. ISRO has shown the way for Indian technology to be developed

* ISRO launch centre SHAR, Sriharikota, 24 March 1987

and used in production. We are looking to other such organizations which are at the cutting edge to spread the technology that they are developing amongst our industry.

One of our major problems still is that of developing a full scientific manpower, scientific temperament, scientific temper as Panditji had visualized. ISRO again shows the way in this area.

Let me congratulate everyone who has worked with ISRO for the tremendous progress, the tremendous thrust that ISRO has given to India's industry, India's scientists and India's technology.

❐

29

Science and Technology for Peace and Prosperity

I am sorry I could not be with you at your inaugural session. I hope you have enjoyed your stay in Delhi. You have been very busy, but in the midst of your preoccupations you may have had some time to have a glimpse of an ancient society trying to come to term with the modern age. India is full of contradictions, but it is also full of vitality, of the urge to change, to remake our social life so as to free it from the inequities of the past.

When one speaks of the past, one is inevitably drawn to the immediate past - our experience of colonialism. Colonialism did many things to us. It was destructive in a profound historical sense. But its incalculably harmful impact was to instil the belief that science was European and that India and the East were mystical spiritual and, therefore, anti-science. There could not have been a greater distortion of our history. Yet our people were made to believe it. Even our intellectuals came to accept it as an axiom. Thus the spiritual East stood in contradiction to the dynamic science of the West.

I need not invite the attention of this learned assembly to 'what that great savant of science, J.D. Bernal, called the West's arrogant ignorance of the rest of the world".

* Valedictory Session, International Symposium on Science, Technology and Development, New Delhi, 25 March 1987.

Needham's monumental work on China has exposed the hollowness of the claim that science is an essentially European phenomenon. The political purpose behind these theories of colonialism was obvious. It was to instill a deep-seated sense of inadequacy among the colonial people. Our colonial masters seemed to tell us that we were backward because we were incapable of doing science and our only hope lay in imitating what they had done in their own societies.

The scientific heritage of India has thus been deliberately and consciously obscured. The architect of modern India, Jawaharlal Nehru, was often exasperated by this falsification of our consciousness. He knew that behind much of the talk of spiritualism lay the fear of change. He knew that the identification of the Eastern civilization with mysticism was a weapon in the hands of those who wanted to preserve the status quo. He, therefore, campaigned all his life to develop what he called the scientific temper.

When India gained independence, we were faced with gigantic problems of poverty, unemployment, social and economic backwardness, and vast inequalities. We were also faced with the problem of unifying our nation on the basis of modern concepts of democracy and secularism. Looking back at this distance of time it seems amazing that we should have attempted to do what we in-fact did. We were trying to build a modern society at a time when the country had been divided on the basis of a mediaeval, theocratic notion that religion was the essence of national identity.

Jawaharlal Nehru realized that only on the basis of science and technology could we move ahead. It was not that science was some kind of modern mantra. There is undoubtedly an attitude of this kind. And it is precisely this kind of belief in the omnipotence of science that had led to the crisis of modern civilization. We have become helpless spectators of the tragic drama of the misuse of science. I shall come to that later.

I was talking about the colossal problems that we faced at the dawn of Independence - the problems of hunger, disease and ignorance. It is to these problems that the sensitive mind and spirit of Jawaharlal Nehru sought solutions. And the solutions that he sought were in the domain of science and technology. Science had expanded man's powers to control his own destiny. Now it was possible to feed, clothe and house millions and millions of our people. It was no longer possible to blame fate, nature or any other abstract entity for the injustice that one found in the world. It was no longer possible to persuade people that their miserable condition was ordained by cosmic laws which they might not understand but which were designed to bring them everlasting happiness, if not now, then in the future.

In India, then, from the moment of our freedom we linked science with development. For us science was the liberator, not the destroyer. For us science was the enhancement of life, not its extinction. Therefore, in our vision science was an ally of peace. Here we come across a somewhat agonizing question.

We live in the midst of starting paradoxes. We have it within our power to abolish hunger, yet we feel nobler organizing charities for starving children. We have the power to banish ignorance, yet we feel virtuous in buttressing ancient prejudices and hatreds. We have the power to heal the sick and bring health to all, yet we feel righteous it devising increasingly complex methods of spreading diseases. We have the power to liberate people from the fear of unexpected death, yet we are busy making people afraid of modern science and industry. We have the power to let peoples and nations come together in peace to realize the true potential of humankind, yet we are busy spending trillions of dollars on arrangements to separate them in fear and hatred. Survival of the human race itself has become a question mark.

Should the revolutionary upheavals of our times, the amazing explosion of human consciousness, lead to this utter helplessness in the face of the human predicament? Should the transformation of life by science bring us to a situation where, as Marx said, "all that a solid melts into air", Have we, in other words, lost control?

I do not think so. This impressive gathering of scientists is an evidence that thousands upon thousands of people who care about life, who care about the future, who care about humanity, do not think so. We have been taking things apart in order to understand them. It is time to put them together again. The human condition demands no less. It demands that we reintroduce ethics and morally into our consideration of the fundamental questions facing humanity. So far ethics and morality have been side shows in the drama of restless change. They have been mere appendages. Now they have to step on to the centre of the stage. This is what we attempted to do in a small way in the Delhi Declaration of November 1986.

We need a new vision of humanity, a vision based on truth and nonviolence, a vision that will nourish life in all its myriad beautiful forms. That vision can have no place for nuclear weapons. That vision can have no room for the mass human suicide represented by nuclear weapons. In the unfolding of this vision the spiritual experience of humankind must play its part. It is an experience of love, of breaking away from one's own narrow grooves, of reaching out beyond oneself, of exploring the infinite possibilities of Self. Science must begin to answer the questions that real men and women pose, not only in one country but in all countries. In seeking to do so, it will inevitably assist the yearning of the human spirit for peace, for harmony, and for truth.

Then and then alone will science lead us, as our scriptures remind us, from ignorance to knowledge, from darkness to light and from death to immortality.

Is that too utopian? I submit it is not. For me and for millions of my fellow citizens in India problems of poverty are real, problems of illiteracy and disease are real and the problem of creating a society which gives equal opportunities to all are real. We are battling with them everyday. We are putting all that we have into solving those problems. We are making progress. If you had come to India in 1947, you would have seen an altogether different picture. We lived at the margins of hunger. The great famine of 1942 had occurred barely five years ago, carrying away three and a half million people. Today we grow enough food to provide at least minimum nourishment. We have to do much more to achieve a healthy and balanced diet for our people but famines are a story of the past.

This is a dramatic change which people tend to take for granted because it has become familiar. But only as recently as 1966-67 we knew what lack of food meant. It raised the specture of starvation. It also meant loss of national pride because we had to import from those who had the means to give and did not give it without strings.

Whichever fields we choose to survey - education, health, industry, transport, communication - we find evidence of unprecedented change. The colonial stagnation has given way to a steady movement for socio-economic transformation. This transformation is taking place through the application of science and technology.

More than anything else we need peace, peace in the world and peace in our region, to complete the revolutionary tasks we have on our hands. Ever since Independence, we have consistently striven to build a peaceful world. We eschewed the confrontation of the military blocks. We put forward an alternative vision in which the big and the small, the powerful and the weak, the rich and the poor could work together to create a world free from want and fear. At first it appeared to many that we were not sufficiently cognizant of the realities of power. To some, we appeared immoral, refusing to take side between good and evil. But we persevered because we knew that good can defeat evil only in a world safe from the death and destruction of atomic weapons. In a world devastated by the nuclear bomb, good will perish along with evil.

Our vision has found increasing acceptance. The search of the Six Nations for peace and for nuclear disarmament is a powerful expression of the deep urges of the entire people of the world for a new human order. The Non-aligned Movement is striving in the same direction. It has been worth trying. The Soviet Union, alive to the horrors of war, put forward far-reaching proposals at Reykjavik. Although no agreement was reached, these proposals are a watershed in the history of negotiations on nuclear disarmament. The search for agreed solution must continue. There is no resting for our generation which carries the awesome burden of nuclear arms. We have to shake off this burden and walk erect without fear.

To help humankind to do so, men and women of knowledge have to come forward to revolutionize our consciousness. Today, thought process are being controlled and distorted. People are told that nuclear weapons are necessary for their security and freedom. If they do not have nuclear weapons they would be enslaved and would lose their liberties. A powerful mythology has been built up to ensure that people understand reality not by looking at facts but by imbibing irrational dogma. It is as if we were back in the Middle Ages. The powerful hold of the theology of the arms race has to be broken. We can see the strings of a new enlightenment. Millions of people are participating in peace movements. They are proclaiming that they want this earth, this life. They are pointing out that more bombs do not mean more security. This process has to be helped by the men and women of science who must ceaselessly educate the people all over the world that what is said in defence of the nuclear weapons in untenable. It is unacceptable to reason. It is against the dictates of morality.

I am aware of the difficulties inherent in this enterprise. The structures of power do not respond easily to the prompting of reason and good sense. These structures have created a world of arcane logic which is impervious to the demands of survival of the human race. But the modern age is characterized above all by the vast expansion of human consciousness. It is further characterized by the capacity for decisive action on the part of the million who were formerly objects of history but are now its makers. These two revolutionary trends give us confidence that we can change the course of history. It has been done before and it can be done now. We have the experience of our own freedom struggle where we challenged the mightiest empire on the earth. It is this faith in the power of non-violence that has sustained us in India in working for peace, disarmament and development.

I applaud the efforts, the World Federation of Scientific Workers has made to oppose the misuse of science and technology and to bring together scientific workers from all countries to work for a new and better world. I recall the words of a famous French physicist who said "If I stopped my scientific research it will, sooner or later, be taken up by others; however if I refuse to fight fascism there may be no science left." The situation today is poignantly similar. Scientists have to fight against the menance of nuclear war, because if they do not, it will be the end of science. The priesthood of mass destruction will take over.

Thank you very much for asking me to be with you this evening. I am in sympathy with the draft Resolutions and the Declaration that you have adopted. Your deliberations here will help the cause of peace. They will also help the developing societies to better understand the rule of science and technology in promoting development and human welfare.

❑

30

New Technologies and Industrial Growth

South India's Business community has always played a vanguard role amongst India's industrialists. It has helped in the making of a strong and self-confident Indian industry. We can look back to stalwarts such as Chidambaram Pillai, who played a breathtaking part in shipping at a time when it was required to point towards self-reliance which has become our credo, which has become one of our major goals, for our planned economic development.

On the platinum jubilee, my congratulations to the South Indian Chamber of Commerce and my best wishes to all of you. You represent many commercial and industrial houses which have made our economy strong and self-reliant. My tributes to M.A. Chidambaram, your former President in whose honor the platinum jubilee building has just been named. During these past years we have seen a new buoyancy in the Indian economy. We have shifted from a decade long three and a half- per cent growth rate to a long-term growth path of approximately five per cent. Major contributions have come from agriculture, which has stablized in spite of three or four years of bad monsoons. A major thrust has been given during these two, three years by a much more vigorous infrastructure. The railways have put in

* Platinum Jubilee Celebrations of the South India Chamber of Commerce and Industry, Kalavivanar, 27 March 1987

specially commendable performance. Other transport sectors have improved and, perhaps most important, the energy situation is much better today, though much more needs to be done with plant load factors.

Steady agriculture and sound infrastructure give a foundation for industrial growth. During the past three years, we have averaged over eight per cent which is the highest in many decades and certainly the highest if you consider the much wider industrial base. But no economy can be an island to itself. And India's good performance has to be seen in the adverse conditions that have existed in the world during these years. The hostile international environment has made it difficult for our industry but in spite of that, our growth rates have been good. Prices are under control although there are pressures on certain consumer prices which is a bit worrisome but we feel that we can keep them well within limits. There has been steady increase in real incomes and this has helped stabilize the other elements of the economy. Some of our policy directions, two years ago, have set the economy on an even keel. The direction that we have given has been good and we would like to maintain that direction. The investment climate is good, saving has been unprecedented, the capital markets are ready for tapping, a little too much. The public is ready to invest and industry needs investment. The time is to act now. We will shortly be bringing in legislation to regulate the stock markets, to make them more dynamic and curtail illegitimate manipulation in the stock markets.

Four decades of industrialization have seen very wide-ranging developments in our industries, the most impressive perhaps, amongst the developing countries.

Today, our industry is poised for leadership in certain areas. In certain areas, our industry is doing very well. This morning I was in Bangalore, looking at the Defence

Research and Development Organization and asking them not to limit their R&D and production to Government, but to spread out to other public sectors and also to the private sector industry. We feel that it is essential development of industry, both public and private, that such R&D efforts are used to help bolster our industrial growth and, normally in most cases it helps in reducing the cost of production also. A number of cases were brought to me today where certain public sector units, defence public sector units, were charging vast amounts for certain items. Sometimes when the items were handed over to other industries the prices have dropped to almost half and sometimes very much less. So, what we have really to look at is the total growth of industries in India, without being too particular about what should be in the public sector and what should be in the private sector or what should be in the defence sector. I would also like to reiterate that there are certain areas which must remain in the public sector, certain strategic areas, certain areas where private industry does not feel that there are adequate returns, where we feel that investment is necessary. But the public sector, we feel, must be at the cutting edge of the industrializations of the country, and it must move along with the cutting edge as we move along. It must not remain behind. Some areas can be passed on to the most efficient management; not that the public sector cannot be efficient; it has been efficient. But if it is used at the cutting edge. It is used to open up areas, it is used to develop. If it is used to develop expertise and manpower, then there is a cost to that. And that cannot then be counted as part of the efficiency of the system.

Today we need to look at the cost efficiency of our whole industrial system. The balances are somehow just not working out. Perhaps the markets are too causey, whether it is for the private sector, or perhaps more so, for the public sector where the markets are almost entirely reserved. We have to make our industry more efficient. It is not a question of efficient just for the sake of efficiency. Because if our industries are inefficient, we pay for it through cuts in other programmes. If we have to spend more for capital goods, if we have to spend more for setting up industries, it comes out of other programmes or it comes out of reducing the same programme in size. So efficiency has to be a key word and we must bring much more efficiency into our industry.

With efficiency is linked quality. The quality of our products is by and large not upto the required standard. An Indian consumer has seen the quality of products from other countries, and he is more and more reluctant to accept the quality of Indian goods. For exports too quality is important. Quality cannot be built in just by putting in more quality control or by more checks. It is the ethos that must permeate the entire process, in the management in the workers, in the system. Only then can quality come in. But while saying that I would lay the responsibility squarely on the management. It is upto the management to see that labour is productive, labour is efficient, and I believe that labour in the South is more productive than labour in many other parts of the country. And I would like to congratulate both management and labour for their productivity. But productivity in labour and efficiency in the industry must come with improving the training standards of labour. I feel that too often, in Indian industry labour is not upgraded over the years, it stagnates with a particular level of technology and perhaps then it becomes a vested interest not to upgrade the technology. In industry it becomes a sort of chicken and egg situation. You do not train labour, so they get stuck with a particular technology. When you want to change the technology, then they dig in their heels and say that it should not be changed because they feel that they would get replaced with the new technology. We must break out of this. Training for human development must be a continuing process. It must go on throughout life.

With management normally the training process continues. But unfortunately where labour is concerned, and perhaps here our unions are to blame more than anyone else, we tend to demand more and more salary and more money without demanding a better life for the man, better working standards for the man on the shop floor, on the machine. Upgradation must become part of the system. It is only then that better quality will come in. And it will be only then that our industry will be able to rise to the challenges that it will face as we move into the next century, in the next phase of industrialization. Technological upgradation is very very important and it must relate to the cost of our products. Too often we get stuck with a particular technology. Perhaps some of our government policies also help you to get stuck. We have tried to ease those a little bit. We have began looking at the problems industry-wise. We will continue this process. We have looked at a number of industries, looked at every aspects of the industry, to determine measures to help you improve, to help you expand, see how our Government policies, whether licensing, excise duties or customs duties or other controls are constricting your growth, give you additional incentives, at whatever levels they are required in the specific industries, targeting growth rather than first aid, or direct help. We have looked at a number of industries - electronics, textiles, cement, plastics, food processing capital goods, some are in the pipeline some have already started doing quite well. We have already listed out a number of other industries which we are going to look at this year. Well, it is a continuous process. As we complete one, we go to the next. We are open to suggestions from you on the order of priorities, suggestions for specific industries. As we go into each industry we will be involving people from these industries in the process. But ultimately we want to cover all of our industries in the manner. And one of things that this will do is to give a certain amount of stability to the system.

We have opened out a lot in the Centre, on licensing, on easing up, I do not claim that all the cobwebs have been cleared, but much has been done. The number of licences that have been issued in these past two years is very much more than we have issued in any of the years before that. This is apart from the very many areas that we have removed from the purview of licensing. Increased opportunities have thus opened up for industries but we do not see industry expanding at the same rate as the licences or opportunities that have been given. Perhaps this is due to certain constraints at the State level. We look forward to the State Governments also opening up in a similar manner and allowing industries to expand.

Industry is a very major area for tax collection for us and for State Governments. And I do not say for a minute what we should be doing is not stifling you to degree that you cannot breathe. We should be allowing you growth, and we should be collecting more taxes out of much higher growth than higher rates of taxes. We have seen its result. It has happened in electronics, and it has happened in cement. Wherever we look at the industries within the package we have opened, there has been high growth. We have collected more money. Industries have been happy and we have been more happy. But it requires just an initial breakthrough and perhaps a bit of gamble in the first two or three years. Unless we look at industry in a long time frame, we will not allow industry to grow and we will not be able to collect even what we are collecting now. So we have to be more practical and more farsighted in relation to the problem. Perhaps State industry ministries can involve the industries in their States, public as well as the private sector, to see how these blocks can be removed and industry can grow faster.

Lastly, let me once again congratulate you on your platinum jubilee. 75 years of contribution to India's industry, to industry in Southern India. During these years we have witnessed a complete transformation of our economy from a stagnant, declining growth economy to an economy which is becoming more and more dynamic; it is growing, reaching cutting edge in certain fields and I have no doubt that it will move into more and more area in the cutting edge of technology. The challenges ahead are even greater and I have no doubt that India's industry, both private and public, will rise to this challenge. The challenge is to move ahead. Thirty years ago the challenge was to industrialize. Today the challenge is to move into the area of new technologies, not to get caught in old technologies. The challenge is to be able to grow with the new technology and not get caught up at each step. The challenge must be not just to import technology but to indigenise; not indigenise in a retrograde fashion, but indigenise with a view to aggressive growth so that industry does not stagnate but grows from the technology that you have bought. The next generation must be ours. We must expand. Other countries have done it, smaller countries have done it but no developing country with our base has been able to do it. But I have no doubt that our industrialists will be able to do it.

My best wishes to you for this challenge ahead. Congratulation for the contribution you have made to the growth of industry in the country and in Southern India in particular.

❐

31

Environment and the Industrialization

You represent the global concern for environment. We have learnt in the past years that disregard of the environment can be crippling to development, and that reckless industrializations brings about irretrievable spoilation. Man, with modern technology at his command, has for the first time the power to destroy the environment around him and create a situation from which he will not be able to come out, no matter how technologically advanced he may be. We must utilize technology for protecting the environment and not for abusing it.

The WCED report shows that without environmental preservation there can be no sustained development and that for accelerated economic development we need environmental conservation. We welcome Prime Minister Brundtland and her colleagues as fellow campaigners in a worldwide movement to link development concerns with environmental issues. I should like to give a special welcome to all the Ministers and other who have come from various countries of Asia.

The ancient Indian tradition points out that man can be happy only if his life is in harmony with the environment. The modern technological civilizations has

* World Commission on Environment and Development, New Delhi, 6 July 1987.

in fact waged a war on the environment. We must get back to the state of harmony between human beings and nature.

The old civilizations of Asia have supported vast populations. Over the years, we have used just about every square inch of land for cultivation. Our large population have put pressure on lands on which forests grew. There does not seem to be any virgin forest any longer. The need for conservation is that much greater.

If the environment is to be protected the world over and within our own countries, we need to have a re-look at our developmental priorities. We cannot develop if we do not see the large picture. We can develop only if we see humanity as one, without any barriers, without putting pressures on each other. This applies to relation between industrialized and developing countries. Within developing countries it applies to relations between the richer and the poorer.

Conservation strategies have been worked out for ecologically fragile zones. We have 127 agro-climate zones for which we are setting up National Agricultural projects. For endangered plants and animal species, we have established biosphere reserves and taken many other measures. We are making the planning and implementation agencies responsible for environmental consequences of their developmental activities. It is also necessary to see that work that has already started does not further damage the environment. We shall, I am sure, benefit tremendously from international cooperation in protecting the environment. We ourselves are ready to contribute what we can to international cooperation in building a movement that will protect the environment and link environment to development and to a new economic order.

Your report describes the seamless web of cause and effect which weave together an area's economy and ecology.

Environmental degradation is not limited by man-made frontiers. The environmental chain, such as atmospheric pollution, pollution of the oceans and river systems crosses political boundaries. It cannot be switched off and on at international borders. Secondly the international economic system impinges on global environment and the national environment. Poverty in developing countries and excess in the industrialized, both lead to depletion of natural resources without renewal of replacement. The rich countries and the rich in developing countries consume far beyond their needs in resources and energy, and that in turn puts pressure on the poor. Unless we are able to balance both and work at both ends we shall not be able to come to a satisfactory solution. What is needed is an integration of the global environmental system with an international economic order which is more just and more equitable.

For protection of the worldwide environment, we need high rate of growth in developing countries. As Indira Gandhi said in Stockholm in 1972; "Poverty and need are the greatest polluters." Until we can remove poverty, until we can give the basic minimum needs to all, the poor will feel no stake in the environment. Fuel and fodder are two basic requirements of the poor. In the old days, the environment provided them freely. But today they are becoming to scare that women have to go very long distances to get what they used to obtain at their doorstep. The women in the villages, especially in hill areas, are spending almost their whole day in getting fuel to cook their food and fodder to feed their animals.

In many region, the poor have lived in forests for centuries without damaging them too much. In our system of development and modernization, we have brought roads into these areas and have opened up the areas. But these roads do not help the poor so much as they help the rich to send away the products of the region for their own greed.

This is true of the international scene also. Development must not mean that the rich countries develop at the cost of the poor. The flow of resources to developing countries must be adequate. The debt burden today is pushing many countries to exploit their resources and their environment in order to repay those debts. The terms of trade are skewed in such a manner that the value of primary goods is going down. Larger quantities of resources are being taken out of the ground to get the same amount of earnings.

Technology is not parted with easily. It is given when it becomes second level or on very harsh terms. It makes it harder for the developing countries to use technologies which will protect the environment. Such measures are not conducive to self-reliance or to protecting the environment.

What we need is a global commitment to eliminating poverty. Low growth rates mean accentuation of environmental degradation. In developing countries, environmental problems arise from poverty, from pressures of population. The question is of survival. We almost ask a man or a woman in the village if he or she wants to survive or let the environment survive. Only if we are able to improve the quality of life of our poorer people and our more backward regions, shall we be able to protect and regenerate the environment. The people will cooperate, if the burden is not intolerable. So the promise of growth will encourage conservation. Poor growth will give little incentive to protecting the environment. What we need is a widening of options, to prevent the abuse of the environment by poor households who are obliged to do so for their immediate needs. The human element cannot be ignored. Those affected must be protected and cushioned from the steps that we take.

Those affected invariably are the poor. If for example, our legislation to conserve forests is to be effectively implemented, we must provide alternative employment, alternative income, alternative supply of food, fuel, fodder, and building material to the poor. We have tried to build these things into our forest policy.

On the same analogy, international conservation measure should also display a similar understanding of the imperatives of development in the poor countries. As Indira Gandhi had remarked, "Twenty per cent of the world's population consumed 80 per cent of the natural resources of the globe and produced about 90 percent of world's waste and pollution". The industrial world is primarily responsible for depleting the world's ecological capital. For development, the developing need a bigger share in global consumption. Resources must be distributed more equitably between the rich and the poor. What is required equally is that the rate of consumption of the resources of the global must slow down. Otherwise there will be no resources left for the developing countries when they become more developed. For effective conservation, we need an equitable international pattern of consumption, specially of scarce natural resources and of energy.

Development generates major environmental problems. The consequences of industrialization are global, cutting across political and religious boundaries. There is another boundary that is affected. We must consider whether we have the right to deprive the future generations of their future. Can we deplete the ozone shield, which affects the food chain in oceans, and the health of every living being? Can we promote acid precipitation that kills forests and lakes? Can we allow the carbon dioxide green house effect to change our climate? Are these not part of the heritage which must be handed down to the coming generation or can the present generation claim the sole right over such heritage? We have seen in the past years how just a light change of temperature in the lower depths of the Pacific has affected the climate in Northern Africa, leading to droughts and famines as in Ethiopia.

This perhaps is a portent of what could happen everywhere on the global in the future. The realization must come that everyone is affected. There are no boundaries, no barriers. Every action affects every human being, whether in an industrialized or developing country. We must see the environment from that point of view. Yet we treat environmental policies, as national policies or regional matters. What we need to evolve is the involvement of the entire international community on a footing of democratic equality. We look to your Commission in helping to bring about such an awareness in the world.

We need greater commitment from the international community. The UN is the right forum to undertake corrective action. The effects of pollution and degradation hit poorer nations and poorer households disproportionately harder. We have seen what happened in Bhopal in 1984. We have seen how the rural poor have suffered from floods and droughts. Our relief work given a rough measure of the way the environment is degrading. The relief that we provided in the first two years of the Seventh Five Year Plan has been of same order that we provided in the whole five years of the Sixth Plan. In such a short time, we had to increase the relief two and a half fold. We have reoriented our relief programmes in such a way that they build up rural assets and regenerate the environment. This year the drought in some areas has been even more severe that in the past. But the effects of that drought have been less because of the drought-proofing that has been done.

National programmes must look at the weaker sections and focus on those who bear the heaviest burdens and have the least resilience. Relief measures should be conceived in such a manner that environmental upgradation takes place. Conservation of the environment is important in itself but it is also crucial to our development. It is imperative for national stability and for international peace. Indiscriminate deforestation destroys cultivable land, marginalised small farmers and swells the ranks of the landless labour. The poisoning in rivers deprives our fisherfolk of their livelihood. The poisoning in rivers area development leads to waterlogging and turns an asset into a liability. Unchecked urbanization gives rise to expectations which turn into discontent. We need to seek similar international cooperation to ensure that countries and people who are affected most by degraded environment are protected.

The threat of instability is not only national but international. To the pressures created by poverty, add the pressures of armaments, the pressures of vested interests in maintaining a system of blocs in international politics, and we end up with a very unstable peace. If we have to tight this, we must see where to begin. The environment is an area where there is very little difference of opinion. Perhaps it is the area where international cooperation is most promising. So conservation can provide a good start to the much needed effort of building a new world.

I once again congratulate the World Commission on Environment and Development for the report it has provided under the leadership of Mrs. Brundtland. I have no doubt that the debates that you have started all over the world will help in building our common future. We shall follow with interest what other Governments will be doing. Your report, I have no doubt will lead to an international programme to safeguard the environment through faster development of both, the industrialized and the developing countries, both the rich and the poor. I thank you on behalf of India for giving us this opportunity to play host to you. ❐

32

Science in India–Today and Tomorrow

I would like to first congratulate CSIR on completing forty-five years and wish you a very happy birthday and many more to come. My congratulations also to all the young scientists who have won the new awards that have been instituted on this occasion.

Forty-five years in the history of any institute of national importance is a significant event. With the CSIR completing forty-five years, we must think back to Indian science through the ages. In the short presentation that we were given, aspects of India's technology in ancient times were shown to us. India had always been at the forefront of science and technology till we were colonized. It was with colonization that our science and technology started falling behind. But in recent years, we have once more seen a revival of that tradition of science and technology and being at the frontiers of knowledge. Today, we also recall the many scientists who have given new life to India's science and technology in recent years. Perhaps, among the most famous are the Noble laureate Prof. C.V. Raman, the mathematics genius Srinivasa Ramanujan whose centenary we will be very shortly celebrating. Prof. Jagdish Chandra Bose, Prof. Saha, Dr. Bhatnagar, Dr. Homi Bhaba and many others in that line.

* Foundation Day Celebrations of the Council of Scientific and Industrial Research (CSIR) New Delhi, 26 September, 1987.

Forty-five years is also a time to reaffirm our commitment to science. Our commitment to using science and technology to build a new India, an India with a scientific temper whose conscience is dedicated to the reduction and elimination of poverty, an India in which science will reestablish its historical role, an India back in its old place at the vanguard of development of science, of knowledge.

Our freedom struggle was not limited to only political freedom. A basic essence was also the effort at removal of poverty and the uplift of our people. The first phase was of political independence. The second phase of removal of poverty, the uplift of our people, involves a massive input of science and technology. By definition, development is the use of high technology by the average person in his daily life and those who try to convince us that development is not using better technology are doing a disservice to the nation and are keeping the nation backward. Jawaharlal Nehru repeatedly emphasized that only through science can we modernize the Indian mind and only through science can we give the poorest and the weakest the instruments for the economic betterment of their life.

As I said, our stagnation in science and technology began with colonizations. Prior to colonizations, India was the goal that was sought by the countries right across the globe for our wealth, our knowledge, our science and our technology. And it is in that place that our scientists and our technologists must put India back. After forty years of Independence, we are today at a phase, in a position, where we can reach out. We have developed the expertise, the know-how; the human resources. We have developed the capabilities to put India back into that place. The challenge is now with you. We will give you whatever support is needed from us. We must in a sense win back the honour. The glory that was India by closing the gap in science and technology. This is a national task. CSIR is a major weapon in this task, in this war on poverty, in this challenge of development.

Over the years, the CSIR network has grown. With almost 8 per cent of our total R&D efforts going into CSIR projects, it is one of our major institutions. Today, CSIR is unrivalled in the range of opportunities that it gives and the range that it spans, in the spectrum of science, in different technologies, in the range of technicians and of many learned doctors of science.

One of the biggest challenges that we are facing this year is that of drought and, in some areas, very severe floods. These underline the need to link the scientific efforts with the reality as it exists on the ground. It is important to do research at the frontiers, in blue-sky areas, in esoteric areas, and we must continue that. But it is equally important for us to concentrate on those areas which will affect the life, the livelihood of our people today and our indigenous scientific effort must look at the challenges that the country is facing now. Science is needed to mitigate, perhaps eliminate, the consequences of the vagaries of the monsoon on our agriculture, whether that means very high levels of work on tissue culture, on genetics or in a more mundane manner in irrigation system, in balancing our environment so that we can get the best out of it in making the best use of our water resources.

Drought-proofing is important. Weather forecasting is equally important. I find that in many of these areas, we are not putting in the effort that is required to be put in today. There was a period when a lot of effort was put in but that seems to be wanting and it is necessary for us once more to concentrate on these areas because these are the areas which will make a major difference to the life of the average Indian.

Perhaps, one of the biggest challenges for Indian science is the next leap, the quantum leap, in our agricultural production. A breakthrough perhaps in dryland farming could be what we are waiting for and looking for. We must remember that it was Indian science which effected the Green Revolution. It was Indian science which has made possible the transformation and development of the post-Independent India. And, it was Indian science which has made us self-sufficient, which has given us a political strength to be able to make our position, our views known in the world, without fear of being suppressed or bullied or pushed in any way. One of the major strengths of the country today in international affairs has come about because our scientists and our technologists have given us that strength to be able to stand up and speak our minds.

Another major area of great relevance to the average person is that of health and how our scientists can help improve the health of our people. We are proud of the achievements that we have already made in wiping out many killer diseases such as malaria, smallpox, cholera and others. We have started an immunizations programme in Indira Gandhi's memory to immunise all children against major diseases. We note that there has been a drastic reduction in infant mortality which is the key to population control. Health care must be one of the priority areas for our scientists. Indian science and our scientists have shown that we can hold our own in the world. We can and are producing scientists who are equal to the best in the world. Sometimes this is evidenced by what is popularly known as the brain-drain, with a lot of our scientists leaving the country. I myself prefer to look at in a different perspective. I do not see the education process ending with graduation or ending at any particular time. I see it as a continuing process of gaining knowledge throughout one's life by work, by research by different inputs and in that idiom, I see the going out of scientists as only one more phase in gaining that knowledge provided we can get them back to work for us when we are ready to have that knowledge and employ that knowledge. And it is for us to create an environment where scientists start coming back. We should not worry about their going because they are only gaining knowledge for the country. We should worry about getting them back after they have gained that knowledge, creating an environment where they can work, where they do not have to worry about petty problems but can concentrate their minds on the research, the development that they are engaged in.

But, our objective must not be to develop only a small group of top scientists. We must broaden the base of the pyramid because it is from that broader base that we will be able to get even more top quality scientists and that means going down to our educational institutions to see that proper training is given in those institutions and not just the quality of training but also the type of training, the spheres, the sectors in which we need to develop. We must identify those areas in science and technology where we will need more people and those are the areas that we must strengthen in our institutions. If our institutions concentrate too much on highly esoteric and frontier areas, then we will not be able to give adequate work to those scientists, because, we are just not in that phase of our development and if we cannot give them employment, they will go away and we will not be able to utilize them even at a later date. So some sort of work on what directions, what sort of course are needed, requires to be thought about. This has to be done not just for the top level but also for the lower educational and higher educational institutions so that the right type of scientists emerge.

We have, and it has been said many times, a very large scientific and technical manpower. Different numbers are quoted. Some people say we are third. Some people say, we are tenth. But the question is not just of numbers. It is also a question of quality. It is a question of how good they are. If one looks at the number of papers that are produced, this is perhaps amongst the highest in the world, but if one looks at the number of papers that are quoted by other scientists, then I believe the number is definitely smaller. We must be more careful about quality, especially in science and technology. There is no place for mediocrity in science and technology, because by definition, there cannot be, if you are going to protect mediocrity in any bureaucratic or other form, then you are going to kill scientific development and high technology. We have to move out of this phase of a very bureaucratized scientific structure into a much more dynamic structure where those who are really at the frontiers, those with good minds are benefited or allowed to use those minds for science, for development and for the betterment of our country.

Science has no political boundaries. It flows across all boundaries. Ideas, concepts and the consequences of various scientific endeavors are a common heritage for all humanity and it is therefore, for our scientists not to be cocooned in the knowledge that is available only with certain boundaries. We must encourage our scientists to reach out for knowledge that is available elsewhere. We must assist them to interact with other scientists, especially in new area of development. This is most essential. We have agreements for scientific development and cooperation with many countries including the USA and the USSR, and this will help us broaden our outlook, the interaction will help our scientists and perhaps equally help the scientists of other countries. We must have much greater cross-fertilization of ideas, of experience, of expertise. This is essential for fully releasing the scientific wealth and talent in our country. Science can be nothing without excellence. Already we have an established reputation of excellence, meriting international respect and recognition in fields such as geophysics, radio-physics, catalysis, modern biology and many others. We are at the scientific frontier in superconductivity, in semiconducting materials, in non-conventional sources of energy and in certain areas of defence electronics. Yet, as I said, notwithstanding such pinnacles of achievement, there is too much mediocrity in our scientific effort. We must work toward reducing this and improving the percentage of excellence that is available. It was to this end that the Government had appointed a Committee to review the CSIR. There is always time to improve and correct and perhaps the 45th birthday is a good time to do just that. We shall continue all our efforts to give a better deal to our scientists, better working conditions, better access to professionals, better equipment and improved career prospects.

Once more, my congratulations to CSIR on completing forty-five years of great and useful service to the nation. In return, the nation pledges better living and working conditions for all those who are engaged in promoting India's progress and scientific progress.

❐

33

Rural Telecommunication

Your report on 36 months of C-DoT is most encouraging Your accomplishments demonstrate the possibility and the potential of developing new technologies which are geared to our particular needs and which are suited to our environment. This shows what developing countries can achieve in sophisticated areas like telematics. More importantly, it is a practical demonstration of the viability of the basic philosophy of self-reliance. Your work has reinforced the nation's confidence in pulling ourselves up by our bootstraps. For this considerable achievement, I would like to congratulate Sam Pitroda personally and everyone who has been involved in C-DoT.

C-DoT's development of the indigenous switching systems that we have seen are even more important when we look at the manner in which it has been done, because that is something which would hopefully flow into other areas as well. Within the stipulated time, without any cost overrun, within the budgeted amounts, quite unlike most other government projects where we seldom see things happening on time, and where we seldom even know or have any wild idea of what it is going to cost us by the time the scheme is anywhere near completion.

Another major contribution of C-DoT is to the work environment within the organization. The work environment means a fuller involvement of everyone who

* Speech after the presentation of C-DoT's report to the Nation on its First Technology Mission, New Delhi, 1 October 1987.

is participating. It means getting the best out of the people whom we are using. It means not using a lot of redundant people to make it seem as if we are giving a lot of employment, whereas in fact we are only handling out a dole. If we want to hand out a dole, there are better ways of doing it than through public sector units.

Unfortunately, there has been a view held in many parts of the country and amongst many groups that technology is something that is for the elite and not for the poor and not for the rural masses. I have always disagreed with this point of view, and I have held that poverty by definition is the lack of use of technology by the average person. And as long as we prevent the average person from using better technology, we are either inadvertently or deliberately continuing his level of poverty and not allowing him to get out or break free from that burden of poverty. Whether that technology is the type of technology that we have seen today in C-DoT, which is perhaps amongst the front-runners in the world in this particular field or it is the other technology like tissue culture, genetic engineering which again is a frontline technology, but without which our farmers will not be able to break out of their poverty, of their low productivity, it is only with better technology that we will be able to break the back of poverty in our country, and we must know how to use this technology. The danger, of course, is in getting carried away with the more esoteric and the glamorous areas which do not necessarily benefit the average person. So, we must see that our concentration is in the right place, and then push ahead with the most advanced technologies. It will not work to talk merely of appropriate technology. Appropriate technology is only appropriate to those who are exporting it to us and those who are trying to get rid of old, redundant units which they cannot use any more anywhere else, and it is appropriate for them and not appropriate normally for us.

Again, I would like to congratulate C-DoT for getting its priorities right, starting off with the rural exchange which is a major breakthrough. For the first time, we have seen equipment designed for our own conditions, our own situations, where we do not have to put up very expensive air-conditioned, clean air units to run normal equipment, where maintenance can be done from a distance and the various components are standardized so that with just a few selected components, you can have quick efficient maintenance. Perhaps, with these rural exchanges we will be able to rectify the imbalance in our telephone system which has so far been too much weighted towards urban areas. Better rural communications are essential for infrastructure development, for modernization, and perhaps most of all, if we are to get timely assistance in times of stress or tension or natural calamities. With efficient rural communication, perhaps our administration also, especially in the districts, will enter a new phase of much more efficient and quick reaction to the problems as they come up.

C-DoT has shown that by developing our own technology which is compatible with the older imported technology which has been installed in the country, we can, as a country, fulfil our own needs even in very high technology and frontline areas. It vindicates the attention that the Government has paid to science, technology and research and development in many fields.

In our present state of development, it is not enough to substitute imported products by domestic production. We have gone past that stage. That was the first stage of development where we replaced specific imported components with those developed by ourselves. We must now step beyond and go not just to replacing imported technology with our own but we must replace it with technology that matches the imported technology in performance, in cost and in trouble-free service. Self-reliance will become a reality only if we are able to bring this basic change in our thinking process. Even more important, we have to start thinking even beyond, because even today, although we are now in the process of thinking in terms of replacing complete systems with our own development, we are still thinking in terms of developing basically what has been developed in other countries. We read in a magazine or we read in reports about particular developments in a field and then we try to match those developments.

We have to break that barrier as well. This is the time when we have to think of what we need and give those challenges to our scientists and our technologists so that they can develop beyond what has been conceptualized anywhere else. This must be the next phase. C-DoT has broken some ground in that. But we must have a much more widespread thinking in every area of research and development if we are to break out of this colonial mentality that we have got where we keep thinking that we have to achieve what others have achieved. This is the time where we have to achieve beyond what others have achieved and that is the challenge that we must give to our young scientists if their full capabilities are to be used by us. If we do not give them this challenge, they will only, most likely, leave the country and use the capability for others. It is for us to put this challenge to them, to give them the freedom to rise to the challenge and meet the challenge and then show the world that India is not what the world conceptualizes, with lots of elephants and maharajas but India is a developing country, ready to meet the challenge of the modern world.

C-DoT now faces perhaps the most difficult part of its work, and this is where we have always been found wanting. Invariably, our scientists do well. But when it comes to the point of changing over from the laboratory to the factory floor, to the production process and to translate a few prototypes into a product which is mass produced, efficient, competitive, that is the area where we have not been able to really rise to the challenge. And I have no doubt that C-DoT will continue breaking new grounds and will show that in this area too we can switch over to an efficient competitive production process, produce equipment which is equal to the best in the world at competitive prices, at competitive reliability, and this new ethos could then spread to our other manufacturing units as well.

We have during these past years opened up many areas in the communication and electronics fields. We have liberalized to allow non-government organizations to come in and with the ground that C-DoT is breaking. I hope that this challenge will be accepted by many manufacturers who will come in and open up these areas, take full advantage of the liberalization that we have done. During these years, we have also seen a much better performance in the telecom sector, as a whole and I would like to congratulate all our people involved right from the top level administrators down to the people who are running the factories, to the linesmen, for making this possible.

I believe the success rate on STDs, has gone up from about 20 per cent in 1986 to almost 70 per cent in 1987. I hope they will maintain the same level of achievement in the coming years as well. International Subscriber Dialling has reached out very deep into the country and remote communication, through satellite, going to peripheral and inaccessible areas, have really helped open out many parts of the country. We have also achieved good production and progress in the range of telephone instruments, switching and transmission equipment, PABXs gellical cables and, I hope that we will not get stuck at gellical cables, and we will be moving on to areas of higher technology with fibre optics and other fields. We should not, at this point in our development, get bogged down with old technology and put up new facilities to produce outdated equipment and outdated technology.

Following C-DoT's success in indigenous digital switching technology, the next challenge is the technology for digital transmission. To show that the present success is not just a flash in the pan, C-DoT must continue to adhere to its time schedules and to its financial estimates and establish efficiency and economy as a norm in our system. C-DoT can thus made a lasting contribution not just to telecommunication but also the ethos in government departments and they can bring about a new work culture, new work standards, new environment, new accountability and it can be an example to all our R&D facilities.

Economic stagnation and the gap between the developed and the developing is primarily due to technological backwardness. Till a few hundred years ago, India was at the forefront of technology, of development. There was no gap and there was no backwardness. Now the national imperative must be to make up for those couple of hundred years that we have lost in being colonized, to get back to the frontline where we were, before we went under. This requires leapfrogging that gap. This is possible only with self-confidence in our ability, in a single-mindedness in pursuing our goals. It is possible with a highly motivated leadership at every level and is every institution, and most of all with dedicated hardwork. Indeed, this is the chief characteristic of our five thousand years old civilization, having confidence in ourselves, enough confidence to absorb, to synthesis and to accept whatever is best without feeling that it will overwhelm or overcome us. We can close the gap that has developed between ourselves and the vanguard and we will restore India to its traditional place in the front rank of nations. C-DoT has given one demonstration of the nation's unflinching resolve to do so.

34

National Water Policy for India

I would like to welcome you to this second meeting of the National Water Resources Council. The main task before us is to finalize the National Water Policy.

The Working Group, established by us at our last meeting under the Chairmanship of the former Union Minister of Water Resources, Shri B. Shankaranand, has done commendable work and produced a valuable document which has been circulated for consideration today. The report has been prepared in consultation with the experts. There are valuable insights and deep perceptions in the main elements of the draft policy before us.

First and foremost is the reiteration of the view, which we unanimously agreed to last time that water should be treated as a scarce and precious national resource. The planning, development and conservation of our water resources must be conducted on this premise and in this perspective.

It follows that the formulation of a National Water Policy for ensuring optimal use of water resources in the overall national interest need not be confined to State boundaries as the unit of planning and development. The draft policy before us recommends that the drainage

* Second meeting of the National Water Resources Council, New Delhi, 9 September 1987.

basin should rationally constitute the basic unit of planning and water resources development. There was a consensus on the issue not only in the Working Group but among all those whom the Group consulted. I commend its endorsement by this Council.

Another significant conceptual achievement is the recognition that the development of river basins need not always be directed only at the people living within that basin. Our rivers are bountiful and if properly harnessed, many of these rivers can meet adequately the requirements of the people living in the basin and still have something left over for others less fortunately placed. There is, therefore, scope for transfering water from one river basin to another with a view to meeting the requirements of water short areas. This gives real content to the concept of water as a national resource.

These are important principles. For want of adequate recognition of these principles, we have found ourselves caught in prolonged inter-State water disputes. While the arguments have gone on, this precious and scarce natural resource has run into the seas, benefiting no one. We must therefore, establish clearly and unambiguously the fundamental principles which will guide our country in using our abundant water resources for the good of the people, the good of the nation. It is in this spirit that I would request you to endorse the principles set out in the draft before us.

The endorsement of the basic principles will, however, constitute but a beginning. Without a beginning, there can of course, be no further development. At the same time, the starting point must not be confused with the end of the question. After endorsing the principles, we need to proceed expeditiously to drawing up action plans for the development of each of our river basins, their interconnection and, possibly, their inter-linkages.

These action plans should cover every facet of development, not only water resources development and better water management, but also the conservation of the environment, forestry, animal husbandry, navigation, etc. The approach adopted in launching the mammoth Narmada Project contains valuable lessons for the integrated development of our river basins.

The action plans also need to take an integral look at the entire system. Irrigation planning must be fully integrated with agricultural planning for the watershed. This is not always the case at present. It is unfortunate but true that most of our engineering talent is concentrated on the main project with inadequate attention to the command system and conveyance system. This produces sub-optimal results. The skills and technologies going into the construction of the dams are not so evident when it comes to the construction of canals and water courses, and their maintenance. Seepage occurs, the water table rises, salinity spreads, and instead of the irrigation system greatly benefiting agriculture, the land becomes virtually uncultivable. We, therefore, need to see in the action plans provision for suitable engineering skills all along the line as well as systems of monitoring which ensure quick action to counter the deleterious consequences of irrigation, such as increased salinity. Operational and extension work must, from the planning stage itself, take into account the terrain and capabilities of the farmer. This will promote the optimal utilization of available water resources, minimizing losses, maximizing retention and providing for recycling and reuse.

Another matter which needs to be carefully taken into account in preparing development plans for water use is the proper evaluation of the real choices available. Advanced techniques of planning are necessary— and are available— to deal with difficult questions of choice such as the right spread of investment, the optimal level of modernization, and optimal design for conjunctive use of ground water and surface water. Making the correct choice and ensuring the best mix of options will be crucial to the most economical and cost-effective utilization of this scarce and precious natural resource.

Irrigation must lead not only to economic growth but also to equity and social justice. Too often, some farmers have gained disproportionately through the chance factor of their geographical location, while others have been treated less than fairly because of their location on the periphery. In our irrigation planning, the emphasis should be on benefiting as large a number of farmers as possible within a given area.

Such rational irrigation planning will be greatly facilitated by a rational system of water rates. We have recognized that water resources are not merely a precious asset but also a scarce asset. Therefore, water rates must reflect the scarcity value of the resources. Hidden subsidies militate against efficient use. Also, because of unrealistically low water rates, irrigation revenues have been so low that-- leave alone recoveries of fixed costs-- it has not even proved possible to meet the annual maintenance and operational charges. The result is neglect and deterioration of irrigation systems, harming all concerned in the long run.

I am also impressed by the proposal in the draft paper that farmers should be progressively involved in the management of irrigation systems, and that the assistance of voluntary agencies should be enlisted. In irrigation, as in so many other aspects of our national life, there is an unnecessary hiatus between the administration and the beneficiaries of administration. It would be reasonable to expect far greater attention to matters like maintenance and repairs and the equitable distribution of water if all the beneficiaries are to be responsibly involved in the sound functioning of the system.

Similar attention is needed to flood protection works. The degradation of catchment areas and increasing encroachment on the natural flood plains of rivers are aggravating the problem. Urgent action is needed for improved flood forecasting and warning, as also the demarcation and enforcement of flood plains zones.

I have only touched upon some of the major points in the draft document before us. There is nothing inevitable about our being buffeted by natural disasters like droughts and floods, not being confronted, as we are today, with the tragic irony of severe drought in most parts of the country and heavy floods in the east and north-east. Such disasters can be forestalled or mitigated by the rational use of our national resources of water.

We need to fully utilize the potential we have created. We need to step up investment in irrigation. We need to give first priority to the completion of the projects on hand. We need to prevent anomalies like the establishment of water-intensive industries in water-scare areas. We need to take continuing advantage of developments in irrigation planning techniques and technologies. We need, in short, to take quick action to translate the principles set out in the document before us into concrete action on the ground.

I have pleasure in inviting you to give your comments on the draft paper before us. I also invite you to pledge yourselves to early action for moving from general principles to specific action. I would also suggest that as most Chief Ministers and Ministers have brought written speeches, we might take these on record and have a more fruitful discussion on issues rather than monologues on issues. We might be able to come to some more fruitful conclusion, specially on those issues which are a little bit more contentious. ❐

35

The Earth is One, but the World is not

The miracles of modern science and the towering achievements of technology have given us a measures of mastery over nature. Economic progress has, however, engendered a callous disregard of the harmony within the ecological system. Therefore, we have to consciously remind ourselves, we are a part of nature. We are a strand in the single fabric whose warp and weft link together all that is of the earth, the water and the air.

We have learnt to our cost that development which destroys the environment eventually destroys development itself. And we have learnt to our benefit that development that conserves the environment conserves also the fruits of development. There is, thus, no fundamental dichotomy between conservation and growth.

Yet, striking the right balance between the environmental imperative and the demands of developments is not that simple. Conservation imposes an escalation in costs. When resources are limited, the increased cost of any one project necessarily means less investment for others. This appears to imply a curtailment of economic growth. When the environment is not protected, damage to the environment will extract its

* UN General Assembly, New York, 18 October 1987.

price-- from those living in the vicinity, from others at a distance, or even from coming generations.

We do not know enough about the impact on the environment of development decisions. We also do not know enough about how best to offset damage to the environment. There are no easy solutions. Yet, we cannot ignore environmental considerations. We have to strive for the optimum mix through increased knowledge and increased awareness.

In India, we are seeing a growing awareness of the symbiotic relationship between the protection of the environment and sustainable development. There is the renowned Chipko Movement in the Himalayas, where women prevent the wanton felling of trees by throwing themselves protectively around tree-trunks. Island communities join hands to stop the coral mining which destroy their lagoons. Villagers hand together to stop goats from grazing on the bramble planted to halt the advance of the desert. Environment groups are active. In our Parliament, Members are increasingly receptive to environmental concerns. They are beginning to demand that the conservation of the enviornment be guaranteed before major development projects are undertaken.

At one time, environmental issues related mainly to the quality of life of the affluent. Today, in developing countries like ours, we are primarily concerned with the lives of the poorest. When village ponds and wells go dry, it is the poor who trek to ever more distant sources for water. When forests are destroyed, it is the poor who go farther and farther afield in the search for fuel wood. As lands are degraded and forests recede, it is the poor and their animals who, in the dry season, trudge hundreds of kilometers in search of grazing lands. It is the livelihood of the poor and their hopes that shrivel in the arid anguish of drought and are drowned in the raging fury of floods.

It is also the poor who suffer most from pollution. When water borne epidemics strike the urban slums, it is the poor who are afflicted by disease and even death. When factories spew harmful gases into the air, it is the workers in the nearby housing colonies who suffer the contagion, when industrial units discharge their effluents into the rivers, it is the poor fisherfolk who are deprived of their incomes.

Although they bear the brunt of environmental damage, the poor are themselves little responsible for any of that damage. For centuries they have lived in harmony with nature. The problem is caused by large scale commercial exploitation, which garners the profits but escapes the consequences. Yet, when laws are passed and rules are made to conserve the environment, the burden falls on those who have gained the least and suffered the most. The people of the forest cannot suddenly be cordoned off from its boundary. Fuel and building materials must be made available at prices they can afford. Shepherd and cowherds must be found alternative pastures or provided fodder, to be effective, conservation must be humane. That is the challenge before us.

A large number of animal and plant species are seriously threatened. Apart from the ethical and aesthetic case for protecting these disappearing species, it is possible answers to unsolved problems of health and survival might be found in the yet undiscovered secrets of these gene pool reserves.

We in India are now developing mechanisms to control pollution and check the deterioration of the environment. We assess the environmental impact of development work so as to harmonize development with the environment. We carry out research and take the results out to the field. We promote environmental awareness among the people. We hope this will lead to greater vision, concern and care in the planning, designing and implementation of development projects. We learn as we go along.

We are trying to integrate these complex environmental issues into our design of development. There are no easy or readymade answers. In principles, we would wish to give equal priority to the development and conservation. In practice, there are major gaps in knowledge, many intangibles and unknown quantities. Experts disagree and assessment vary.

Conservation is not a national task alone. Even as peace is indivisible, so is the world environment. The one world which Jawaharlal Nehru spoke of so often from this very forum, is a world which already exists in the physical laws governing the environment. The environment everywhere is jeopardized by the noxious fumes and life-killing wastes of industrial pollution. The poisoning of the rivers and the seas deprives and endangers all of us, all over the world. The accumulation of carbon dioxide in the atmosphere and the threat to the ozone layer put the innocent to as much risk as the polluters themselves.

Worst of all is the passing on the pollution and environmental hazards beyond one's boundaries. There is no political boundary which delimits the spread of poisonous gases, no line on a map which radiation cannot cross, no national frontier at which effluents can be turned back. All those affected by such transnational consequences of environmental damages must have an equal say in the resolution of problems. We must also keep the global commons and space free of environment depredation. The conservation of the earth's environment has to be ensured through democratic discussions and decisions in International forums.

The conservation of the world's environment also requires concerted international action to reduce disparities between countries. The compulsions of development and limitations of financial resources tempt many developing countries to exploit their natural resources beyond endurance, ignoring environmental safeguards. If the world economy is to move to more sustainable paths of development, the crucial requirement is to widen the options available to developing countries for growth.

A world economy which denies itself the benefits of interdependence is both unjust and inefficient. Growth in the developing countries is being hampered by protectionism, by the deteriorating real terms of trade, by the unfavorable conditions for the transfer of technology and by the curtailment of the flow of development assistance.

Programmes of conservation must, therefore, address themselves to inequities in International economic order. For example, the lion's share of the world's natural resources has been pre-empted by few countries. The average citizen of the industrialized countries consumes ten times more fossil fuels and minerals than the average citizen of developing world. The world's resources just cannot sustain such profligate consumption of energy and materials.

Neither can developing countries be denied the right to develop nor are the world's natural resources sufficient for all to follow the greedy path to growth. What then is the answer to the conundrum? The answer lies in more rational patterns of consumption, more efficient utilization of depletable resources by the developed countries, and more equitable access to these resources for the developing.

The international community must also address itself to safety measures in high-risk industries. Bhopal, Seveso and Chernobyl have shown how vulnerable we are. It is incumbent on the management of such industries to ensure the utmost vigilance in design, operations and maintenance. Valuable lives cannot be lost due to inefficiency, indifference, negligence or worse.

All other environmental dangers pale in comparison to the ever accumulating stockpiles of nuclear weapons. We must remove the threat of thermo-nuclear war wiping out, in a wink of history, life as we know it from our common planet. All nuclear weapons must be dismantled.

The report, Our Common Future, is both a document of high technical excellence and a call to concerted political action. The report reminds us that **"the earth is one, but the world is not".** We must recognize that even as development which degrades the environment is self-defeating, so do impediments to development endanger the environment. We must also recognize that environmental issues are closely linked to the larger issues of peaceful co-existence and international cooperation, disarmament and development. Any unidimensional perspective on environmental would be gravely misplaced. Environment as an international issue, has to be placed in the context of international cooperation, to be pursued through international institutions, to be linked to all aspects of international relations. Conservation is each nation's task, but a task which can be accomplished only in the setting of a cooperative world order.

In one of his most famous slokas, Guru Nanak Dev, the founder of the Sikh religion, sang:

"Air is the vital force,
Water the progenitor
The vast earth is mother of all"

The verse sums up the Indian tradition of respect for nature, respect for all that gives us life, respect for the sources of our well-being on the earth. In our tradition, there is no arrogance towards nature, no desire to dominate it. Our ancient wisdom teaches us to seek harmony with all creation. All creation is inter-dependent.

The core of the Brundtland Report is recognition of that interdependence. Everything in our experience, from the centuries old teaching of our seers to our contemporary experiments in development, endorses the essence of the message given to us by Prime Minister Gro Harlem Brundtland and her colleagues. We thank them in all sincerity for their deep insights and sage advice.

The report of the Commission is the culmination of an important phase of the task. The international community will have to carry forward this work. As experience grows and lacunae in knowledge are filled, answers will slowly be found to the complex questions of development and the environment. The search for the right answers must go on relentlessly. It is a worldwide endeavour to which India pledges her unstinting support.

❐

36

Science and Technology for the Rural India

This year we have from the Jawaharlal Nehru Memorial Fund chosen a topic which we thought, would bring back into focus the thrust that Jawaharlal Nehru had given to India's development. While Panditji looked at every aspect, his mind was always focussed on the villages, on the rural areas, on the poorest people in the country and how their life could be ameliorated, how we could help them break out of their poverty and into more modern life.

Jawaharlal Nehru had pegged all his hopes on two areas. His first love was children and perhaps the second was science and technology. And, it is only by going to the children, by developing their minds that we can help our people break out of the systems and the vested interest into which they have got locked. And perhaps the only way that this can be done is by inculcating what he called 'a scientific temper' in the minds of our children, of all our people.

Science and technology is sometimes, especially in India, seen as something very sophisticated which is meant only for a few people to use. That is not so. Science and technology that is so sophisticated and only for the very few, is really for the laboratories. When we talk of science and technology, we talk of the application of that

* "Science and Village" exhibition, New Delhi, 14 November 1987.

in our everyday lives, in methods which become so mundane that we do not even realize the type of technology we are using when we are doing something. For example, when a farmer sows a seed today, especially the wheat seed in India, he does not know what has gone behind that seed, what sort of genetic engineering of tissue culture of what levels of science have gone in to produce that seed. But he uses that technology even in his simplest tools and it is only when he began using that technology that we have been able to have a Green Revolution and our farmers have been able to break out of poverty.

Other parts of the country still need such a Green Revolution, and we are trying to do that now. But, basically the point is that development, progress, by definition must be measured by the amount or level of science and technology that we use in everyday life. Only when we start using much higher levels of technology, can we really call ourselves developed. Anyone who claims that there is development without the use of better technology is ensuring that India remains locked in its backward state.

Those people who today criticize many of the steps that we are taking to bring science and technology to the villages, to the workers, to every section of our people, are from that same section that criticized Jawaharlal Nehru when he stepped out on the line of science and technology. When Jawaharlal Nehru spoke of heavy industries, there was a huge lobby saying no. India should not be doing this. At every step, he was opposed, and opposed by the most vociferous groups in the country, but he persisted and we will persist along the same path that Jawaharlal Nehru has shown us.

Today the challenge is to bring science and technology to the poorest areas. It is a double challenge. On the one hand, the challenge is to create an awakening in our people in these areas so that they can accept such technologies. If they are put to him in a proper manner, and he is made to understand, he accept them, he uses them and once he has had the taste of using better technology, then it is very difficult to stop him from going further ahead. On the one hand, the challenge is to create this awakening. This is a challenge to the education system to all the human resource elements that are linked to it. On the other hand, there is also a challenge for our scientists. They must look more at the problems of the villagers, and science, specially when it is turned into usable technology, is of use only when it is cost-effective. If it is very expensive, then it is not ready to be used yet. When we talk of higher technologies going into normal everyday field, they must go in a manner whereby they increase productivity, they increase efficiency and they are cost-effective. We are still not able to do this fully. I have not seen the exhibition, I can see bits and pieces sticking out over the kanaat. Many of the things that I see are not fully cost-effective yet, and that is where the crunch comes. When we try and take something which is not fully cost-effective to a villager, his common sense is much too strong to accept it. His gut reaction is that this is a wrong thing. It is only when we make it right, we make it cost-effective for him, that he will accept it and we have seen it happen in our villages. So, the challenge is from both sides.

Sometimes, we do not go into the simpler things. One of the biggest problems the country is facing today is that of the damage to our environment. We cannot forcibly stop that damage because much of that damage is caused by wood being used for fuel and structure. But have we concentrated enough in giving fuel at competitive prices or giving structural material at competitive prices especially in those areas where wood is very easily accessible. We have not managed to do so. The thrust that we must give, and sometimes it is not that easy for our scientists because these are not the glamorous areas of frontier sciences, where our scientists have made tremendous progress and have taken India to the frontiers. But equally, perhaps even more important, are those areas which reach out to our people, reach out to the poorest people and the poorest areas. This is where we must concentrate more.

The two challenges-- one of developing the minds of our children and the other of targetting the thrust of our scientific research— must be given the highest priority. We have done a lot for children but sometimes we have seen these programmes from a grown-ups view-point: when you are questioning about what we have done, the office immediately produces a long list of statistics of schools, immunization, mid-day meal programmes. But we have not looked at the mind of the child. We have not seen things from the point of view of the child.

We must target our programmes to develop and open out the mind of the child, to allow him to think freely without being afraid or threatened. This is the real challenge that the country faces today.

Just one word about one of the books. About three years ago, when the book on the letters to the Chief Ministers, was being prepared and the letters were being read -- and that was the height of the problem of 'Operation Bluestar' in Punjab-- Indiraji called me to her room and showed me a draft of a letter-- which at least to me looked like the draft of a letter, which was a typed copy-- and I read it without paying too much attention to the date and I said, "it is a very good letter and of course, you must send it to all the Chief Ministers", and then she said, "that was the letter that Panditji had already sent to the Chief Ministers on Punjab when the problem on Punjab was going on in the earlier phase." So although these books are historical records in a sense. They relate very much to India today, the direction we are taking, the problems we are facing, and perhaps in them are also ideas or solutions to our problems.

I would like to thank the Jawaharlal Nehru Memorial Fund for the Exhibition. I am sure that it will bring a new awareness amongst children and I hope that through the questions children raise, it will bring a new awareness amongst our scientists as well.

❐

37

New Biology and Biotechnology

I would like to start by paying tribute to all those who have been involved in the CCMB and in these few short years have enabled the Centre to collect such an outstanding galaxy of scientists from all over the world, who have created an institution with the potential of carrying out research of the highest order.

In India, we have been trying to push our scientific research into the frontier areas. This is one of the field where I believe, we have made good investment. I would like to thank all those who have been involved in this process and for what they have achieved. When we invest in science and technology, specially when it is a developing country, our mind is invariably on the results that will come out and how they will relate to the national struggle against poverty, disease and malnutrition, how it will uplift our people.?

Thus for biology has been mainly a descriptive science. It is now becoming a fundamental instrument in technological change, transforming the basic parameters and constraints that nature has given us. While the question of what exactly life is still remains a mystery, we are gaining much greater understanding of the mechanics of life's processes, of the transmission of characteristics from one generation to the next, of

* Centre for Cellular & Molecular Biology, (CCMB) Hyderabad, 26 November 1987.

modifications of genetic characteristics through cross-breeding, hybridization and other techniques of genetic engineering. This has become possible by inter-disciplinary cross-fertilisation of biology with other sciences: mathematics, physics, chemistry, and perhaps more.

The result is that modern biology is on the threshold of doing great good to humanity. Evidence of the good that is possible is there for all to see in India. It is reflected in the Green Revolution. It is reflected in areas of health and medicine, in bio-based industries and in the industrial application of enzymes. So important is this revolution that it could transform the human condition, perhaps, even more dramatically than the Industrial revolution of few hundred years ago,. At the same time there is immense potential for an evil to be let loose. Biological or chemical warfare is perhaps as dangerous as, or more dangerous than, the devastation of nuclear weapons. So, the question of which way we go, the way of good or the way of evil, depends crucially on the moral sensibilities keeping pace with scientific discovery.

The CCMB is our earnest intention to keep India at the forefront of modern biological research and bio-technology. Till a mere hundred years ago, India was at the vanguard in many sciences. Then we fell behind. The gap in technology very quickly translated itself into a widening gap of poverty. Ridding ourselves of poverty essentially means closing that gap in technology and science. This is the gap that we have to close. We have the required traditions of learning, we have the required human resources and we are clear about our objectives. Yet, there are some financial constraints and inequities in the international intellectual order which act as artificial barriers to the flow of scientific knowledge across frontiers, but by remaining as open to the world as the world will allow us to be, and by dint of our own effort, we are determined to recover our national historical place at the high table of the world science.

No scientist, whatever his discipline, can escape his social responsibility. What is needed is a tangible link between the pursuit of science and the welfare of society, especially in developing countries like ours, since science costs money. Therefore, in determining the mix between basic research and applied research, the balance in countries such as India must be heavily weighted in favour of research with immediate applicable potential. But we would be very short-sighted if we did not work out a proper mix between basic research and more practical applied research. Too small a component for basic research would make it difficult to fuel the research that could follow. What is needed is perhaps a critical quantum of basic research so as to further develop what we have absorbed and adopted and together with that to generate our own breakthroughs. Therefore, there is no dichotomy between basic research and social needs.

Indeed a strong indigenous fundamental basic research base is essential for our long-term social needs. The CCMB is a prime example of our endeavour in this direction. In a society such as ours, there are urgent and compelling demands for limited resources. You yourself have voiced some. It is, therefore essential that institutions like the CCMB become and remain centres of excellence. But what is excellence? Results, of course are very important but in fundamental research activity, specially at the frontiers, it is difficult to lay down time schedules or criteria of achievements that must be met. Perhaps, a more important criterion in determining excellence is the ethos of the organization and the institution, not judged just by numbers but by the sincerity and the zeal of scientific pursuit in the institution, planning and concentrating of effort within the institution, and the prevalence of a scientific temper.

These qualities are evoked in a large measure by the leadership that is given. Excellence is neither a function of individual inputs or material inputs, nor a function of results scored, but a function of your success in harnessing the individual's creative talent in a common endeavour, with a high sense of social responsibility. We are convinced that if the ethos is right then it is inevitable, that brilliant new concepts, unexpected new technologies, unexpected benefits will accrue to India and the world. You have told us of the ethos in your organization and while we expect that many of the bugs that you might be developing in your labs do not escape from your test tubes, perhaps, this is one that you could allow out into the open filed to infect some other areas of administration. But if the ethos is wrong then it is inevitable that the research will be imitative and repetitive. By definition, good science must be the pursuit of the unconventional. As scientists working at the frontiers of human knowledge, you owe it to yourselves and the world to reflect deeply upon your ethical responsibilities. It is easy and dangerous to slip into illusions that you are dealing with life itself. Long before words like genetic engineering and biotechnology entered our vocabulary, the masters of science fiction had envisaged dangers of your vocations. For more than a century in fantasy and literature there existed the Frankenstein syndrome, now an imminent possibility in every bio-lab around the world.

Genetic engineering, without caution, inherently carries horrendous consequence over which we might lost control. As Adlous Huxley foresaw in the *Brave New World,* we could have indeed a very sad, cruel, inhuman world. The ultimate ethical choice is faced by the scientists in the loneliness of the laboratory. If he has flowered into a rounded personality with a keen awareness of social and ethical responsibilities he will make the right moral decisions. If his brilliance is only of scientific talent, to the detriment of the higher human attributes, he could make wrong moral decisions. So, in the ultimate analysis, what is needed are not only good scientists but perhaps, even more important, good human beings. Also essential is the collaborations between the frontiers of research and the social sciences and humanities. One single genetic breakthrough or genetic mutuant can render a stick of sugarcane, perhaps, 5000 times sweeter than what nature has given us or make every cow into a *Kamadhenu* which could give us unlimited supply of milk. We must associate biology and biotechnology with the social sciences to mitigate any adverse short-term consequences in transmitting laboratory results into socially beneficial action, so that we do not throw millions out of work or create destitution in countries, disrupting vast regions.

It is necessary that knowledge must surge forward, productivity must increase, quality must improve, nature must be made more beautiful. At the same time we must associate these advances with those of the humanities, those of the social sciences, to maintain our value system and not to destabilize larger human considerations, to give the correct ethical perspective to laboratory work. In the West, after the outset of the industrial and technological revolution, there grew a chasm between the two cultures, the human science on the one side and scientific and technological research on the other. Fortunately in India, thus far, by and large, we have avoided such a rift. But we must think whether we have avoided it because of our old traditions of having a synthesis between science and the humanities, or perhaps it is just a relative lack of science and technology in our daily lives. Yet recognizing the possibility of a rift is more than half the battle won and therefore, I am particularly delighted that so advanced a scientific Centre as the CCMB, has maintained such close links with the world of art.

I see many in the audience who are distinguished torch bearers of contemporary Indian culture. We need such synthesis between science and culture, between scientific compulsions and ethical considerations, between advances in our knowledge of nature and knowledge of ourselves. India pledges its support to science. It is an honour for me to formally declare open and dedicate this laborarory to the noble cause of science and to the largest service of the nation.

❒

38

Environment Links with the Development

Indiraji was perhaps the one person most responsible for converting the concern about environment from a concern of the affluent and elite to the concern of the poor and for the poor. Her path-breaking address at the UN Environment Conference in Stockholm in 1972 swung away attention from the peripheral issues of the environment to the real issues of the environment, that of the relationship between the environment and development. It is a testimony to her contribution to protecting the environment and to raising an awareness about the environment.

Today, we need much more systematic study about how the environment links with development. The inter-linkages, although they are there, are not known precisely enough. The connection between the specific causative factors such as degradation or deforestation and how that affect the long-term prospect or how that really affect the environment is till not known precisely enough to be assigned a specific economic value so that it can be measured and countered in each plan or in each project. No further study is required to see that degradation of the environment also reduces development and degrades development. That is known and established and nobody today needs convincing of that.

* The Indira Gandhi Paryavaran Puraskar for 1987 to the Bombay Natural History Society, New Delhi, 19 November 1987.

Need for Greater Awareness

What we need to look at is to see how conservation consolidates and reinforces the process of growth. And this must become the basic parameter of our measurement. Instead of looking negatively, we should start looking positively and see how environment contributes to the development process. We must both increase scientific knowledge on environmental matters and at the same time, we should enhance awareness amongst planners, technocrats, bureaucrats, all our people at large.

In Parliament, there is already a very clear and unambiguous sensitization to the issue. Just a few years ago, the environment was something that stopped development, that caused problems for all MPs. Today, that has changed and it is in fact just the reverse with MPs raising questions on clearance of projects where there are still some problems on the environmental side.

Today, there is a much greater recognition amongst all sections of our people about the cost of degradation and the cost of not protecting the environment. But, what must be realized is that there is no escaping this cost. Sometimes, it is only seen as a cost that is added on to the cost of the project-- so many hundreds of crores or tens of crores for environmental protection or whatever that might mean. But, what we do not count is the long-term cost that we will pay if the environment is not protected. We might pay it, the next generation might pay it, perhaps a neighbouring community might have to pay that price. But, that price is there and it will be paid, it will be extracted and our not including that cost in the cost of a particular project or development work does not remove that cost or hide that cost. It remains there. Somebody has to pay. And, the more we develop, the more we realize that many of the steps that we had taken in our earlier phases of development where this cost had not been totalled into the cost of the project, we are having to pay that price today and the price that we are paying is very very heavy.

Droughts and Floods

It is very difficult to link things specifically, but almost everyone will agree that the droughts and the floods that we have had this year are influenced very substantially by the degradation of the environment, by deforestation, by various steps that we have taken without caring enough. This year, it will cost us close to Rs. 3,000 crores— just in one year; that is, if we do not include the loss of production, it is still Rs. 3,000 crores. With the loss of production, it would be a vast figure. So the price is being paid. It is being paid in different places, by different generations, by different communities. We can't dodge that price. The decision and the studies that are required are on how to include that price in the initial conceptualisation of the project so that we know what we are actually getting in terms of value for money for a particular project. We still don't know this accurately enough. We took one step in the South Asian Association for Regional Cooperation when we asked for a regional study on the degradation of the environment— its effects, its causes and its cost. We hope that we will be able to make progress in this direction. We hope that the Society will help us in looking into these aspects.

Pioneering Initiatives

The Bombay Natural History Society deservedly has been awarded the first Indira Gandhi Paryavaran Puraskar. The Society for over a century has taken remarkable pioneering initiatives, decades ahead of its time, in making continuing and invaluable contribution to our knowledge of India's flora and fauna. The society has undertaken fundamental research. Its collections constitute a repository of basic knowledge about ourselves and our country.

You will all, I am sure, agree that today this award should have been handed over to Dr. Salim Ali. Unfortunately, he is not with us. He is perhaps the greatest single personality that we have had in this field. He embodied great qualities of head and heart, and a lot of the work that he has done goes into the awarding of this prize to the Bombay Natural History Society. Today we pay with this award our highest tribute to Dr. Salim Ali also. The greatest tribute that we can pay him is to continue the work that he had done, continue the thrust that Indiraji had given for the protection of the environment. From the government, there will be every effort to do so.

My congratulations to the Society, to Prof. Bole and his colleagues on this award.

❐

Study of Astronomy in India

The presence at this seminar of some of the greatest contemporary astronomers is both a matter of pride for us in India and perhaps equally a challenge for us. Pride, because their presence is a tribute to the remarkable contribution of Indian civilizations to the world of astronomy. Challenge, because, we owe it to independent India to resume the place that it had many hundreds of years ago, at the front rank of world astronomy. India has probably the oldest living tradition of astronomy. Thousands of years ago our ancestors began gazing at the stars, working out the mysteries of the vast universe. Some of their insights were so perceptive that even today, thousands of years of scientific enquiry later, they still hold true. For example, we have just been shown, in Vedic times we had the concept of the *Adhik-Mas* or intercalary month which is periodically added to the lunar calendar to bring it in line with the solar year. *Jyothish Vedang* of about 700 B.C. or perhaps even earlier charts the *Nakshathra Yatra* or the path along which the moon moves identifying the clusters of stars which fall in its path on successive days of its motion around the earth. While Greek astronomers were declaring, "The centre of the universe is here, not there," our *Puranas* give evidence of an understanding of the rotation of the Earth round the Sun.

Indian astronomy came into a new maturity through the work of Aryabhatta in the 6th century A.D. Aryabhatta explicitly set out the theory of the rotation of earth, of the

* International Seminar on Ancient Astronomy, Hyderabad, 22 December 1987.

Earth as a sphere and the reason for eclipse nearly a thousand years before Copernicus and Galileo. He was followed by Varahamihra, the Ptolomy of Indian astronomy who compiled the immortal *Pancha Siddhantika*. In this ferment of scientific enquiry, discovery upon discovery followed in rapid succession. The system of decimal numeration and many other innovative mathematical methodologies expounded by Bramhagupta, in the 8th century, were carried to Baghdad by the renowned scholar from Ujjain, Kanaka, around 750 A.D. Baghdád of Harun-al-Rasheed, proved to be the confluence of separate streams of Indian and European thought. Indian numerals got rechristened as Arabic numerals and entered the European thought-process. As the French mathematician La Place said: "It is India that gave us the ingenious method of expressing all numbers by 'n' symbols each receiving a value of position as well as an absolute value... Its very simplicity, and the great case which it has lent to all computations is what puts our arithmetic in the front rank of useful inventions."

As Indians, we are grateful for this great heritage. At the same time, it is incumbent upon us to recognize that for the better part of the next 1000 years, initiative passed from India to Europe. America or elsewhere. We remained more or less where we were. Even Maharaja Jai Singh's Jantar Mantras in Jaipur and Delhi were grand in themselves but were rendered somewhat obsolete by the invention of the telescope, which had happened earlier.

Such a seminar should, therefore, serve as an incentive to renewed endeavour. In Dr. Narlikar and others, we have restarted producing astronomers of world repute. But thus far, this has been a matter of chance. Now under the New Education Policy must commence a systematic search for such talent that we can then scatter around our labs because what makes institutions centres of excellence, is much less the quality and not the amount of equipment but more the brilliance of the minds that are in such institutions, and they must constitute the core for developing such institutions. In his provocative survey of European astronomy, Arthur Koestler suggested that scientific discovery arises less out of a logical chain of circumstances than scientists, like sleep walkers groping in the dark. Perhaps, we neither should nor can remove an element of sleep walking from the scientific process-- especially as path-breaking innovation needs not only reason and ratiocination but also the imaginative leap into the unknown and a little bit of luck. But we can try to create conditions in which, while walking awake in the day-light, is at least as productive as wandering through the night.

India is well placed to do this. Although the last few centuries have the benefit of important astronomical observatories, some, as the one in Madras are nearly 200 years old. Recent astronomers like Vainu Bappu, the only Indian to have a comet named after him, Dr. M.N. Saha and Dr. D.S. Kothari, have begun putting India back into the forefront. Recently at Kavalur, I saw for myself the fascinating new telescopes that have been installed. We will encourage our research efforts to interact at all meaningful levels with work being done elsewhere in the world. Science does levels with work being done elsewhere in the world. Science does not and should not, know the artificial barriers, or national boundaries. Of course, there is the reality of narrow nationalism and vested interests which attempt to build barriers to block the free flow of knowledge. While some governments are disposed to constricting flows of knowledge, most scientists would prefer knowledge to flow unimpeded. So we shall continue, as in the past, to make astronomy both an Indian contribution to the world and the world's contribution to India. In this, as in all other national endeavors, our aim must be self-reliance which does not mean autarchic self-sufficiency but a capability perhaps, more important, a confidence in ourselves, to interact with the world on an equal footing.

Where, however, does one look for the great astronomers? The Narlikars and Bappus of tomorrow are today children in our schools, to some extent indistinguishable from their companions. Before they can be spotted, their interest has to be aroused. Every night of course provides the same canopy of stars which brought out the ancient Babylonians and Egyptians, Indians to peer into the infinite expanse of the universe and speculate about its origins, contours and what is signifies. Our children too can peer into the infinite expanse of the universe. But what is needed is an inquisitive mind, an enquiring mind, a mind that will ask questions, a mind that will be sparked off by the education system. We have to build a system which will do that. Apart from that we have modern educational aids to touch the imagination and to spark and nurture interest, such as this planetarium and many others. Such planetariums should be encouraged to reach out to arouse interest and perhaps even to spot the brilliant minds that are left unseen.

I would like to thank Sir Fred Hoyle for his presentation this evening and the other distinguished speakers for having made this evening a memorable and educative experience. Too often formal inaugurations deteriorate into repetitive speeches where the organizers are congratulating themselves rather than enlightening the unenlightened. This has been an evening with a difference. We have learnt in detail, about the contributions of India to ancient astronomy, the contribution of other civilizations, a glimpse of the challenges of the future and I thank all those who have made it possible. Our first Nobel Laureate in science was Dr. C.V. Raman, and I would like to let him have the last word, I quote:

> "Let me declare here and now my belief that there is no science so grand, so elevating, so intensely interesting as astronomy."

❑

40

New Frontiers of Science and Technology

I am delighted to be here with you in this historic city which was a nursery of the spirit of Swaraj and is a nucleus of intellectual endeavour. Pune is linked with the names of Chhatrapati Shivaji, Lokamanya Tilak and Gopal Krishan Gokhle. At its best the city symbolizes the synthesis between modern sciences and ancient wisdom. I am pleased to be able to say that the University Grants Commission has decided to set up an Inter-University Centre for Astronomy and Astrophysics here.

It is appropriate that Pune plays host to the Indian Science Congress during the celebration of its Platinum Jubilee. Professor C.N.R. Rao drew our attention to the congruence of these birth centenaries - of Ramanujan last year, C.V. Raman this year and Jawaharlal Nehru next year. These three men, each in their very different ways, epitomize the rebirth of Indian science after centuries of dormancy.

The founding of the Indian Science Congress in the early years of this century went hand in hand with the rejuvenation of Indian Science and I would like to commend you on the role that you have played in this awakening.

I have heard Professor C.N.R. Rao's presidential address with deep interest. As is only to be expected from

* Inaugural Address, 75th Session, Indian Science Congress Association, Pune, 7 January 1988.

a scientist of his distinction and experience, he has made a number of suggestions which call for careful study and thought. I would like to assure you that the Government will give the most careful consideration.

The theme that you have chosen for your session is an exciting one. All of us who are dedicated to building a better future for our country must constantly think of frontiers of science and technology in the Indian context.

You as scientist will bring your own perspective to bear on the subject. Actuated by the urge to know - as Johannes Kepler said "why things are as they are and not otherwise" - you would tend to interpret the concept of frontiers as the limits of knowledge, limits that have to be tenaciously pushed forward. I shall define frontiers in a somewhat different way, interpreting them as the constraints in our lives and endeavours.

In my view, the most critical one is the frontier of human well being. Addressing the Indian Science Congress 40 years ago. Nehru said: "Surely, science is not merely an individual's search for truth. It is something infinitely more than that... Its objective must be to remove the ills of the community. It must have a social objective before it."

In India the number one social objective is and must be, for the foreseeable future, the elimination of poverty. Our scientists have already achieved much. They have contributed to the trebling of foodgrains production since the early 1950s, helped to raise yields, diversify cropping patterns, introduce new occupations and relieve distress. They have rid us of killer diseases and increased our life expectancy.

But so much more needs to be done, Mahatma Gandhi pointed out that if the villages of India perish, India itself would perish. You must take science and technology to the villages and tackle most of our problems, providing nutrition, health, housing, energy and communication. Your most difficult challenge is to find effective, fall-safe and socially acceptable means of reducing our population growth to the point where we have a net reproductive rate of one. We have to study recurring floods and drought, the patterns of rainfall and the changes that we are witnessing. We have to drought proof our agriculture. The farmer wants more answers from the scientists. The progress that has been made in foodgrains has now to be given a new momentum. More important, it is still to be duplicated in other crops. And we need to turn our attention to other cereals which are the staple food of large sections of our people.

Scientists need to look at the way we use our water resource. India is one of the most favoured regions of the world in the amount of rainfall it receives. True, the rain is concentrated in a few months. But we must learn why, in spite of this, we are now short of water even in those areas which receive normal rainfall. Dryland farming and water management should be near the top of the scientists agenda.

This brings me to our bruised and battered environment. We cannot go on depleting our environmental reserves, destroying scarce forests, polluting our waters and atmosphere. This must be reversed. The task is a gigantic one. It calls for the combined efforts of scientists, administrators, planners and managers. We don't know enough: we need a better understanding of the problem that we are up against, and that calls for a rapid growth of the environmental science.

We must study the impact of our policies and programmes on our natural heritage. Science and technology must tell us how to protect our soil fertility, how to create the correct balance and distribution of forest cover, and the right kind of cropping patterns. It must warn us, when warning is needed, of the implications of pumping pernicious wastes into the atmosphere and using chemicals to increase crop yields. These are but a few of the areas to tackle. If we do not take action disaster will surely overtake us. Science must squarely face the challenge of sustainable growth.

I have devoted considerable time to the problems of poverty and development because they are central to our concerns. The scientific community should not forget the message of development contained in our Scientific Policy Resolution of 1958, which says: *the creation and adoption of new scientific techniques can, in fact, make up for deficiency in natural resources and reduce the demands of capital. Science and technology can make up for deficiencies in raw materials by providing substitutes or indeed, by providing skills which can be exported in return for raw materials.*

I would describe the next challenge as the frontier of self-reliance. I have already spoken about agriculture where our scientists and farmers together in the space of just one decade pulled us away from large scale imports into the realm of self-sufficiency.

Our scientists have done us proud in other fields as well. Our atomic scientists have enabled us to explore the peaceful use of the atom, almost entirely through our own efforts. We design and build nuclear reactors of our own, we are among the handful of countries in the world, with a mastery of the complete nuclear fuel cycle.

For us, the peaceful use of nuclear energy is no abstraction. It serves us in industry and medicine, in food and in energy, and we are proud to have done it ourselves. Our space scientists have given us the ability to fabricate and launch satellites and probe the mystery and the promise of space. They are developing larger and more powerful launch vehicles which will put commercial satellites into space before long.

We have progressed towards self-sufficiency in another crucial area because of the excellent work done by our defence scientists. Thanks to the R&D work done in a range of defence fields - from aviation to electronics, to communications- we have a sophisticated defence production industry which meets a substantial proportion of our needs.

The lesson from experience is that if we concentrate on our effort, put our brains where our needs are, we can do it. What restrains us is our timidity, our tendency to continue with the old and the familiar.

We must not be inhibited. We should boldly seize what is new, examine the opportunities and adopt what suits us. We should let the adventure of discovery and spirit of invention take us forward to meet our goal.

We can do and we have done a great deal on our own: yet the challenges and possibilities of science are far too vast for any one country to master single handedly. But there are fields where we can save time and resources by cooperating with the international scientific community. As long as this is done sensibly, with our own interests uppermost in our minds, it will not compromise our goal of self-reliance. True, self-reliance has to reside in our minds. If our minds are free from fear and hypocrisy, we will have the self-confidence to take wisely from others and the confidence to know that we ourselves have much to give.

In this spirit we have to approach to new areas of science and technology that are opening up the world over. We cannot be left behind in such fields as bio-technology, super-conductivity, faster computers, renewable energy sources, new composite materials, lasers and a host of other fields and products.

We must not only be in tune with research in these areas, we must know how they are being harnessed in the service of society. Ultimately it is such harnessing that compels attention and gives science its raison d'etre. The nation looks to its scientists to help policy makers to determine scientific, time bound objectives in major areas of national endeavour. We must then bend all our energy to the achievement of such goals and that is the only road to self-reliance.

The third challenge we face is that of the frontier of excellence. You Professor Rao, have referred in your address to these key issue and unless we focus on them we will never make the sort of progress of which we as a nation are capable.

As scientists, you will recognise that genius does not occur in isolation. For every one Ramanujan achieving his full flowering, there will be other who are enable to break the bonds of social neglect or the inadequacies of our education system. It is revealing that two geniuses of this century, Einstein and Ramanujan came to their calling from humdrum occupations, the former a clerk in the Swiss Patents Office, and the latter a clerk in the Madras Port Trust.

The challenge of today is to refuse to accept the strait-jackets that our existing systems force on us. The founding President of the Indian Science Congress, Sir Ashutosh Mukherjee, recorded his pleasure at being able to persuade C. V. Raman to give up what he described as "a lucrative official appointment with attractive prospects for a university professorship, which I regret to say does not carry even liberal emoluments".

Ashutosh said this gave him a hope that there would be "no lack of seekers after truth in the temple of knowledge which it is our ambition to erect."

We need to make it much smoother for today's seekers of truth to enter today's temples of knowledge. For instance, higher science and technology are still largely the preserve of the urban elite. They are effectively taught only in the English language. Surely the social base of science cannot be allowed to remain so narrow.

We have a lot to learn from the popular response such as the Bharat Jana Vigyan Jatha, which was convened in Bhopal from five different directions on Raman's 99th birth anniversary. The Jathas travelled 26,000 kms made 500 stops enroute and brought the message of science directly to 50 Lakh people.

Mathematics is the underpinning of the physical science and technology. The teaching of mathematics requires no great capital investment as in the other sciences. Its present neglect is a manner of great concern to me. We must also re-examine the way in which we organize the teaching of science to ensure that talent is encouraged and high standards of scholarships are fostered.

The fourth challenge is what I would describe as the frontier of peace. It was Einstein who said that "concern for man and his destiny must always be the chief interest of all technical efforts, never forget it between your diagrams and equations."

With the signing of the treaty to abolish intermediate nuclear forces, we have at last a ray of light from under the darkness of the nuclear cloud. That, at least, the concern for man and his destiny is not quite dead.

We have to remember that eventually we are of one world, For from being insulated from it, we are a part of the global scientific environment. Nor are we immune from the mistakes and madness of others. Science and technology have taken us to the brink of nuclear war. We must pull back, Science must warn humankind of other precipices of destruction and dissolution. We need to be cautious about bio-engineering, experiments in genetics, in creating or unleashing certain new forces and materials.

As scientists, you have the power to show us the way. You are not only men and women of science, you are citizens of the human race endowed with unique ability. You are able to understand the physical world better than others. You have the means to transform it. You owe it to humankind that this special gift is used in the service of peace.

It is not enough to accumulate scientific knowledge and the technology that comes from such knowledge. Humankind needs a deeper wisdom to judge the moral and ethical implications of scientific effort. Our ancient seers have shown the way. The larger vision of human destiny must inform the scientific quest. The very survival of humanity depends on that.

After 40 years of freedom the time has now come for us to take stock and see what we need to do to quicken the pace of our progress. We need to do this across the board. We must therefore, do this in the context of science and technology as well. As you ponder the issues you have set out, I would urge you to consider what the scientific community and the authority must do in the coming years to meet the challenge of the four frontiers I have spelt out.

The task is to lift ourselves into the forefront of the global community within the span of one generation.

In conclusion, I am reminded of the words of the Nobel Laureate Sir Peter Medawar who drew attention, tongue-in-check, I think, to our two professions. He said: "If politics is the art of the possible, research is the art of the soluble. Both are immensely practical minded affairs. Good scientists study the most important problems, they think they can solve. It is after all, their professional business to solve the problem, not merely grapple with them."

❐

41

Agriculture–Our Success in Self-Reliance

First of All, I offer you a very hearty welcome to this meeting, especially because agriculture holds a very important place in India's development. Three-fourth of our people live on agriculture even today. One-third of our GNP comes from agriculture, and, for that matter, our growth-rate and development also depend on agriculture. If there is good crop in a year, things go well; if crops fail for two or three years, problems surface.

In a way, our success in agriculture can be counted as our success in self-reliance. We achieved great success in the Sixth Five Year Plan. Our foodgrain production crossed the 150 million-ton mark; it tripled during the 37th year of freedom; that was why we set up a target of about five per cent growth rate in the Seventh Plan-- five per cent in foodgrains and four per cent for the agricultural sector as a whole. But we have not achieved full success. We made a lot of effort in many spheres. In irrigation our effort was to see that on-going irrigation schemes were brought to completion. Specially, it was noticed that the big schemes attract people's immediate attention but, then, in their completion the pace falters. Huge dams are built, large canals are dug out, but the channels which can take the water to the farmers fields are neglected. This needs attention.

* The Chief Minister's Conference on the Special Foodgrains Production Programme, New Delhi, 18 March 1988

We have also tried to help the small and marginal farmers. Our efforts were directed to helping those engaged in dry-land farming and those toiling on rain-fed land. We had a special programme for peddy, in the Eastern region, and we devoted attention to the leguminous crops.

We also initiated a technological mission on oil-seeds. But when we look at the actual performance, it is not all that encouraging, the main reason being the failure of monsoon. It has failed us for four years. Two years were the years of terrible drought and in another two, we had too little rainfall. So, in a way, we can see some excuse for our inadequate performance, we can tell everyone; we can even convince ourselves by saying that a great crisis impaired our hopes, what could we do? But the fact remains that the needed development did not come about. Now we should accelerate it. We have to meet the situation promptly and review why we could not make progress despite the drought. Ten years ago, we had a drought which was not so terrible but it made our situation precarious. But now despite the drought we have had development and at least, we are moving ahead, we are progressing. Now India has the strength, we have progressed sufficiently enough, to ensure that adverse weather conditions do not make so much of a difference. That is why, I thought we should get together and modify our strategy, accelerate things and draw up a programme to give our agriculture the potential to remain undamaged by droughts; our farmers should remain unfettered. Even if the rains fail, the crops should not be deficient.

We will have to attend to many things. We have to develop the necessary strength to remain unaffected by drought. We should look back to the last 10-20 years to find out what has been tackled correctly and what went wrong. Only if we pay full attention to everything will correct answers emerge.

The first question is whether we have made full use of irrigation? Has there been full utilizations of our investment in irrigation? Have the small irrigation channels been go ready? Have we taught the cultivators the appropriate use of water? Have we deliberated upon the optimum utilization of our limited resources of water, of its proper distribution? For example, if we begin to grow paddy everywhere, in the desert areas, let us say, then there can never be enough water. So, there must be a suitable plan whereby we ensure not only the distribution of water but also its appropriate management. In our desert development, we have dug out canals to get a lot of water there and there have been very good crops. But other countries had a similar problem and they tackled it in another way. They took to drip-irrigation, to make do with less water, and yet they achieved as much production. Thus, we have to think whether we did the right thing or whether they did the right thing, or if there is a third course? Is there a via media which is still better?

Again, we have to review with seriousness what has been happening and what has to be done with reference to the resources and the funds. Were the resource earmarked for agriculture fully utilized for agriculture or were there diversions? If there are diversions, with resources going elsewhere, then this cannot be termed proper development. We have seen that often agriculture has not really received all the funds meant for it. Irrigation schemes have remained incomplete. While old schemes have not been completed new ones have been taken up. Quite often foundation stone is quickly laid and a new edifice is raised, but then canals are not dug out. Thus, we do not succeed in making the schemes fruitful. If we go on like this, we will never see the desired development in agriculture.

We have seen that, for a number of reasons, our foodgrain production has reached a kind of plateau and is not registering any appreciable increase. We have to give very serious thought to this problem, how we can get out of this situation and begin moving forward again.

Indiraji's strategy was basically a very sound strategy. And it is because Indiraji laid the foundations for our agriculture that the nation has really survived these last two years of severe drought. If she had not done that, we would have been in very serious difficulty. That strategy has worked effectively. It has given us a substantial increase in output. It has enabled us to build buffer stocks, which have seen us through this difficult period. It has given us a resilience to take difficulties and calamities in our stride. But that is not enough. That strategy was launched twenty years ago, and perhaps over this period the attention paid to it has gradually diminished. Are we concentrating enough on agriculture? Are our hearts and minds really set at pushing agriculture as we should? Agriculture has lost momentum. We have two more years of the Seventh Plan still left and we can still achieve the targets. It is still possible to reverse the trend and achieve what we had targeted for the Seventh Plan. But that can happen only if we really put our full efforts into the task and we have will to do it. We have seen that whenever India has shown her will, there has been tremendous strength and we have overcome the most formidable of odds. This is just such a challenge. We can meet it through the collective efforts of all of us gathered here and of lakhs and crores of other people who are in the field in various capacities-- farmers, labourers, extension workers, scientists, technologists. There is need for a concerted and consolidated efforts by all of us, and from the Central Government's side, we have taken certain steps to this end.

When we carried out the mid-term review of the Plan, we found that the agricultural sector had not done as well as we would have liked it to. I directed the Planning Commission to constitute a task force to give a new impetus to foodgrain production. The task force has interacted extensively with the State Governments. It has prepared a report which outlines the proposed Action Plan to ensure the highest and the best level of production in the coming years. This Action Plan should lead us to our target of over 175 million tones by the end of the Seventh Plan. We have no doubt that this can be done. However, the first and foremost requirement is a total commitment to this objective and for that, we need to give overriding priority to agriculture. It will require a deep and high-level political commitment to impart the political will, to rationally-- and I want to emphasize the word rationally-- deploy resources for agriculture, and to prevent the diversion of resources from agriculture to other sectors as also from key areas within the agricultural sector to more secondary areas in that sector. The Action Plan focuses on five major crops; rice, wheat, maize, *chana,* and *arhar.* Here I would like to say one more thing. We must also have much better cropping management. What tends to happen is that if a farmer gets a good earning from one crop, then farmers all over the country want to grow the same crop and the State Governments all over the country want to try and give the farmers the same sort of return on that crop. The fact is that this cannot happen. The climates are so different, the soil is so different, the water availability is so different that there cannot be this sort of standardization.

We must develop a system where the farmer earns the right earnings irrespective of the crop, and we must somehow have the crop targeted to the agro-climatic region, that the farmer in a poor agro-climatic region is not penalized because he is told to grow a particular crop. A lot of thinking has to be done in this regard. I don't expect quick answers but perhaps in the next few months, we should develop some new approaches.

Sugarcane is an example. Farmers want to grow sugarcane everywhere because it gives a very good return. But only in a few areas of the country does sugarcane give really good economic returns. We should have a strategy where the country gets the maximum returns from the agro-climatic situation in a particular areas and the farmer does not have to suffer the consequences of the fact that he happens to reside or do farming in such a zone.

The Action Plan then goes on to suggest better water management. This is a very crucial element in this strategy. As I said earlier, water management must mean not just the distribution of water, which is important, but it must also mean the education of the farmer in better utilization of water for his particular crop bringing in better technology so that he uses less water more efficiently and gets a higher yields. One hundred and sixty-nine districts have been identified where favourable irrigation possibilities hold the best immediate prospect for increasing production. For the optimum utilization of available water resources, we need an Action Plan on several related fronts like command area development and utilization of ground water resources. Six lakh tube-wells and dug-wells have been planned per year in identified districts, by recasting the NREP and RLEGP to earmark perhaps, one third of the fund for irrigation wells. This would work out to 3.48 lakh wells in 1988-89. Again, in the 20-Point Programme there are so many areas that relate to agriculture, but our concentration within the 20-point Programme seems to have been on NREP and IRDP, with a sort of lack of effort on the other equally important points. So, perhaps, from the Centre we need to reorient our thinking on the 20-Point Programme and to give a greater push in areas where we have become a little weak.

With the efficient implementation of the Jal Dhara Scheme, which was announced in this Budget, we will be able to give pump sets to small and marginal farmers at very low rent and lease charges. We must also complete before the last year of the Plan irrigation projects that are nearing completion so as to ensure proper utilization of the irrigation potential in a package of inputs comprising high yielding seeds, increased fertilizers and pesticides and increased flow of short-term and long-term credit. For each district, specific problems must be identified, which will help push yields to the maximum realisable in the shortest possible time. It is essential for district officers to ensure the operationalisation of all these programmes, while looking at the agro-climatic and agro-economic problems in each area and to go into the details of the micro-implementation of these problems.

The reality hit me hard when I asked the Planning Commission, during the last meeting, as to what they expected to be the total crop and they gave me a figure. I asked them to give me a break-up-; how much in which State and in which district? What is the basis of this number that you are giving? Then we suddenly discovered that it was a sort of overall estimate. Nobody had gone into the problems of a district. Which meant nobody had really bothered to go into the problems of the farmers. Unless we go down to that level and start asking ourselves what is going to be the plan for this crop in this district, we are not going to be able to help the farmer. The district is more convenient administratively, but, perhaps, correctly, we should not even go by district but by the agro-economic zone.

The fertilizer has to be available at the right time. The seeds have to be available, we must have a certain in-built flexibility in case of late or early rains, in case of less rain or more rainfall, and there are other problems, like a pest problem or some shortage. So all these things can be taken care of only if we have gone down to the micro-level. They cannot be solved from the Centre, but certainly by you in the State. We don't want to attempt to do it from there, but we want to push you to do it. Only when you do that, shall we really be able to help the farmer.

As I said earlier, within the 20-Point Programme, we need to put new emphasis on agriculture-related areas. One of the reasons that IRDP and NREP have done very well in the 20-Point Programme, is that we have started a very systematic, thorough and a continuous evaluation process. Perhaps we need just such a continuous evaluation process for the entire agricultural sector. But if we look at the micro aspect of this in the district, in the same way as we have done for the 20-Point Programme for IRDP and NREP, we could develop the scheme for the whole agricultural sector. The scheme must not be a bunch of papers landing up at the Centre or at the State capitals totally fouling up all work that is going on. The parameters should be well thought out. They must not be the kind of indicators that we so often ask for and the DMs so often give us. I was told in many of these DMs' conferences, and they were very honest and outspoken about it, the parameters you asked for, have been spelt out honestly, but the parameters are wrong. They are not relevant to the people in our area. But because that is what you wanted we have done what we could. So we need to choose these parameters very carefully and see that we really are asking for the right answers. Our administrative system, no matter how loose it looks at times, has always delivered when it is asked to do something specific. I have every confidence that if we ask the right questions, we push in the right direction, the system will rise to the occasion and deliver perhaps even more than our expectations.

The extra effort that has been outlined in the Action Plan will require additional funds. So additional funds have been made available by additional allocation to the agricultural sector in the Central Budget. But perhaps much more will need to be done in all the State Budgets if the required thrust is to be given. Additional funds really means not just more money; it can also be generated by better utilizations of the money that has already been allocated. If we can be more efficient in that, we can generate more funds for agriculture without actually asking for more allocations. But the real answer is in doing both. There is a very definite need for better management of the existing resources. We need to re-prioritise our resources and we need to give additional resources to ensure a proper funding for the Action Plan.

Perhaps one of the most important things is that agriculture must once again be accorded the top priority that it had. At the Centre we have not really ever digressed from agriculture. But there is the feeling in the States that agriculture is not as important any more. There was a time when almost every Chief Minister used to be the Minister for Agriculture. It was seen as a visible commitment on the part of the State. Today, there are very few Chief Ministers who are Ministers for Agriculture. This seems to convey a message down the line and administration doesn't pay too much attention to it. Agriculture must be accorded old importance once again. I am not propagating that all Chief Ministers must also become Agriculture Ministers. This is entirely the prerogative of the Chief Ministers.

But I would like that some mechanism, be set up for regular monitoring of agricultural sector by the Chief Ministers and at short intervals they monitor the progress of various parameters. Of course the parameters will vary, depending on the States, the crops or the season. The parameters will require to be flexible to ensure meaningful monitoring. I hope the Chief Ministers will take this up in all seriousness.

Coming down to some of the nitty-gritty problems of the farmer, one of the biggest problems is keeping the input costs reasonable, competitive and low, compared to the price he is getting for the crop. Reasonable input prices are the underpinning of any success in agriculture. This has been one of the basic principles of our agricultural strategy. And this has been one of the basic reasons why we have found success. We must and will see from the Centre that the Central procurement agencies provide the fullest support at the time of marketing and when it is most needed. The stage was set in this year's budget. Fertilizer prices have been brought down, the duty on pesticides has been reduced, import procedures streamlined, and the interest rates on loans for agriculture reduced. The flow of credit has been increased by Rs. 3,000 crores. What remains is effective implementation. It is the interest that every Chief Minister takes and the efficiency with which he reacts that will make a difference to this programme. The Centre will fully back the State Governments on these issues. It is essential to have an appraisal at Governments on these issues. It is essential to have an appraisal at the national, the State and the district level of what has happened, what needs to be done and so on. We need feed-back through the government channel and concurrent evaluation by independent agencies, so that we are not just spoon fed on information.

That takes me to what I feel is one of the most important areas of any development. In agriculture, it is even more so. And that is continuous training. There can be no development or progress if there isn't continuous training right through, not just of our scientists, technologists and extension workers, but continuous upgradation of the skills of the farmers also. And one of the biggest problems, I find, is that there is a dearth of trained and educated manpower in the rural areas. Our development model is such that anybody who gets trained, or who gets educated, who gains knowledge, does not want to stay in the village any more. He goes off to the town. That is why, no mater how much effort we put in, rural areas continue to look the same. Some basic thinking is required for devising ways to keep this trained manpower, these resources, in the rural areas, which are the most crucial areas for the country and its development.

Another point which is perhaps not directly concerned with agriculture ministries, but is directly concerned with agriculture, is the managerial capacity at the grassroots level. Unless we are able to keep educated youth in farming, it is going to be very difficult to improve the quality at the grassroots level.

After all, in the ultimate analysis, that is the key to what we are talking about--by better management at every level and particularly at the field level. That means keeping the bright youngsters in the villages, keeping them interested in the farming. For the son of a farmer, thee should be enough prestige and importance in the village for him to want to stay there willingly,. For that, we have to look not just at the farm sector but also at the development of the rural areas. There are certain minimum basic amenities which all people are looking for. When farmers' children get educated, they go to school, they go to college, they go to an agricultural university, and then when they go back to the village, they should not say: "No, there is nothing here that I am looking for," So, unless we give him something, he is not going to stay. Obviously we can't give him something in every village. That is not possible. So, some new thinking is needed on how to give him what he wants in some reasonable measure. It should not get spread to thin that it is totally invisible and is of no value. We need to really go into this. If we start thinking now, perhaps we will be ready with it for the Eighth Plan. We will be able to pull people back to the rural areas or at least keep them in the rural areas.

One aspect which I think has got missed out in the Action Plan or perhaps been taken for granted is extension work. I feel extension work is a most important areas to ensure the delivery of everything we want to get to the farmer. A lot needs to be done in this area. Here, I feel, the agricultural universities must play a key role. This cannot be left only to government agencies. Just as we have made the bank branches nodal points in the development of villages by making a bank branch adopt 15 or 20 villages in its areas, we should have a very aggressive exercise whereby agricultural universities are given responsibility for extension work and for development work in a region. They should be given freedom of action and should also be held accountable. I have no doubt that we can do this. The expertise is there. The technology is there. The scientists are there. But somehow all this is not spreading well enough on the ground. And while I am on agricultural universities, I have a feeling that the thrust has gone out of our scientific development in the agricultural universities. Do we need to push it harder? Do we need to look deeper? In our research and development are we not engaged in just what we were engaged in ten years ago? We need to think why this is so and then take measures to correct the situation.

To achieve the target that we have set for the Seventh Plan, we now have only four main cropping seasons left, which is not very much. The output has to go up to 166 million tonnes in 1988-89, only then will it be able to go to 175 in 1989-90. The time to start is now. There is no time to wait. We must achieve this result, starting with the coming season. It was because the country at every echelon had focussed on foodgrains that we became self-sufficient and self-reliant in food. Now we must concentrate our attention once again on restoring that momentum in the universities, in the farms and in everybody from the scientists to the farmers. We must harness the country's many talents for this as a priority national goal. By achieving this ambitious but very definitely achievable target, we will once more instil a sense of pride in the rural areas, and in the farmers of our country, and give the thrust that is required to get the country going and moving.

It is to rise to this challenge that we have met here today. I look forward to suggestions and inputs from you on what we can do and how we should to it, how we can help you and how you can help us.

❐

42

Poverty Gap is Essentially a Technology Gap

I would first like to congratulate all the scientists and technologists on whose initiative we have brought together this National Academy. This academy must emerge as a true centre of excellence and as a reservoir of outstanding talent to be placed at the disposal of the country.

The poverty gap is essentially a technology gap. What separates the developed from the developing country is the level of technology that is used directly or indirectly in the everyday lives of our people. Within a country, what defines and distinguishes the better off from the worse off is again, the quantity and quality of technology that they use in their daily lives.

Till the middle of the 18th Century, India was at the vanguard of world technological development in various fields and had held this position virtually without interruption from about the 6th century B.C., perhaps even in the pre-Aryan period, India was on par with Samurai and Egypt.

Therefore, it is no longer a historical perspective in which we see our backwardness or our poverty. It is, in fact, an aberration in our history and our heritage. Our natural place must be at the forefront of development and

* Foundation Laying Function or the Indian National Academy of Engineering, New Delhi, 11 April 1988.

technology as also of thinking. It is to that forefront that this National academy must target or take us in the least time possible, not just as an individual responsibility but as a national task.

We have seen during these last forty years of Independence that the principles and policies that had been enunciated and implemented by Gandhiji, Jawaharlal Nehru and Indiraji, were very much in the right direction and had strengthened and built our foundations. We have succeeded in developing our human resources and in developing a basic trained manpower and our mental resources in the country.

One casualty of our education system has been scientific teaching. Although we have reached peaks and pinnacles in a number of areas, the average is not something that we are too proud of. Very few schools have laboratories or really properly qualified teaching staff. Universities are substandard. Even professional laboratories and institutions leave much to be desired. Despite these handicaps if we have succeeded in building the third largest reservoir of trained manpower it is because of the innate scientific and technological aptitudes of our people. Therefore, with some improvement in our human resource development, we can forge ahead to the vanguard of technological advancement.

To eliminate poverty, we must improve the technology input at the lower levels of our society. A good example is the Green Revolution where very high technology was made available at the farmers level, some of it directly in terms of seeds, some of it in a way which the farmer doesn't see, perhaps a nuclear power plant generating energy for his pumps. But, ultimately, it is the quality of input that we get at the lowest levels which will help us to remove poverty.

We have developed a number of technology missions

to carry out just this task, to direct the highest technology and scientific development towards removing poverty, and the war on poverty. By pulling together all that is required in technology and managerial power and strength, by putting together the best in scientific developments and breakthrough we can meet the needs of the poor. In India today, the prime need is a higher and more sophisticated technology to meet the needs of the poorest sections of our society. There can be no poverty alleviation without technological upgradation.

The academy must keep in mind the basic aim of poverty elimination as a fundamental objective and forum of all indigenous engineering efforts. In the last forty years, Indian engineering has demonstrated its ability to absorb and assimilate imported technology. Good and imaginative adaptation of technology has taken place to make it more useful in our conditions.

But, all is not so well. Generally, we have not been generating our own technology to meet our requirements, or developing imported technology indigenously to eliminate further imports and keeping up with developments in the world. Also, there have been very few real contributions from India at the frontiers of science.

The first step as a developing nation must be to buy and assimilate the technology. From there we must move on to developing that technology so that we can use it better for ourselves. We have gone through both these phases. The next phase must be to breakthrough to the frontiers and show the world that it is not just a question of catching up and achieving what other have achieved, but India can and will break out to the frontiers up ahead of the others.

The major task of the Academy is to chalk out the future course for Indian engineering, using interdisciplinary advantages and the vast and diverse experience that you fellow have in India and abroad. The country expects you to demonstrate that India can be innovative, that India can show imagination and we can orient science and technology to the three basic directions of indigenous development of imported technologies, or indigenous generation of new technologies and of moving to the frontiers to put Indian science and technology at the front rank in the world. Your efforts are needed in Industry to bring about self-reliance which till now has been achieved at a very high cost. Self-reliance must be more efficient. It must produce high rates of growth and a wide range of manufactures. We have to break away from the high cost low, productivity and poor quality that we have got stuck in. In the next phase, we have to achieve in many areas where we are on the verge of breaking through. There are some areas where we are now almost touching the frontiers in many areas of defence electronics, we are at the frontiers in the drug industry, in catalysts. Our remote sensing satellite and the "Prithvi"; all brings us right up to the front-line. But except for the drugs and the catalysts, we are just that scratch behind and that is what we have to break out of now.

It has taken us forty years to catch up to these frontier areas. This is the time that we must show the world that we can breakthrough and give the lead in a number of areas. After two centuries of stagnation we are now on the way to acquiring technological and scientific self-reliance. We have acquired the ability to achieve but we are still to fully achieve. The Academy's duty will be to bridge that gap, between the potential that has been created, between what is achievable and what India must achieve.

My good wishes to the Academy. ❑

* Prithvi – the indigenous surface to surface missile, which was successfully tested on 25 February 1988.

43

Bio-Technology for the Second Green Revolution

Lal Bahadur Shastriji was a close lieutenant of Jawaharlal Nehru. He was a freedom fighter. As Prime Minister in his short and tumultuous period, he faced many challenges. But the two big challenges that he faced were those of aggression and the agricultural crisis. It was from these two problems that he faced that he coined the phrase 'Jai Jawan Jai Kisan. Today, it gives me great pleasure to lay the foundation stone of the Lal Bahadur Shastri Centre for Bio-technology and Plant Protection. In a sense, this Centre stands for the victory of the Kisan.

I do have a comment though, on limiting the role of the Centre by adding the word 'Plant Protection'. I feel that cannot be limited to plant protection; there are many fields that are already available and perhaps will become available when our knowledge and our research in bio-technology leads us down the road. So, I would request you to reconsider the two words 'Plant Protection' and not limit the scope of this Centre that we are starting today.

Indian agriculture can be divided into two phases; the first half of the twentieth century, during which period it was for all practical purposes absolutely stagnant and

* The Foundation-stone laying of the Lal Bahadur Shastri Centre for Advanced Research in Bio-technology and Plant Protection, New Delhi, 4 October, 1988.

stationary, no meaningful development took place at all; and Indian agriculture in the second half of this century where we have seen a stagnant, dormant agriculture blossom into one of the major Green Revolution areas of the world. We have seen during these past two years of drought that our agriculture has gained the resilience to face up to tremendous challenges. What has made this happen? What is the difference between the first half century and the second half of the twentieth century? The difference is basically scientific knowledge, scientific input and equally important their application at the field leave which means it is the team work between our scientists, our extension workers and our farmers that has led to this. But the beginnings, the roots of this growth are very definitely in the science and technology that has been applied to the farm sector, to the agricultural sector. With science and technology, in a very short period, we have transformed India, formerly a country of famine and shortages, into a country that is strong, resilient, self-sufficient. It is a success story for the whole world to see.

We have had major breakthrough in wheat and paddy but this is only the beginning, it must be only the beginning and it is only a base of what lies ahead. We have to look not only at foodgrains but right across the entire spectrum of agricultural production. We have to look for a quantum jump in our output, in our productivity, just like we have done in wheat and paddy. We have to look at pulses and oilseeds, at tubers, at fruits, vegetables, perhaps even at flowers. We have to not only look at how to apply better technology to improve these areas but we have to look at the geographic areas and see where we have succeeded, where we have found less success. We have to see why we succeeded, and we have to find out why we have failed in other areas. The Green Revolution must be taken to other parts of the country, other regions of the country. We must also look at the basic needs of agriculture— fertilizers, pesticides, water-sometimes we have too little and then suddenly we have too much. So, our agriculture must be made strong and resilient and able to face these challenges.

The developments at the IARI and our other institutions do the nation proud and I would like to congratulate all those scientists and administrators who have been involved in these developments not just today but going back to the founding fathers, to the foundations of these institutions. You have made a breakthrough by converting DNA technology into usable technology. This must now be taken to the fields. Toxin producing genes which kill insects have been transferred into crop plants, Genes for resistance to herbicides have become a reality, thus saving nutrients which are depleted by weeds. Coat protein genes have given crops protection against viral infections. Thus, bio-technology is the harbinger of the new Green Revolution in the agricultural sector now.

Indian science must always strive to be at the frontiers of knowledge. That was our traditional place before we got colonized and all our expertise got killed. We must get back to that peak, to that high position. Our science must be innovative and not imitative. It is not adequate just to replicate what others have done, we must effect breakthroughs so that others replicate what we have done. Scientific activity is a creative activity and like all creative activities, it needs the right atmosphere, a congenial atmosphere, for that creativity to take place. We must help develop just such an atmosphere in our institutions to allow the spirit of creativity to flourish. If we are to get top class work from our top class scientists, then we must see that all the red-tape is removed, all the inputs that are required are readily available and that advanced centres of research and development on science are allowed to flourish in every sphere of activity and in every part of our country. But at the same time, scientists must not get locked up in ivory-towers doing their research just for the sake of science, for the sake of research, especially in fields such as agricultural research. That research must relate very actively to the reality of life of the average person in our country, the life of the poorest, to those areas which are of utmost importance to the nation. The linkages between science and its applications, between science in one particular field and science in other fields and even the linkage between science and humanities is very important if science is to fulfil the role expected of it.

Over the years the IARI (Pusa Institute) and all its related institutions have fulfilled this role to a very great degree. They have earned themselves a formidable reputation not only in India, but throughout the world. Now, there are new frontiers of bio-technology and we look to the IARI once again to give the same type of leadership in these new fields. Once again, I would like to congratulate all those who have been involved in this, in building these institutions, in developing and in pushing the frontiers of knowledge further forward.

At the same time, I would also like to put in a word of warning. With bio-technology and biological sciences, we are playing not only at the frontiers of knowledge but we are also playing at the roots of life itself. And there are tremendous dangers if things go awry, if things go wrong. So, tremendous care is necessary to see that a very strict discipline is maintained at all times to see that nothing goes wrong and I look forward to the Institute giving leadership in this area as well.

In a country like India, the demands from the agricultural sector are increasing very rapidly. The demands increase with the increase of population, but the demands also increase because the quality of life has gone up and logically the demand on agriculture has also gone up. We have matched most of these demands with the peaks in our production, but we must remember that every peak in our production is only the base camp for the next summit that we must strive towards. We have seen that in 1986-87, when the country went through severe drought and we were able to impose strict discipline, take up all the slack in the system, we found that our agricultural production did not suffer as much as had been prophesied. So, there is much more strength in our agriculture than is visible in just the production as we see it today. We have started taking up this slack; we have divided the country into a number of agro-economic zones so that more specific action can be taken in each zone and for the first time, we are quantifying and qualifying what will be required for each area, not just in terms of the type of crops but also all the other inputs that are required, the timing, the quantity and all the infrastructure that is required to see that they arrive on time, they are used on time, and they are used to the maximum benefit.

In 1988, we had targeted a hundred and sixty six million tonnes of grain output. We have already increased that target to a hundred and seventy and I have been assured, more or less assured, by the agricultural department, that they are going to go well above a hundred and seventy and I look forward to this massive jump in output that we are envisaging this year. But, let me remind them that if they go up by that much this year, that will increase our aspirations that much more for next year and we won't let them slacken between now and the next year or towards the end of the century, by that time we have to be targeting at close to 250 million tonnes, which will require our looking at new areas- the drylands, the hills, eastern India; it will require at our looking at coarse cereals, at pulses, at oil seeds. This is what the poorer people need and that is why we give so much importance to the technology mission for oilseeds and the national project for pulses.

We must also perhaps start looking at agriculture slightly differently. When we look at industry, we find it very easy to look for tremendous incentives,. All sorts of incentives, but somehow, agriculture is seen as a stepchild when the Finance Ministry looks at things. This has to be changed. We have started doing this, but a lot more needs to be done. If we are to break new ground in agriculture, these old attitudes must change. We have started doing it and we hope in the coming years we will be able to have a major breakthrough in this. The new grounds that we want to cover are fruits and vegetables. The perishable items that have to be discarded and thrown away because they cannot be consumed in time. They will not only give a more balanced diet to our people but a much increased income to our farmers. But to do this, we need to review many things. We need to look at processing, packaging, we need to look at the whole chain that links the farms and farmers with the processing centres, with the markets.

Perhaps, most important, we also have to look at exports and see what can be done to make Indian agriculture more competitive around the globe and that of course means that we must also look at marketing, because marketing is a very important part of any modern nation's economy and if we are not going to be up in that we are not going to be able to compete.

We look to the processing industry, the food processing and agricultural processing industry, as bringing in a second Green Revolution to India and just as the first Green Revolution has completely changed those areas that it has affected, we expect that this second Green Revolution will completely change all aspects of rural India and the lives of our farmers, more specially in giving jobs and employment and development to the areas more distant from the urban centre.

In the end, I would once more like to congratulate all those who have been involved in India's agriculture, the scientists, the extension workers, the farmers, most of all today I would like to congratulate the scientists who have made this change possible in our agriculture, and I would like to remind them that your success have only increased our hopes and we look towards you with much greater aspirations and optimism in the years to come.

This Institution is a fitting tribute to Lal Bahadur Shastriji, one of our great leaders. Let me wish you all the very best for this Institution.

❐

44

Space Technology and the Humanity

I am sorry that urgent work prevents me from being with you personally today. My absence does not in any way diminish the warmth of the welcome we extend to you. We are honoured by the presence here of the world's most distinguished space scientists and technologists.

The 39th Congress of the International Astronautical Federation is being held at Bangalore. This is the capital of aerospace activities in India. Your Congress coincides with the 25th anniversary of the Indian space programme. This international event also coincides with the birth centenaries of two of our greatest scientists, the Nobel Prize winner C.V. Raman and the mathematical genius Srinivasa Ramanujan, as also that of Jawaharlal Nehru, the prime architect of modern India. The theme you have chosen— "Space and Humanity"— reflects the deep belief of these statesman and savants in the development of human society through science and technology.

From time immemorial, men and women have looked up the skies in curiosity and wonder, with fear and fascination. Who of us has not been touched by the romance of space exploration? Who has not dreamt of a journey to the stars? However, the exploration of space is not only the province of scientific fiction writers but deeply associated with the future welfare of humanity.

* 39th Congress of the International Astronautical Federation, Bangalore, 10 October 1988, Speech read in absentia.

India's scientific tradition in the field of astronomy dates back to ancient times. It reached its apogee in the fifth century with the great astronomer and mathematician, Aryabhatta. In spite of such a rich scientific heritage, colonization virtually halted India's progress in utilizing the capabilities of modern science and technology. The credit for revitalizing the scientific tradition after India attained its Independence, goes to Jawaharlal Nehru. He said.

> "It is science alone that can solve the problems of hunger and poverty, of insanitation and malnutrition, of illiteracy and obscurantism, of superstition and deadening customs of rigid and blind beliefs, traditions of vast resources going to waste, of a rich country inhabited by starving millions."

Nehru saw science not just as a tool for economic development but also as a means for the emancipation of humankind. To him the scientific temper was the true religion which had to percolate to the people. Only thus, he believed, could the qualitative transformation of society be achieved.

India has been following the path set out by Jawaharlal Nehru. Considerable progress has been achieved in the field of science. Important strides have also been made in the space programme. Our space programme is closely linked with the development needs. Space technology, when put to use in various areas of development, touches virtually every facet of human life-- communication, meteorology, agriculture, education, industrial growth, resource management, environment, disaster mitigation, health and entertainment. More important still, the benefits flowing from space technology become available to both urban and remote rural areas, as well as to developed and developing regions. Space technology provides instantaneous access to programmes, shrinking both time and distance, helping transcend narrow walls.

Space science and technology have the potential of providing a new perspective of our own planet— that of a single global village. The concept of the oneness of humankind has been an integral part of our ancient heritage. Our great epic the *Mahabharata says:*

> "This is mine, that is another's:
> Such reckonings are for the narrow-minded.
> For the noble hearted,
> The whole world is one family."

The Indian space programme made a modest beginning twenty five years ago with the establishment of a sounding rocket station at Thumba, on our south-west coast. The programme soon became a key instrument for our achieving self-reliance. The focus was on developing this powerful technology to provide practical benefits to the nation in the areas of communication, education, meteorology, and the management of our natural resources. During the last two decades we have launched eleven application satellites, eight of which were built in the country. We have also built a modest satellite launch capability. Today, the unique multipurpose operational INSAT satellites have revolutionized communications, enabling people even in the remotest corners of the country to participate in the mainstream of the life of the nation. Remote sensing applications are providing vital inputs for the management of our agricultural, mineral, environmental, forest, water and soil resources. There has been an innovative use of space technology for emergency communication, rural telegraphy, local specific disaster warning, and search and rescue. Efforts are under way to use space technology for the optimal management of integrated soil-water biomass resources. This will enable us to effectively tackle the massive problems of recurrent drought and flood disasters, which bring untold misery to millions.

To most people , space is still synonymous with interplanetary probes, the exploration of the planets and the pursuit of the enduring dream of discovering infinity. There was world-wide excitement when the first man landed on the Moon and the first pictures from Venus and Mars were received. Studies on the Sun and stellar system have made fundamental contributions to basic advances in cosmology and astronomy. Projects like the Comet Hailey and Phobos missions, which are a necessary part of scientific evolution and hence of concern to all humankind, have been successfully carried out as international co-operative efforts.

International co-operation in science and technology, particularly in the field of space, can go a long way towards ensuring a better standard of life for all humankind. Many important activities such as the monitoring of the environment, meteorological phenomena, and ocean atmospheric dynamic are global in nature. On the other hand, a large number of problems, such as domestic communications, education, rural development, and resource management require the application of space technology based on the aspirations of the people of each developing country and their economic, cultural, social and technical background. At the UNISPACE -82 Conference on the peaceful uses of Outer Space, Indira Gandhi's message said:

> "It is pertinent to ask if such spectacular advances, which in some ways have brought the world together, have also contributed to reducing the glaring disparities which divide people, the rich and the poor, the haves and the heave-nots. The promise of gains from advanced technologies elude the majority of peoples, whose aspirations for a better and richer life remain unfulfilled."

We believe that much greater concerted international effort is required to enable developing countries to have full access to the benefits of space technology. On our part, having derived considerable benefits from international co-operation, we have regarded it as our moral obligation to initiate a new programme on a "Sharing of Experiences in Space" called SHARES. Under this programme we have already trained a number of scientists from developing countries in areas of relevance to them. We reiterate our firm and unequivocal commitment to international co-operation in the peaceful exploration and utilization of outer space, for the development of humanity as a whole.

If, as recognized by the United Nations, Space is to be treated as the "Common heritage of all mankind", its pristine tranquillity must not be jeopardized by extending our quarrels on earth into space. Recent attempts to extend the introduction of destructive weapons into space, are ominous developments, of great concern to humanity. Every step taken with a view to creating impenetrable defences has only escalated the arms race and brought humankind that much closer to its end. More than ever today, human survival depends upon concerted action and immediate negotiations to usher in a world free of nuclear weapons and rooted in non-violence. With this in view an Action Plan was submitted by India to the Third Special Session on Disarmament of the United Nation's General Assembly. The Action Plan calls upon the international community to negotiate a binding commitment, a commitment that is total and without reservation, to general and complete disarmament. The Action Plan seeks the elimination of all nuclear weapons, in stages, by the year 2010 at the latest. We believe that if the nations and peoples of the world act together and with sagacity it is possible for the human race to survive the second millennium and also ensure peace, security and survival into the third millennium and beyond.

I applaud the efforts of the community of scientists belonging to the IAF, which is truly an international organizations representing all shades of political, economic, cultural and ideological systems. I would hope your discussions here will not be restricted to technological developments alone but also cover the larger dimension of the peaceful uses of space technology for the benefit of humankind.

You work in an area often referred to as the "Heavens". The Heavens must remain serene, tranquil and peaceful. While expanding the frontiers of science and technology, you must also provide a new vision of humanity. Your work must serve as a bridge between the East and the West, the South and the North, the developing and the developed, the deprived and the affluent.

❐

45

Better Technology is Better Future

We meet to honour the memory of Shanti Swarup Bhatnagar. He was one of our great scientists, the doyen of modern Indian science. He was a genius with a very original capacity for thinking which he uses to give concrete shape to Jawaharlal Nehru's vision of a modern India based on a scientific temper.

Through S.S. Bhatnagar's efforts, India's scientists have emerged among the leading scientists in the world. They have transformed the image of India from a land of rope-tricks, snake-charmers and elephants to a land that today is the repository of a wide spectrum of science and technological ability in the world.

We must remember that the primary problem that we face in India is one of removing poverty, and keeping that in mind, the litmus test for any national activity is how it helps us remove poverty. That applies equally to science and technology. But when we talk of science and technology, we must look at the broader concepts as directly on the removal of poverty. But, equally important are those aspects of activity which give our country stability, which give our country strength, so that we can protect our Independence to continue the work of

* Presenting the Shanti Swarup Bhatnagar Award for Science and Technology, New Delhi, 17 October 1988.

removing poverty. And sometimes, in looking at the broader picture, we have to look beyond the very limited aspects where science and technology reflects directly on removing poverty.

Our scientists and technologists are the agent of change. It is your ideas, your findings in various fields that you work in, that help us in removing poverty. Your work is transmitted through various extension agencies, various other units. But we must remember that it is the scientist who is at the root of these exercises and it is important for us to so orient scientific activity that it looks more specifically at poverty removal in our country. I would like to congratulate CSIR on the work that they have done in various fields which relate directly to the upliftment of our people.

We have also learnt a lot of lessons and we must recognize the mistakes that we have made. I find that, perhaps, one of the biggest mistakes that we have made is in the way we have done import substitutions. We are always substituting that which is third generation or fourth generation. We are never upfront when we are doing import substitution and invariably, by the time we have breakthrough in substituting that, the next generation or perhaps two generations ahead of that is already available to us readily and that frustrates our scientists and frustrates our technologists. It frustrates our efforts at getting into production with what our scientists have done. This is why we have tried to give a new thrust to science and technology in the country, to target it much more at the frontline, at the cutting edge where our accomplishment can be at least equal to the developments that others have achieved in those areas and that then gives us time and flexibility for converting the work of our scientists into actual production and useful products for our people. This, of course, means that we must concentrate on fewer areas but concentrate very much more in those areas. We have to select those areas very carefully, and then we should not hesitate in backing and funding the work in those areas so that our scientists have whatever is required to effect a breakthrough in those areas.

I am not suggesting that we cut out all the other areas entirely, just that our focus should shift into more definite fields and, in those fields, there should be nothing holding our scientists back in terms of the availability of facilities, of funding, of equipment, avoiding the complications of red tape that we are so fond of creating. Something I find that our technical and scientific administration are even better at producing red tape than our traditional administrators. Well, we must have at least some areas where we can unwind the red tape and unfetter our scientists.

Our national goal must be self-reliance. We have shown, our scientists have shown over the years, that India can become self-reliant in critical areas. In agriculture which has been one of the most critical areas, we are today very strong. We have proved it through these last few years of drought. In the defence field, which is not strictly reflected here, we have, again, shown that we can be the equal of the best in the world when our scientists get the type of support that is needed.

We need to broaden the areas where we are really upfront, widen them, and to look at those areas in a more objective, perhaps more aggressive way. We have to look at things in terms of what we want to make of India. I find that we have been having very inward – looking policies in development areas. We have to look at where we want to take the country, what are the challenges that the country will be facing - may be economic challenges, may be security challenges, other challenges and what we need to do to strengthen ourselves to face those challenges.

The challenges, of course, will depend on what we want to make of our country, where we want to take our country. Today, when international relations are changing very rapidly and very radically, we must take the opportunity to evaluate where India should be in the new scheme of things. If India is to take her due place in the world, then we need to work very aggressively at home to develop in those areas and fields which are essential in the new scheme of things. This is where the role of our scientists, our technologists becomes very much more important than it has been in the past.

If in the current shift in global relationships, we are not able to ensure for India her rightful pace. We may perhaps miss a good opportunity. We may not get an opportunity for decades to come to correct this situation. So, we should not miss this opportunity. It will require tightening up a lot of the looseness that has come into our system, tightening our belts, reducing wasteful expenditure, whether it is in government, or whether it is elsewhere, and focussing all our energies on the main task of removing poverty, of getting India where it should be, to its rightful place in the leadership of world civilization. That is where we were in the past and that is where we would be today. But, again, this will need many scientific breakthroughs, it will require us to be at the frontiers of science in many new fields, and it will require a lot of effort on the part of everybody to give you the support that you need to take us to those front-line areas.

In this past you have done well, our scientists have done well. There were some presentations just outside this hall. I took a few minutes to go through them, and it is commendable that we have achieved what we have. But the challenge that I am putting to you is well beyond that. We have to rise to that challenge. I know that our scientists, our technologists and our institutions have it in them to rise to the occasion. It is for us to give them all the support that is needed for this exercise.

Let me, in the end, congratulate all the prize-winners for the work that they have done. We really look at these awards as an incentive to rise to much greater heights, to do much more work in your specific areas, and to help us build a new India.

❐

46

Managing Science to Build a New India

"I am honoured to be in this legendary city, renowned for its place in India's history as the seat of the Pandyan empire, famed for its contribution to Tamil Literature, home to the architectural wonders of some of our greatest temples and the scientific artistic marvels of the Panchloha casting. Here in Madurai, one savours the fusion of science and spirituality, which Acharya Vinoba Bhave talked of and which Jawaharlal Nehru commended to an earlier Session of the Indian Science Congress.

In choosing Madurai as the venue of this year's annual Congress, you have chosen well. It is even more apposite that you have selected a University named after Thiru Kamaraj. He was not himself a man of much formal education but there was in him a greater education, a profound wisdom and a deep understanding of men and matters which it would profit every scientists to learn from. His simplicity of manner was a useful antidote to the arrogance of intellectual elitism. His concern for the poor remains an abiding corrective for every scientist who regards science as an end in itself. The objective of science can only be the service of human kind. It must be placed at the service of the depressed and the deprived. Kamraj's dedication and tireless hardwork stands as an

* 76th Session, Indian Science Congress Association, Madurai, 3 January 1989.

enduring example for scientists to emulate. For, as Thomas Alva Edison said more than a century ago, scientific achievement is but a little bit of inspiration added to relentless perspiration.

The idea of holding this Congress in the Madurai Kamraj University came from Prof. Krishnaswamy, the former Vice-Chancellor, who was tragically taken away from our midst. We greatly miss his presence here. He possessed a width of vision not always found in the scientific community. Abjuring the narrow compartmentalisation into which scientific study so often falls. Prof. Krishnaswamy sought out linkages in his quest for a holistic approach to science. He worked for the establishment of the Faculty of Life Sciences at this University, combining various intellectual disciplines into one. We extend our sympathies to his bereaved family and to the colleagues he has left behind to the vision of one man, Jawaharlal Nehru, whose birth centenary we are celebrating this year. He described his relationship with science in the following words:

> "I too have worshipped at the shrine of science and counted myself as one of its votaries."

He placed the highest importance on the cultivation of a scientific temper. He saw science and technology as the motor of modernization. Thus, he saw science as holding the key to developing both a better human being and a better society. At this instance, a large number of scientific institutions were established throughout the country and brought under the aegis of the Council of Scientific and Industrial Research. He established a chain of national laboratories, the Atomic Energy Commission, the Defence Research and Development Organization and several other such bodies. He brought science into planned development. A new impetus was imparted to the teaching of science in schools. Universities were groomed into becoming centres of scientific excellence. In 1958, under the guidance of Jawaharlal Nehru, Parliament adopted the Scientific Policy Resolution which, for three decades and more has remained the bedrock of our scientific development.

Indiraji continued the policy adding new dimensions to the thrust of our scientific effort. During her term of office, remarkable achievements were recorded in such frontier areas in Space, Environment and Bio-technology, Ocean Development and Antarctica Research. Our financial outlay on scientific research has increased from a mere Rs. 14 Crores in the First Plan to over Rs. 2500 crores in the current Seventh Five Year Plan. If non-Plan expenditure on science is added to this figure, the total five year expenditure on scientific research comes close to Rs.5,000 crores, that is , to nearly a thousand crores every year. Our expenditure in scientific R&D has now topped one percent of GNP. We do, of course, lag substantially behind the developed countries in this regard but, among the developing countries, we probably have one of the largest, best organized and most productive scientific establishments. For this achievement, the country thanks its scientific community here assembled.

As in all other aspects of our national life, the watch word of our scientific effort has been self-reliance. In frontier areas, where the alternative to self-reliance is outmoded secondhand technology, our scientists have done us proud. In atomic energy, we have mastered the entire fuel cycle and are capable of designing and building our own reactors, In space, we have launched eleven application satellites, eight of which were made in the country.

We have also built a modest satellite launch capability. We are particularly proud of the Indian Remote Sensing Satellite, IRS-IA, which has become one of the most important instruments in the management of our national resources and environment. Space remote sensing is now providing valuable inputs in agriculture, wasteland management, forestry, drinking water, mineral resource mapping, and flood and drought management. Not only is space based remote sensing making it easier to detect underground water acquires, the targeting of specific area for drilling wells has increased the success rate of drilling from 40% to 90%. In agriculture, the meteorological imageries from INSAT-1C have vastly imposed weather forecasting, not only critically useful for increasing cultural productivity but also indispensable for disaster warning. We are managing a satellite system which is crucially responsible for nationwide TV distribution and for adult education, continuing education, development education and the eradication of illiteracy through non-formal education. We have had our failures in launching satellites but such failures are not uncommon in the developmental stage of launch vehicles technology. What is more important is that we have acquired the capability of making powerful liquid fuel engines and large solid boosters constituting a significant milestone in our work toward the Polar Satellite Launch Vehicles. The prime thrust of our space effort is to establish our self-reliance and provide practical benefits to our people in area which directly impinge on their daily lives. In defence electronics, there are some areas where we could be classed among the growing world leaders. Our scientists are doing good work in bio-technology, superconductivity, photonics, modern computational techniques, new materials and non-conventional energy sources.

Perhaps the most spectacular application of science and technology to development has been the Green Revolution. During the colonial period, India's name was almost synonymous with famine. Colonialism began with a famine that wiped out a third of the population of Bengal. It ended, two centuries later, with a famine, which killed over three million people in Bengal alone. Our foodgrain production at Independence was virtually the same as it had been half a century earlier. If in these last 40 years we have transformed ourselves into a country synonymous with self-reliance in foodgrain, it is largely owing to the scientific breakthrough which made possible high yielding varieties of wheat and other agricultural crops.

After four decades of independence, Indian science presents a picture of both development at the frontiers as well as development at the grassroots. Yet, it cannot be gainsaid that the bulk of our expenditure on scientific development has been concentrated on the blue sky research and other sophisticated areas. The application of science at the grassroots, although of fundamental importance to the development efforts, has not received quite the same attention. It is an imbalance that seriously needed rectification. We are now attempting to rectify this through the Technology Missions.

These Technology Missions are directly related to our highest national priority, the war on poverty. Problems of immunization, drinking water and the eradication of illiteracy are receiving not only the attention of the best scientific talent in the country but also the required funding. It is expected that expenditure on the Technology Missions will be of the order of Rs. 5,000 crores, in the next two years, thereby ensuring that spending of this magnitude which was earlier being undertaken in a routine departmental manner is now being spent with focus, purposiveness and much better results. The Mission mode also represents an innovative approach to the management of development. It aims at innovative, low-cost solutions. It meshes the work of the highest scientific talent with the efficiency expected of the ordinary technician. Thus, the drinking water mission marries the remote sensing of acquiries with the plumber, the mason and the electrician who are required to instal, operate and maintain a hand pump. It also marries technological and technical ability with district and village level administration. It brings in the voluntary organizations. It makes the application of S&T to development of a people's movement. It poses to industry such key questions of developmental import as the manufacture of new plastic blackboards, dust-free chalk, cold chain equipment, solar-powered pumps and improved designs for the traditional oil "ghani". It thus breaks out of the bureaucratic mould into which even science has fallen despite the administration of science having been largely vested in scientists and technologists to the exclusion of bureaucrats.

The production-oriented Technology Mission for oil seeds has been complimented by a new mission for Dairying, which is expected to bring one hundred and fifty thousand villages all over India within its ambit, thus sensibly augmenting rural incomes and employment. In addition, there are several S&T programmes being carried out in the mission mode, such as embryo-transfer technologies for improved animal husbandry, the control of iodine deficiency disorders and integrated vector control for malaria eradication.

What we need to establish are adequate linkages between science and technology, on the one hand, and the economic and productive sectors, on the other. It has been estimated that indigenous R&D is contributing to not much more than Rs.10,000 crores worth of industrial production a year. Less than a quarter of the nation's expenditure on R&D is funded by industry. The poor linkage between R &D and industrial applications is also reflected in the virtual stagnation in the numbers of patents field. Science and technology neither experienced an adequate demand pull from industry nor gets an adequate industrial push from scientists. There is a pressing need for indigenous solutions tailored to our particular requirements in infrastructure areas like energy, transportation and communications, including telecommunication.

Perhaps the basic reason for the lack of consonance between the growth of our science and technology and its impact on the development process that our scientific effort has got too diffused. In choosing several different goals at the same time, without adequate prioritizing among them, we are achieving for less than optimum results. It would be far better to recognize that our resources are limited and that, in the allocation of scarce resources, there is no alternative to making hard choices which will result in adequate resources deployment for priority sectors even if this means starving other sectors regarded as less important. The careful identification or priority sectors, both in blue-sky areas as well as at the grassroots, will better enable us to achieve excellence. Excellence in development oriented S&T should be our national objective. We need to create an economic environment in which competitive pressures on industry compel industry to turn to R&D for product development, improve quality and cost efficiency. We also need to orient our educational system in the direction of keeping up with developments in science so that both students and teachers are imbued with a desire to be up-to-date with all that is contemporary and relevant.

This will also incidentally, contribute to reducing professional frustration among the more talented of our scientists. Further, the mismatch between the scientific manpower we are generating and the manpower needs of our science will be repaired. It is, indeed, ironic that the country with the world's third largest reservoir of trained scientific ability, nearly 4.4 million strong should be facing such an acute shortage in important areas of the kind of scientific talent required. In addition, by securing excellence through prioritisation, we will be able to encash some of the resources we have built up in brain-banks abroad among non-resident Indian scientists who would wish to return to their homeland enriched by the experience they have gained in other countries.

If science is essential for development, it is indispensable for sustainable development. The environmental imperative has now fortunately made its mark on the development scene. In many ways, the origins of the recognition of the interface between the environment and development can be traced back to Indiraji's Keynote Address at the Stockholm Conference on the Environment held in 1972. The Report presented to the United Nations by Prime Minister Gro Hearlem Brundtland has focussed world attention on these issues. There is a national and an international dimension to these issues.

The crux of the national dimensions is that conservation has to be regarded as an integral element of the cost of development. There can now be little doubt that the eventual costs of environmental degradation are significantly higher than the cost of conservation. There is also little doubt that the benefits of conservation significantly augment the long term benefits of development. That said, it must be admitted that we know too little about the costing of environmental consequences that the pricing of environmental benefits for us to be able to undertake the truly scientific costs benefit analyses required to make rational choices.

While there is general agreement on the broad causes and consequences of environmental degradation, there is need for detailed scientific work on the causative factors of degradation. We also need detailed scientific assessment of the time related advantages of conservation and the time related disadvantages of neglect.

We depend on the scientist to give us option for policy. He can either show us how to undertake measures of conservation which foretell environmental damage. Or he can fashion for us solutions to the problem caused by such damage. Both options are necessary to facilitate an optimal determination of whether to halt a particular development project in the interest of the environment. Or a combination of the two by way of an alternative option or as a series of alternative options.

National action alone cannot suffice. Problems of development and the environment can only be resolved through cooperative international action. The primary requirement is a new world order which ensures durable peace and reliable security as the backdrop against which the process of sustainable development that is development which is sensitive to environmental security and environmental conservation, unfolds itself. Further, such peace and security need to be associated with equity and justice in international economic relation. This is essential for ensuring that development leads to self-generating growth, for ensuring that the fruits of the development efforts are not lost to crashing commodity prices, crushing debt burdens, and the iniquitous terms of trade so characteristic of the present international economic order. We see world peace and peaceful cooperation, general and complete disarmament, sovereign equally and multilateral democratic decision making, global interdependence and international cooperation as the necessary precursor to sustainable development which benefits all and hurts none, now or in the future, here or elsewhere. The ethic we urge is a recognition of the oneness of humanity cherished through adherence to the principal of non-violence. We call for international scientific endeavour geared not to private profit or the vain glory of narrow nationalism, but dedicated to the general good of all humankind, available and accessible to all without discrimination of advantage. We could particularly want Indian Scientists to profoundly involve themselves in this great cause.

The Brundtland Report has effectively brought out the importance of recognizing that major environmental problems are neither national nor regional but essentially global. The most worrying example of this is the Green-house Effect. It is anticipated that the substantial increase in greenhouse gases in the troposphere, particularly carbon dioxide, could lead to an increase in global mean equilibrium surface temperatures of between 1.5 degrees and 4.5 degrees Centigrade (celisius) within the next 40 to 50 years. The consequences of such global warming could include major changes in the volume, timing, intensity and place of monsoon rain. It could induce significant changes in agricultural patterns the world over. The rise in temperatures could also lead to a rise in sea levels causing innudation of entire archipelagoes, vast coastal areas, and low lying lands. At the same time, it is feared that chloro-fluro-carbon (CFCs) could cause depletion of the ozone layer surrounding the earth leading to ultra violet radiation which could result in skin cancers and seriously affect plant and aquatics life. The global environment and global ecosystems are interlinked at several points. The environment is being perturbed as never before by numerous atomistic actions which are collectively spelling environmental disaster. Awareness is essential. More knowledge is needed. And, a free flow of scientific information is indispensable.

The Green-house Effect is primarily the consequence of the burning of fossil fuels. The consumption of fossil fuels is disproportionately higher in the developed countries than in the developing, but the fallout of the Green-house Effect would be disproportionately more severe in the developing countries than in the developed. Clearly, cooperative international action is necessary to tackle this global problem. Yet, fully accepted scientific data and information on these matters is so little that much more research work needs to be done as the basis for determining the specifics on the international action required. The geographic location of developing countries makes it particularly important that they be fully involved in such research. Our scientists should rise to the occasion.

Research needs to be directed both at possible measure of conservation and at measures to counter the consequences of degradation and repair to the damage done. It would be best for such scientific research to be undertaken as a cooperative international endeavour. If the future of life on earth is at stake, it would be peculiarly narrow-minded and self-defeating to national chauvinisms or commercial rivalries in materials of vital concern to all humankind.

Development is being crippled because of the militarization of scientific endeavour in the world. World expenditure on military R&D is around eighty billion dollars a year, almost all of which is incurred by the nuclear weapon powers and their allies. It is military R&D which is the key driving force behind global militarization. Jawaharlal Nehru warned:

> *"Science today has perhaps begun to cross the borders of morals and ethics. If it gets divorced completely from the realm of morality and ethics then the power it possess may be used for evil purposes. If it ties itself to the gospel of hatred and violence, undoubtedly it will have taken a wrong direction which will bring much peril to the world."*

Unfortunately, large segments of the world scientific community remain mobilized in the cause of war. Military R&D is taking the arms race into dangerous dimensions. Third generation nuclear weapons are promoting the illusion of winnable nuclear war by placing before those who own these weapon the temptation of picking and choosing between specific consequences of the use of nuclear weapons. Binary technology is fuelling interest in a chemical weapons,

Genetic engineering could have the most dangerous implications for biological warfare. The distinction between conventional weapons and weapons of mass destruction is being barred as innovations in artificial intelligence and informatics, give rise to "smart" weapons and even the misleadingly misnamed "brilliant" weapons. Most dangerous of all is the Chimera of Star Wars. Scientific scepticism has taken some of the shine off this project but it still remains the most dangerous escalation envisaged in the nuclear arm race. Once space becomes the battlefield, the destiny of our planet Earth will be mortgaged to the fantasies of the military - scientists and the mindless games the computers will play with no possibility of any human intervention.

There can be no effective disarmament unless a brake is put on the use of science for destructive purposes. The scientific community has to be persuaded to stop playing soldier, even as governments are persuaded to stop using scientists as pawns in the games of war.

At the Third Special Session on Disarmament at the United Nations, last June, India presented an Action Plan which comprehensively address itself to these questions. While the basic thrust of the Plan is towards securing a nuclear weapons free world in phases within a specified time frame, the Plan integrally links nuclear disarmament with a complete cessation of the military application of further advances in science and technology. It also links nuclear disarmament with the education of conventional forces and armaments to minimum levels for defensive purposes only. The Plan envisages worldwide cooperation in science and the world-wide harnessing of the global scientific community to promise horizons in S&T but to preclude those achievements from being directed to military applications. The Plan further recognizes that confidence in a nuclear weapons free world would require an international system of monitoring and verification which must have at its disposal the best available scientific talent in the world. Our Plan for a nuclear weapons free world rests, therefore, essentially on a wide-spread and deeply founded cooperative international scientific endeavour to preclude any sliding back to nuclear arms race. We recognize that the non-violent world we seek is possible only if the international community, including the scientific community, eschews the immortality of science for destruction and cooperatively adopts the ethic of science for creativity. We would like to see the Indian Scientific community take the lead in this regard.

Development is not possible without science. Sustainable development is not possible without science. And sustained peace in the world is not possible without the cooperation of the international scientific community. The world looks to the scientific community to give of its best for the future of humankind, for the future prosperity of humankind and for managing into being a world without nuclear weapons rooted in non-violence.

I wish you all the best for 1989 and a prosperous Pongal.

❐

47

Telecom for Nation–Building

"It gives me great pleasure to welcome you to Delhi. We are honoured that you chose our Capital for this Conference. To our neighbours from the Asia Pacific Region, I give a very special welcome.

Effective communication performs two important tasks. It brings people together. It is vital for optimizing the management of administrative institutions and growth and development programmes. For optimum management, we need rapid collection, collation and transmission of information.

Efficient telecommunications are a powerful tool in a nation-building. They are a tool in fostering the spread of new ideas, in dramatically altering the concepts of time and distance. They are vital to the transformation of traditional societies into modern societies. They are indispensable for involving and getting the people to participate in national policies and programmes. And it is for this reason that we have given such high priority to telecom in our development programmes.

I shall not go into the details of where we are and what we have achieved. It has already been told to you. But let me just say that in these years, and especially in these

* Asia and Pacific Telecommunications Development Conference, New Delhi, 22 Feburary 1988.

last few years. India has made tremendous progress in just about every area of telecommunication. In developing telecommunications, we have kept the watchword of self-reliance, not self-sufficiency but self-reliance. Self-reliance does not mean an autarky, but rather seeking cooperation from others while avoiding dependence by emphasizing our own technology and indigenous manufacture. We have, therefore, stressed Research and Development and product development.

Our focus naturally is on certain aspect which are unique to us - the climate for example, the environmental conditions in which the units will be used, our economic capabilities, our special consumer requirements and our network needs. These are quite different from those of a developed country. They are quite different if you look at rural areas in India and urban areas. And it is with these points in mind that we have looked at the development of telecom. It is with a consciousness of our conditions that we look at technology from developed countries. We keep in mind the difference in conditions.

We have progressed from manual to fully digital exchanges, from open-wire to coaxial microwave. We have brought in satellites and optical fibres. The reach of our telecom is now spreading beyond the metropolitan cities and urban conglomerates to more remote locations, to the islands which are spread out in the Bay of Bengal and the Arabian Sea, scattered populations in the desert areas and isolated districts in the hills and the mountains.

Our public sector units are manufacturing a complete range of telecommunication equipment. Industrial units around the country are manufacturing subscriber terminals, PABXs, and many other components. Our technology has made a notable contribution to rural exchanges, digital switching, transmission equipment, radio system, and optical fibres.

The measures of our achievements is also perhaps a reminder of how much further we have to go. Some 5,40,000 villages are still without direct access to a telephone network. The waiting list is well over a million. The telephones cover only one tenth of the people in rural areas - and three quarters of our population live in the rural areas. The efficiency leaves much to be desired. Ironically, it is quicker and easier to get a call to Sydney to Tokyo than it is sometimes to just get across to Delhi or Bombay. It is almost impossible to get to a village or a remote location.

We have geared our objectives to our needs. Our overall target is to put the entire population of 800 million to within five minutes walking distance of the telecom. It is a very ambitious target and a number of unique steps would have to be taken, taking our environment and these needs into consideration. First, we would like one public paid-phone in each of 5,70,000 villages; a million paid-phones in towns and cities - one at each major street corner. A six-fold increase in the telephone connections from the three and a half million that we have now will take the number to approximately 19 million by the turn of the century. We would like a national package switch data network. We would like greater access to remote areas through satellites. We needed to put all these together and we have done that in a Telecom Mission– an integrated national network, which will give increased accessibility to all and special attention to the more remote and rural areas. We shall forge the missing links in our communication system. Our national network will reach out to those who feel left out of the mainstream of our society. It will provide a telecom infrastructure for economic and social development. This requires a self-confident domestic efforts which will stretch indigenous capabilities to their limits. But it also means that we must not shrink away from international cooperation where that is required. The tasks are so large.

Our telecommunications development over the last forty years has benefited from assistance from several friendly countries, from the ITU, from the UN Development Programme and the World Bank. Our capacities have increased. The need for support and encouragement in these areas has also increased as it has in other sophisticated areas. Conversely, the building of our capability increases our ability to share our experience, our expertise and our equipment with others who are less fortunate. Within the Asia Pacific Region, some countries are much more developed than us, many are like us, developing. We seek to cooperate with the developed where that adds new dimension to our efforts and we offer to cooperate with fellow developing nations who might find something useful in what we have learnt. Cooperation amongst the developing is far below its potential. Perhaps it is because we know so little about each other. There is some interaction and an exchange of views at high political levels and at the higher bureaucratic levels, but at the professional and technical levels, there are vast gaps of knowledge. Our experts know so little about each other that they look first well beyond when they have problems or when they are looking for solutions. We must encourage exchanges at professional levels between our countries. That is how real cooperation within the region will grow. We must make a habit of cooperation and we must nurture it. In our own immediate neighbourhood we have discovered, through the South Asian Association for Regional Cooperation telecom programme, that once we put our minds to it, there do indeed exist many areas for mutually enriching cooperation. Our technology and equipment are designed and developed for our own needs, just as designing and engineering in developed countries are done for their needs which are significantly different from ours.

Global telecom is vital but it is very capital intensive. Hence we find that developing countries creep along and are not able to move as rapidly as they would perhaps like to. We must make the quantum jump, ignoring the intermediate technologies and going into the technologies which will be appropriate for the time when we really come on line with the developed countries. Perhaps that is what Mr. Sathe was talking about, when he spoke about pole-vaulting.

We must ensure that the technologies that we use are cost effective, that they are reliable, and that they are maintainable under our conditions. Recent developments in technology have made this possible. Our need to be alive to these opportunities. Our endeavour is to harness them for our requirements. Our hope is to get organizations such as yours to elaborate a system of international cooperation which will give the developing a just and equitable access to the latest technologies. We look for opportunities for developing countries to make their own contributions to the development of modern technology.

The Arusha Declaration provides a setting for your consideration of world telecom development and the report of the independent commission with the delightfully provocative title of the Missing Link, sets our series of exciting new prospects. Based on these documents your deliberations will be of high importance in telecom development within our respective countries and the promotion of telecommunication cooperation among ourselves.

Our commitment to cooperating in telecom goes back to 20 years from the time when India joined the ITU in 1968. Many changes in the world have taken place since then. But the need for telecom cooperation has only been strengthened.

I hope that this Conference will lead to much greatest and more just access for the development in our region of new technologies and frontline technologies in these areas. We hope that it will bring about a much needed increase in cooperation between the developed and the developing countries. It has given me the great pleasure to be with you today.

❐

48

Strengthening Agriculture for Inclusive Growth

Thirty-seven years ago, speaking in this House, Pandit Jawaharlal Nehru said:

"*We certainly attach importance to Industry; but in the present context we attach for greater importance to agriculture and food and matters pertaining to agriculture. If our agriculture foundation is not strong then the industry we seek to build, will not have strong base either. Apart from that, the situation in the country today is such that, if our food front cracks up, everything else will crack up too. Therefore, we dare not weaken our food front. If our agriculture becomes strongly entrenched as we hope it will, then it will be relatively easy for us to progress more rapidly on the industrial front, whereas if we concentrate only on industrial development and leave agriculture in a weak condition we shall ultimately be weakening industry. That is why primary attention has been given to agriculture and food and that. I think, is essential in a country like India at the present moment.*"

Thirty-seven years later, the time has come for us to reiterate that the highest national priority must be given to the farmer, to farming, to food and agriculture as the cornerstone of our economy. Much has happened in these 37 years. No longer are we threatened with famine. No longer is the begging bowl waiting to be taken out of the

* Statement on the Agricultural Package, in the Lok Sabha, 12 October, 1989.

cupboard. The agricultural policies followed by successive Governments over four decades of freedom have set the stage for the epochal transformation that has taken place in Indian agriculture. True, there was a severe setback during the three-year tragedy of Janata rule, but the agricultural economy was set on course after Indiraji and the Congress came back to the Treasury Benches.

Now, our kisans and khet mazdoors have rendered us self-sufficient in food. They have given us this year the highest-ever output of foodgrains and most other agricultural products. They have given us the inner strength to withstand the rigours of drought and the ravages of floods. They have given us honour and self-respect. They have reinforced our Independence. They have proved the first line of our defence. It is on the basis of self-reliance in agriculture that we have been able to build a self-reliant economy, a deeply democratic domestic polity, and an independent foreign policy. Had we at any time created upon the food front, as Panditji put it, the whole country and everything we stand for would have cracked up too. It is because of our buoyant agriculture that this has not happened. That is the depth of the debt of gratitude that the country owes to the kisan and the khet mazdoor.

During the last nine years, GDP and per capita income have risen as never before. This has led to an upsurge in demand for food and other agricultural products. This is a wholly welcome development. It means an improvement in nutrition levels and living standards. We must gear up production to meet this explosion in demand. Therefore, we are determined to accord the highest priority to agriculture in the Eighth Five-Year Plan. Agricultural growth must be accelerated. Agricultural income and employment must grow faster than they have in the past. Our kisans are concerned at the process of determining support prices for farm produce. We shall ensure that two major modifications are introduced in the methods of computing the cost of production while fixing support prices for agricultural produce. First, we shall determine the wage costs on the basis of the statutory minimum wage for agricultural labour notified by the State or the actual wages paid, whichever is higher. Second, we shall include in the cost of production the labour input of the kisan at a higher wage reflecting the managerial and entrepreneurial role of the kisan.

In order to enable kisans to rationally determine their cropping pattern, support prices are being notified by Government in advance of the sowing. However, this system leaves out of account the increases in costs taking place between the point of announcement and the point of harvesting. To remedy this, we are instructing the CACP (Commission for Agricultural Costs and Prices) to work out suitable escalation formula. Meanwhile, Kharif 89 support prices will be increased at the beginning of the marketing season to take into account increases in the prices of inputs and the general price rise, since the commencement of the sowing season.

The procurement prices per quintal of common variety paddy will go up from Rs. 175 to Rs. 185 and similarly fine and superfine varieties of coarse cereals like jowar, bajra, maize and ragi will go up from Rs. 155 to Rs. 165 of kharif pulses like tur, moong and urad from Rs. 400 to Rs. 425/- groundnut in shell from Rs. 470 to Rs.500 of black soyabean from Rs. 305 to Rs. 325 and of the yellow soyabean from Rs. 350 to Rs. 370, of the sunflower seeds from Rs. 500 to Rs. 530, of the F-414 and H-777 cotton from Rs. 540 and of H-4 from Rs. 650 to Rs.690 and, finally, of the Jute (TD-5 Assam variety) from Rs. 280 to Rs. 295.

These rates will also apply to those farmers who have already sold the produce in the current kharif marketing season. The farming community had also been concerned at the terms of trade for the farm sector in relation to other sectors. The adverse movement of the terms of trade has been rectified to some extent in the Sixth and Seventh Plans. In the Eighth Five Year Plan, we shall ensure favourable terms of trade for the farming sector.

Many farmers are not able to obtain the advantage of minimum support prices because procurement centres are sometimes at a considerable distance from their farms and villages. We intend to increase the number of procurement centres so that, eventually, every kisan will have access to a procurement centre within 10 Kms of his village. The rural roads network will also be strengthened in a phased manner. Kisans, particularly those engaged in the farming of perishable farm commodities, are often denied a fair share of the value of their produce because of the very perishability of their produce. The only answer lies in expanding rural godowns and cold-or cooled-storage facilities. To this end, a special programme is being instituted for the extension of institutional credit on attractive terms for the establishment of cold-or cooled-storage facilities in rural areas.

There is scope for substantially improving credit facilities for the farm community. We propose four specific steps in this regard:

First, we must rectify the problem of credit not being available to members of cooperatives to which they belong, having become ineligible for NABARD refinance. We have decided to open, with effect from the ensuing rabi season, a special line of credit of Rs. 100 crore through cooperative and commercial banks which will be earmarked exclusively for Scheduled Caste and scheduled Tribe farmers. **Second,** scales of finance for short-term production credit will be revised annually so that the credit made available to the farmer fully meets the recommended doses of input at current prices to meet his cultivation requirements.

Third, a special credit regime is being instituted for kisans in rainfed farming areas covered by watershed development programmes. The new regime will operate on the basis of ensuring the availability of credit through a three to five year cycle so as to even out the inherent risk involved in good and bad monsoon years appearing in a cycle in such areas. The special credit regime will take into account problem of overdues which arise within cyclical period to ensure an adequate flow of credit in support of viable crop production and other allied activities. This regime will be reinforced by a major programme of watershed development in rainfed farming areas. The **Fourth** step we propose is essentially a procedural one but which kisans will immediately recognize as being of utmost importance to their requirements. Pass books and agriculture credit cards will be extended to kisans so as to enable the easy drawal of production loans from cooperative and commercial banks.

The National Agricultural Credit Relief Fund will devise a comprehensive relief policy based on the special characteristics of production and the severity of damage in different agro-climatic zones. Through the rescheduling of loans and waivers of interest and principal in defined circumstances, the credit needs of farmers in different zones will be kept in view. While we have invested astronomical sums of money in land improvement and irrigation, our management of land and water resources has been so poor as to render the benefits secured far below the optimum achievable. We propose to take a number of steps to improve the management of our land and water resources.

During the next five years irrigation waters will be made available on an assured basis to an additional one crore hectares of land in the command areas of canal projects. The authorities concerned will be held responsible for, reaching water to farmers in assured quantities and at the right time. Also, ten lakh tubewells and dug wells are to be constructed every years. And five lakh hectares will be covered annually for the programme of desilting and maintenance of village tanks, beels, bunds and ponds. **Second,** the productivity of unirrigated land is to be enhanced through effective watershed development and *in situ* moisture conservation. This programme will extend to 50 Lakh hectares during the next five years.

Third, 25 lakh hectares of usar and barani land will be reclaimed at the rate of five lakh hectares a year. We need not wait for the commencement of the Eighth Plan to take up these projects. A beginning should be made this year itself. Plastic-culture holds vast potential for increasing agricultural productivity. The uses of plastic are many, especially in irrigation, storage and packaging. Existing plasticulture schemes will be substantially expanded. It is proposed to extend incentives for the installation of sprinkler or drip irrigation systems to all farmers. During the next five years one lakh additional sprinkler systems and one lakh drip irrigation systems will be installed to optimize the use of scarce water resources.

Good seeds are the basic foundation of higher agricultural productivity. The new Seed Policy is under implementation and the buffer stocks being built will ensure that kisans have access to high quality seeds and planting material at reasonable prices. We are particularly concerned about small, marginal and SC/ST farmers. With effect from rabi 1989-90, mini kits for the supply of improved seeds will be ensured, under the existing centrally-sponsored schemes to 20 Lakh such farmers. Agricultural research is simply not getting the attention or priority it needs. We are reconstituting the Indian Council of Agricultural Research and I shall take over as its President. We have two major objectives in mind: **First,** we propose to generate appropriate technologies for each sub-zone of the 15 agro-climatic zones so as to be able to modernize our agriculture in each of the zones. **Second,** a special time-bound programme in research and development of hybrids is being taken up to cover rice, maize, jowar, bajra arhar, cotton and oilseeds. Results will be demanded within five years and the implementation of the research programme will be monitored at the highest level. To promote the manufacture of agricultural machinery and implements of improved design, particularly those using new and more efficient materials, a Special Fund is being established to extend credit for the manufacture, fabrication and marketing of such machinery and implements, as also for the leasing or custom hiring of such machinery and implements, plant protection equipment and sprinklers.

For adding value to primary produce, as also expanding employment opportunities in rural areas, it is necessary to encourage agro-based industries, particularly food processing. A special extension and infrastructure package is being put in place for the development and processing of fruits and vegetables in suitable areas. Also, incentives are being given to industrial units to enter into contracts with small producers individually or through cooperatives, For the diversification of rural economic activity, Fish Farmers Development Agencies are being established in all coastal districts to encourage pisciculture and aquaculture. Special attention will be given to poultry development and sheep farming, including reduced costs of feed, market support for the stabilization of egg prices, incentives to establish processing complexes in rural areas linked to small farms, and support to the export of processed products.

Agriculture has the potential of becoming a major export sector. Our kisans will benefit from linking agricultural production to lucrative export markets. In order to realize this potential, we propose to extend incentives to expand the production base of exportable commodities as also the range of non-traditional agricultural exports.

In this connection and in view of the expected bumper crop of cotton. I am happy to announce that we have decided to permit the export of three lakh bales of cotton (one lakh bales of Bengal Deshi cotton and two lakh bales of extra-long staple cotton). As regards the import policy for agricultural commodities, these will be so regulated as to ensure that our farmers are assured of remunerative prices for their produce.

Major institutional reforms are required to support this package. We have two important programmes in hand in this regard:

First, we are initiating a programme to update and computerise land records so that farmers can obtain documentation on demand:

Second, we propose to reform, revamp and rejuvenate the cooperative movement which, in many parts of the country and in many ways, has failed to play the central role envisaged for the cooperative movement in our strategy of socio-economic transformation.

This is a priority task for our next term in office. The interests of agriculture are the interest of the nation. There is no dichotomy between agricultural development and national development. The former is the foundation of the latter. We are confident that the agricultural package, I am now placing before the House, will herald a bright new era for our kisans, khet mazdoors and for the whole farming community.

❐

49

Vision of India: A Dream Anchored in 21st Century

History has seen the rise and fall of many States. Each conducted itself on the principles of first, struggle for survival and, then, expansion through domination. Many eventually fell by the same instrumentalities through which they had emerged, survived and expanded.

Mahatma Gandhi's India represented a new point of departure in history. Without recourse to violence, the Mahatma had brought into being a free country. This was the first time ever that history had seen non-violence used successfully as a political instrument.

That same India, under Jawaharlal Nehru's stewardship, advocated a revolution in the mindest that had hitherto guided international relations. Where, since the dawn of history and before. The quest for dominance had been regarded as normal and natural. Nehru's India advocated an end to dominance in any form and the opening of an epochal new era of peaceful coexistence. Panditji's Non-alignment challenged every conventional assumption of international relations and every conventional goal of diplomacy. Instead of confronting the rival blocs with an alternative bloc, Panditji set before the world an alternative vision of an international order

* Nehru Centenary Memorial Lecture, New Delhi, 13 November 1989.

or equality in place of dominance, co-operation in place of strife, co-existence in place of deterrence, non-violence in place of violence.

Within the country, the domination of the vested interests was frontally challenged by the application of the revolutionary principles on which Gandhiji and Panditji founded our modern nationhood. Democracy took political power from the grip of feudal chieftains and placed it in the hands of the people. Secularism undermined the domination sought by sectarian zealotry. And socialism uprooted the comfortable domination of the economy by large land-owners and a handful of capitalists.

No wonder then that during these 42 years of independence, India has seen many challenges, that would have fragmented nations of lesser intrinsic strength or lesser will. We believe that far from imitating models, developed elsewhere, it is the mission of India to build, in the light of the percepts given to us by Gandhiji and Panditji, a society and a nation which would serve as an example to the world on how to deal with the post-nuclear world and the new technology that now lies in human hands. Nuclear technology has given humankind the power to destroy itself and our planet Earth in the briefest wink of history. Technology has also opened unparalleled opportunities for a fulfilling and bountiful life for all the citizens of planet Earth. How is one to avoid the former fate and ensure the latter? The answer lies in the human mind.

Gandhiji and Panditji advocated an entirely new global mindest to deal with an entirely new global reality. India, by its example, can show the world the path to not only global survival but also to the most glorious era ever in all human history. This noble goal we can realize only by remaining true to the principles of Gandhiji and the vision of Jawaharlal Nehru.

We are uniquely placed to undertake this role because we, in India, are the inheritors of a great historical experience in organizing a multi-lingual, multi-ethnic, multi-religious, multi-caste, multi-regional society. The global village of the new technology has to learn from our experience the basic lesson of how humanity is to live together not as segregated States but as one human family.

The chief characteristic and strength of our civilization have been its unity in diversity. As a civilization, we have never attempted to impose uniformity, we have never attempted to dilute diversity. We have been open to the best of influences from outside, even when such influences came in the wake of military conquest. We have refused to let the spread of human genius be limited by artificial barriers. The continuing theme of our civilizations has been synthesis, that is, the fusing of numerous cultures into a composite culture, where individual identities are retained while common traits are shared. It has bred in our thought processes a sense of tolerance, a ready acceptance of that which is different, a celebration of the diversity of humankind. Panditji ascribed the continuity of our civilization to its "tender humanity, a varied and tolerant culture, and a deep understanding of life and its mysterious ways."

These values and traditions, which constitute the running threat of our civilization, are the explanation for its cultural continuity. More than any other single factor, it is the Indian tradition which has enabled us to face contemporary challenges.

We have had the immense advantage of the idea of India - Bharatvarsha, as our ancients called this land-having predated modern concepts of political unity and having survived all manner of vicissitude, military, political and economic. Going at least as far back as the Rig Veda some five thousand years ago, Indians have recognized the contours of their idea of India, an idea which is always above the shifting frontiers of political entities. The natural frontiers of the idea of India were given us by Nature itself. Ranged along the northern rim was the immense massif of the world's highest mountains. Surrounding the Indian peninsula were the vast oceans. Twelve hundred years ago, Adi Sankara, the unifier of the Hindu religion and the exponent of some of its greatest metaphysical insights, established four places of pilgrimage in the north, south, east and west of India. Pilgrimages to these dhams deeply ingrained the idea of India into our national psyche. The other great religions of India - Islam, Christianity, Sikhism, Jainism, Buddhism, Zoroastrianism, and others - also established places of pilgrimage around the country. They too transcended shifting political boundaries to enter the national psyche and contribute to the evolution of the idea of India. We have benefitted enormously from this idea of India.

The idea of India has not only risen above passing political divisions. It has also risen above the racial, linguistic, cultural and religious diversity of the country. Every ethnic group, ranging from overwhelming religious majorities like the Hindus to numerically small minorities like the Zoroastrians, finds it natural to coexist with the other ethnic groups.

From time to time through our history, there have been attempts to build on narrower identities. But such attempts have not endured. In the long run, the larger idea of India has marginalised those who, in political terms, have attempted to build themselves on narrow identities.

Above all, the continuity of our civilization has been based on an implicit recognition of the entire gamut of values comprised in the single word "non-violence. The roots of the Indian concept of non-violence lie in the philosophy of the Buddha, further developed by our civilization over the last 2500 years.

The philosophy of non-violence originated in our civilization as a moral percept for individual conduct. Mahatma Gandhi retrieved the concept from our millennial tradition and transformed it into a programme of political action. In his autobiography, Panditji described the transformation of this ethical principle into a political instrument as "the spiritualization of politics". Confronted with the mightiest military empire known to history, Gandhiji brought that Empire to its knees by confronting arms with argument, force with reason, injustice with truth, and violence with non-violence. He showed us, as Panditji said, "that the human spirit is more powerful than the mightiest of armaments". He opened the human mind on to an entirely new perspective - of a world of sovereign equals dealing with each other in peace and cooperation, consigning to historical oblivion the vain coveting of the territory, wealth and human resources of others, the ending of the quest for dominance which had hitherto been the leitmotif of world history.

Panditji stressed that violence is ultimately conquered by the dawning of the recognition of the futility of violence. That which is gained by violence is of necessity volatile and transient. Those who have been compelled to submit to brute force do not long accept such submission. The struggle goes on. It ends only when domination and submission give way to equality and honourable cooperation. In this nuclear age, Panditji said, the fall-out of violence would be the extinction of humanity. On the other hand, the fall-out of non-violence would be the blossoming of a common humanity, tolerant of diverse ways of life, with compassion at the heart of its moral outlook, and an abiding belief in the brotherhood of humankind. In his justly celebrated speech to the commemorative fifteenth anniversary session of the United Nations General Assembly -

Panditji said:

> *"In ages long past a great son of India, the Buddha, said that the only real victory was one in which all were equally victorious and there was defeat for no one. In the world today that is the only practical victory. Any other way will lead to disaster."*

The ethical roots of Nonalignment lie in this perception. When India became free, we sought to translate the basic principles of our nationhood into a political testament enshrined in the Constitution.

Thus, democracy we regard as essential to a society which reconciles differences among its members through non-violent means. Democracy is the answer to political domination by class, community, caste or any other criterion.

Secularism is our answer to those who seek religious domination, to those who demand a position of privilege for the dominant religious community as the *quid pro quo* for letting the minorities even exist. As there are those who contest this view even now, let me recall Panditji's definition of secularism.

> *"It means freedom of religion and conscience, including freedom for those who may have no religion. It means free play for all religions, subject only to their not interfering with each other or with the basic conceptions of our State. It means that the minority communities, from the religious point of view, should accept this position. It means, even more, that the majority community, from this point of view, should fully realize it. For, by virtue of numbers as well as in other ways, it is the dominant community and it is, its responsibility not to use its position in any way which might prejudice our secular ideal."*

Panditji conceived of socialism as the third great pillar of our contemporary nationhood, as our answer to attempts at economic domination. When Indiraji saw that the struggle to serve the people was being thawrted by legal legerdemain she brought socialism into the Constitution.

We are one nation and not a union of nations precisely because our nation has room for all manners of diversity. By preserving and promoting all our cultures, we have evolved a composite culture. By transcending ethnic identities without dissolving them, we have created a higher loyalty to the nation, preventing ethnic, linguistic, religious or regional differences from consolidating themselves into divisive political boundaries.

Another pathbreaking innovation which Panditji and his colleagues brought into our Constitution, under the guidance of Mahatma Gandhi, was its enshrinement of affirmative action in favour of traditionally dis-advantaged sections of society. We pioneered the concept that it was not only necessary to end discrimination against the disadvantaged, it was equally essential to empower the dis-advantaged through special access to the legislatures, educational institutions and government jobs, to translate the assurance of equality given in the Constitution into a political, social and economic reality.

This Constitutional innovation was in sharp contrast to the practice of the older established democracies.

For nearly two centuries after Tom Paine's affirmation of the Rights of Man and George Washington's victorious War of Independence, the U.S. Constitution effectively succeeding in disenfranchising the Black population of the country and depriving them of fundamental human and civil rights. In the United Kingdom, notwithstanding the six hundred-year-old Magna Carta, the Catholics were denied the vote till well into the nineteenth century and women till well into the twentieth century. Our country commenced its march into modern democratic nationhood by consigning centuries of discrimination to the past and embarking on a process of special privileges for the most seriously dis-advantaged so that they could make up the leeway of millennia.

We have consolidated and reinforced our unity, integrity and democracy through our processes of planning for development. Two basic principles have informed our system of planning: self-reliance and priority to the poor.

We understand self-reliance to mean paying our own way, standing on our own feet. As Panditji pithily put it:

> *"Nobody can bear our burdens for us: we have to bear them ourselves."*

We hold ourselves responsible for our own development. We are not prepared to mortgage that responsibility to others. We are not prepared to put in jeopardy our hard-won independence nor restrict our freedom of action. We are not prepared to abnegate our responsibility to build, on the basis of the quintessential values of our civilization and the vision of our founding fathers, an India which stands as an exemplar for the world. Therefore, nearly 83 per cent of the investment we have made in development over the last four decades have come from our own resources.

However, self-reliance, in our view, does not mean isolation from the international community or the global economy. That is why we have willingly sought - and given economic and technical cooperation. We have, however, stressed that such cooperation can only be on terms compatible with our honour as a nation, our independence as a State and our self-reliance as an economy. We recognize the essential inter-dependence of the economics of the world. That is why we affirm the need for an international economic order based on cooperation and justice, not exploitation and domination.

Panditji described this as:

"enlightened self-interest, releasing that if some parts of the world do not progress, remain backward, they have an adverse effect on the whole economy of the world and they tend to drag down those parts that are at present prosperous."

The other key element in our planning has been priority to the poor. That too has helped hold the country together and place us in a position to fulfil our larger global responsibilities. I recall Panditji's words in the Lok Sabha in a speech made early in our experience of planned development. He said:

"We often go off at a tangent on grounds of provincialism, communalism, religion or caste. We have no emotional awareness of the unity of the country. Planning will help us in having an emotional awareness of our problems as a whole. It will help us to see the isolated problems in villages of districts or even provinces in their largest text."

The poor constitute the vast majority of our country. They constitute the majority of even ethnic, linguistic and religious group in the country. Poverty cuts across every category. In making the poor the focus of our planning, and in ensuring that the poor of any one ethnic group are neither favoured nor discriminated against, we have pressed planning into the task of uniting the nation and given our people a common stake in political stability and economic progress.

Poverty eradication is not merely a question of specific programmes. It is, above all, a political mindset. In his own inimitable way, Gandhiji called this the worship of daridra-narayana as the highest form of worship. Panditji, in a rather more down to earth way, made the poor the focus of all planned development. He made us understand, that whatever the specific task at hand, the emphasis on eradicating poverty in the shortest time possible has to permeate one's consciousness. Let me illustrate this proposition with regard to industrialization and technology as they affect poverty removal.

Science and Technology

Jawaharlal Nehru was "convinced that the rapid industrialization of India is essential to relieve the pressure on the land, to combat poverty and to raise standards of living, for defense, and a variety of other purposes." The short cut might have been to concentrate industrialization where infrastructure was readily available. This we did not do. We spread it in two ways: one by undertaking different types of industrialization ranging from cottage, village and small industry to more sophisticated larger units. Second, by extending industrialization to remote, backward areas through incentives and Governmental fiat. In particular, the public sector has played a notable part in opening out the hinterland, in bringing all of India within the purview of industrialization. We have thus avoided any unbridgeable chasm widening between industrial India and agricultural India, between rural India and urban India, between modern India and traditional India, between one part of India and any other part of India.

Jawaharlal Nehru defined the role of science and technology in terms of the poor and the people at large. He said:

> *"It is science alone that can solve the problems of hunger and poverty, of insanitation and malnutrition, of illiteracy and obcurantism, of superstition and deadening customs of rigid traditions, and blind beliefs of vast resources going to waste of a rich country inhabited by starving millions.*

The Green Revolution, which brought the prospect of progress to millions of our farmers, was in essence a revolution of science and technology, taking the results of the most sophisticated genetic sciences to the farmer tilling the soil. In the rainfed areas, we have a Technology Mission on Oilseeds and Edible Oils, as well as a National Project on Pulses. A White Revolution - dairying and milk products - is now sweeping parts of the nation. In the hills, a horticultural revolution is in the making.

In a similar vein, we have started a new initiative to harness technology to the service of the drinking water, flood control and the eradication of illiteracy.

Mahatma Gandhi had stressed that democracy would be meaningful to the vast millions of our people only if it were based on village panchayats, the ancient village republic of India. In 1959, Jawaharlal Nehru launched Panchayati Raj in rural India as a great revolutionary measure to systematically transform the Indian polity.

What has happened to that Dream?

As I travel around the villages of India, I feel the seething tension of expectations being totally at variance with reality and realistic possibilities. Because our young men and women have been brought up to look to governmental authority as the provender of all things, good and bad, there is a kind of abnegation of responsibility for one's own development or the development of the local community to which one belongs. There is, therefore, little appreciation, in terms of resources mobilization and resources development, of what is required for the development, process to proceed a pace. Unrealistic expectations are encouraged and then matched to a widening belief that development is a matter of establishing the right contacts, and hoping that nepotism will bring results since the outcome does not appear to be related to merit. It is an explosive situation. The only way of preventing the explosion from taking place is to end the present allienation of the individual citizen from the development process. Paternalisitc planning must give way to participatory planning. Implementation from above must yield to implementation in cooperation with the people and their representatives. There must be representative institutions at the grassroots, entrusted with real powers and real responsibilities, for administration to be truly responsive to the people's felt needs and articulated aspirations.

In every village I visit, I see a glaring contrast between the vast sums of money being spent on development and the spectacle before our eyes on the ground. Much of the money, it seems, is being spent on the delivery mechanism rather than on the programmes. We must substantially augment the share of resources actually reaching the beneficiary.

Our people are exploited at many levels, subjected to petty dignities, often denied a fair hearing, often denied justice. For almost all their problems, they have to turn to officialdom which, however benevolent, is no substitute for a locally elected authority, representative of the people, accountable to the people, and responsive to their needs. The answer to these problems does not lie, indeed cannot lie, in making change here or some adjustment there, some improvement here or some correction there. The system itself has to be changed.

Deep-seated transformation of inegalitarian economic and social structures cannot be undertaken without deep-seated political transformation. We want to create at the grassroots a responsive leadership which, because it is directly and intimately responsible to the people, cannot hide behind the tired cliche and wells worn formulae of the poor but has to find new solution relevant to the new challenges. We intend to endow these bodies with maximum democracy and maximum devolution.

What is really important is that consensus on social change and change itself must be secured by argument, persuation and other non-violent and democratic means, not by violence, deceit or other unethical methods. For the first and the last rule of our political life must be that right ends can be secured by right means alone. As Panditji, under the tutelage of Gandhiji, repeatedly stressed, only the right means can lead to the right ends. In a broadcast made during a visit to the United States– a few months after the martyrdom of Mahatma Gandhi, Panditji, said:

> *"I have become more and more convinced that so long as we do not recognize the supremacy of the moral law in our national and international relations, we shall have no enduring peace. So long as we do not adhere to right means, the end will not be right and fresh evil will flow* from it. That was the essence of Gandhiji's message."

We have also learned from Panditji and the other founder of our democracy that Constitutional and legal provisions have to be reinforced by certain norms of political and administrative action.

The democratic process results in a party being elected to power. But once it has formed the government, the government must be run as a government for all the people and not only as a government for those who have voted for that party. Where leadership in narrow, insensitive and rigid, the available instrumentalities of promoting harmony and peace are of little use. That is why it is essential for the political leadership to be personally and deeply involved in not only setting broad goals but also in the detailed work required to attain these goals. Jawaharlal Nehru showed how enlightened leadership could lead to the resolution of seemingly intractable problems.

Panditji's vision of India encompassed our millennial past and looked out to a millennial future. It was not conditioned by immediate problems and immediate concerns. Rather, it drew its inspiration from the essential continuities of India's civilizations. It charted its perspectives from the need to restore India to its position in the vanguard of all that is of the best in human civilization. Panditji's solutions to problems of everyday politics and everyday administration based themselves on the fundamental moral values of our tradition - truth, nonviolence, tolerance compassion, one humanity and one world. He was the very personification of synthesis, of the composite culture of India, of its unity in diversity, When he looked to the future, he did not limit his vision of India's destiny or India's role in the world to statistical measures of rates of economic growth and other such material indices. He visualized resurgent India as giving the moral leadership to the world, or leading the world in thought and philosophy, in culture and the arts, in science and technology, in equality and justice, in human dignity and human rights, in morality in public life and probity in personal conduct. It is that vision of India which I share. It is that vision of India which the country shares.

Our true celebration of the birth centenary of Pandit Jawaharlal Nehru would lie in building a kinder India in a kinder world, a strong and stable India, an India without poverty, an India which is just and humane, an India in which knowledge flourishes and wisdom is respected, a secular India which is above all narrow parochialisms, an India in which all the weaker sections of today - the Scheduled Castes and the Scheduled Tribes, the other backward classes, the minorities, women, youth are assured equal opportunity and a life of fulfillment.

We seek this India in the world order of Panditji's vision, a world order in which the quest for co-existence among sovereign nations, a world based on equality, democracy and constructive cooperation among countries, a world order which guarantees sustained peace and sustained development, a world beyond nuclear weapons, anchored in non-violence.

❐

Appendices

Vital Statistics: India 2004-2005

Selected Science Indicators

- The national investment on R & D activities attained a level of Rs.18000.16 Crores in 2002-03. The same is estimated to be Rs. 19726.99 Crores in 2003-04 and Rs. 21639.55 Crores in 2004-05.
- 0.80% of the Gross National Product was devoted to R & D during 2002-03. Most of the developed countries spend more than 2% of their GDP on R&D activities.
- Sector-wise percentage share of national expenditure during 2002-03 was: Central Government 62.6%. State Governments 8.5%. Higher Education 4.1%, Public Sector Industries 4.5% and Private Sector Industries 20.3%.
- In the Institutional Sector about 17.8% of the total expenditure was spent on basic research. 41.7% on applied research. 34% on experimental development and the rest 6.5% on supporting activities.
- 79.7% of the total R&D expenditure was met from the government sources and 20.3% came from the private sources.
- 84.1% of the R&D expenditure incurred by the Central Government sources came from 12 major

scientific agencies - CSIR, DRDO, DAE, DBT, DST, DOS, DOD ICAR, ICMR, MIT, MNEs, MOEn and the rest come from other central ministries/departments/ public sector industries. Amongst the major scientific agencies, Defence Research and Development Organisation accounted for 30.3% of the expenditure.

- State sector spent Rs.1528.39 Crores on R&D activities during 2002-03. About 92.9% of the total investment on R&D activities by State sector was on the development of agriculture and allied areas. R&D institutions located in the States of Maharashtra, Gujarat, Karnataka and Punjab incurred more than one third of total State sector R&D expenditure.

- Industrial sector spent Rs.4457.19 Crores on R&D activities during 2002-03. The number of R&D units involved were 1,477 in the private sector and 93 in the public joint sector besides 248 Scientific and Industrial Research Organisations (SIRO).

- Industrial sector in India devoted 0.47% of their sales turnover on R&D in 2002-03.

- The Extramural R&D support increased from Rs.286.71 Crores in 2000-01 to Rs.444.96 crores in 2001-02 and further to 448.69 Crores during 2002-03. The Department of Science and Technology (DST) has played a major role in Extramural R&D funding.

- Academic sector received 50% of the total Extramural R&D support during 2002-03.

- The plan outlay of six scientific agencies has doubled from Rs.12073.12 Crores in Ninth plan 1997-02 to Rs. 25243 crores in Tenth plan 2002-07.

- India's per capita R&d expenditure was Rs.169.38 (US$ 3.5) during 2002-03.

- As on Ist April, 2000, nearly 2.96 lakhs personnel were employed in the R&D establishments in the country including in house R & D units of public and private sector industries 31.7% were performing R&D activities, 30.4% were performing auxiliary activities and rest 37.9% were providing administrative and non-technical support.
- There were 11,304 women directly engaged in R&D activities, i.e. 12% of the total R&D personnel.
- India had 110 researchers per million population during 2000. Only 0.10 SET per thousand population were employed in R&D during 2000.
- Doctorates in science form 67.0% of the total 6,714 S&T doctorates produced by the educational system in the country during 2002-03.
- 2469 patents were sealed in the year 2003-04. Out of which 1078 patents were sealed by Indian's. The maximum number of patents field by Indians were from the State of Maharashtra with a percentage share of 28.6%. United States of America topped the list of applications for patents filled in India by foreign countries with a share of 33.3%.
- There were 302 universities/deemed universities.11 institutes of national importance and 16,885 colleges during 2003-04 imparting higher education in the India.
- India's contribution to the world publications on science and technology was of the order of 2.16% Research papers on agriculture were 7.4% of the world total during 1994-2003.

The National Development Council, on 9 December 2006, has approved the allocation of more funds to the agricultural sector for achieving higher agricultural growth/productivity and incomes of all farmers in both crop and non-crop agriculture, during the Eleventh Five Year Plan, 2007-12.

India-Economic Survey Data

Indicator	Year	Unit	Numbers	Sources
POPULATION AND HEALTH				
(a) Population	1950-51 2003-04	Million Million	359 1073	Economic Survey 2004-05
(b) Birth Rate Per Thousand Population	1950-51 2001-02	Number Number	39.9 25.0	--do--
(c) Death Rate Per Thousand Population	1950-51 2001-02	Number Number	27.4 8.1	--do--
(d) Female Population per Thousand Male	1951 1991	Number Number	946.0 927.0	--do-
(e) Registered Medical Practitioners (R.M.P.)	1950-51 2000-01	Thousand Thousand	61.8 575.6*	--do--

(f)	Registered Medical Practioners (R.M.P.) Per Ten-Thousand Population	1950-51	Number	1.7	Economic Survey 2004-05
		2000-01	Number	5.6*	
(g)	Beds All Type Per Ten Thousand Population	1950-51	Number	3.2	--do--
		1990-91	Number	9.5	
(h)	Expectancy of Life at Birth				
(i)	Male	1950-51	Years	32.5	--do--
		2000-01	Years	63.9	
(2)	Female	195C 51	Years	31.7	
		2000-01	Years	66.9	
AGRICULTURE PRODUCTION					
(a)	Foodgrains	1950-51	Million Tonnes	50.8	--do--
		1990-91	Million Tonnes	176.4	
		2000-01	Million Tonnes	196.8	
		2003-04	Million Tonnes	212.2	
(b)	Oilseeds	1950-51	Million Tonnes	5.2	--do--
		1990-91	Million Tonnes	18.6	--do--
		2000-01	Million Tonnes	18.4	
		2003-04	Million Tonnes	25.1	

(c)	Pulses	1950-51	Million Tonnes	8.4	Economic Survey 2004-05
		1990-91	Million Tonnes	14.3	
		2000-01	Million Tonnes	11.0	
		2003-04	Million Tonnes	15.2	
PER CAPITA NET AVAILABILITY					
(a)	Cereals	1951	Gms/day	334.2	--do--
		1990	Gms/day	435.3	
		2000	Gms/day	422.7	
		2003	Gms/day	407.1*	
(a)	Pulses	1951	Gms/day	60.7	--do--
		1990	Gms/day	41.1	
		2000	Gms/day	32.8	
		2003	Gms/day	29.1*	
BASIC ECONOMIC DATA					
(a)	GNP at Factor Cost (current prices)	1950-51	Rs. Crores	9506	--do--
		1990-91	Rs. Crores	503409	
		2000-01	Rs. Crores	1884890	
		2003-04	Rs. Crores	2505707	
(b)	Per Capita Net National Product (current prices)	1950-51	Rupees	254.7	--do--
		1990-91	Rupees	5365.3	
		2000-01	Rupees	1655.4	
		2003-04	Rupees	20988.5	

(c)	Index of Industrial Production	1950-51	(Base:1993-94)	7,9$	Economic Survey 2004-05
		1990-91	(Base:1993-94)	91.6	
		2000-01	(Base:1993-94)	162.6	
		2003-04	(Base:1993-94)	189.6	
(d)	Wholesale Price Index**	1950-51	(Base:1993-94)	6.8	--do--
		1990-91	(Base:1993-94)	73.7	
		2000-01	(Base:1993-94)	155.7	
		2003-04	(Base:1993-94)	175.9	
(e)	Consuemr Price Index**	1950-51	(Base:1993-94)	17	--do--
		1990-91	(Base:1993-94)	193	
		2000-01	(Base:1993-94)	444	
		2003-04	(Base:1993-94)	500	
(f)	Number of Villages Electrified	1951	Number	3061	India, 2001
		1990	Number	460536	
		2000	Number	506920	
FOREIGN TRADE					
(a)	Exports	1950-51	Rs. Crores	606	--do--
		1990-91	Rs. Crores	32553	--do--
		2000-01	Rs. Crores	203571	
		2003-04	Rs. Crores	293367	

(b)	Imports	1950-51	Rs. Crores	608	--do--
		1990-91	Rs. Crores	43198	
		2000-01	Rs. Crores	230873	
		2003-04	Rs. Crores	359108	
EDUCATION					
(a)	Litecary Rate	1950-51	Percentage	18.3	Economic Survey 2004-05
		1990-91	Percentage	43.6	
		2000-01	Percentage	52.2	
		2003-04	Percentage	65.4	
(b)	Number of University/ Deemed University	1950-51	Number	27	University Grants Commission
		1990-91	Number	179	
		2000-01	Number	240	
		2003-04	Number	302	
(c)	Number of Colleges	1950-51	Number	542	--do--
		1990-91	Number	7346	
		2000-01	Number	12806	
		2003-04	Number	16885	
(d)	Number of High/ Higher Secondary Schools	1950-51	Number	7288	Ministry of HRD (Dept.of Education)
		1990-91	Number	79000	
		1998-99	Number	112438	
(e)	Number of Primary/Junior Basic Schools	1950-51	Number	209671	Ministry of HRD (Dept.of Education)
		1990-91	Number	558000	
		1998-99	Number	626737	

(f) Number of HRD	1950-51	Number	13590	Ministry of
Middle/Senior Education)	1990-91	Number	147000	(Dept. of
Basic Schools	1998-99	Number	190166	
(g) Education Expenditure	1950-51	Rs. Crores	114.4	Ministry of HRD (Dept. of Education)
	1990-91	Rs. Crores	20761.3	
	1998-99	Rs. Crores	61148.8	
RESEARCH & DEVELOPMENT				
(a) R & D Expenditure	1950-51	Rs. Crores	4.7	R & D Statistics 2004-05
	1990-91	Rs. Crores	3974.2	
	2000-01	Rs. Crores	16198.8	
	2002-03	Rs. Crores	18000.2	
(b) R & D Expenditure as Percentage of GNP	1950-51	Rs. Crores	0.1	R & D Statistics 2004-05
	1990-91	Rs. Crores	0.8	
	2000-01	Rs. Crores	0.9	
	2002-03	Rs. Crores	0.8	

Note: 1. * Provisional.

2. ** Figures for the year up to 1993-94 derived by converting the indices on earlier bases into base 1993-94=100.

3. #. Data from Travancore (Kerala) & Goa Medical Councils have not been included.

4. @ Figures for the period up to 1988-89 derived by converting indices on earlier bases into base 1982=100.

5. $ Relate to the calender year 1950.

6. + Data available on website on Registrar General and Census Commissioner (RGCCI), india to projected population of India.

7. c Data refers to average over 1993-97 as estimted by the sample registration system and centred at 1995.

Reference:-

Research and Development Statistics: 2 004-05, Government of India, Ministry/ Department of Science and Technology, New Delhi, September 2006.

Bibliography

(A) Basic Document

Rajiv Gandhi- Selected Speeches and Writings of: Vol. I-V, 1984-89. Publications Division, Ministry of Information and Broadcasting, Government of India, New Delhi, 1987-89.

(B) Books, Journals, Newspapers Articles, etc.

Adiraju Venkateser Rao - Gandhi to Gandhi, See Sathya Publications, Hyderabad, 1986.

Aggarwal Adish – Rajiv Gandhi: An Assessment, Amish Publications, New Delhi, 1993.

Ahluwalia B.K. and Ahluwalia Shashi- Rajiv Gandhi: Breaking New Grounds, Cosmo Publications, New Delhi, 1985.

Aiyar Mani Shankar - Remembering Rajiv, Rupa & Co., New Delhi, 1992.

Aiyar Mani Shankar - In Rajiv's Footprints, Konark Publishers Pvt. Ltd., Delhi, 1993.

Chand Attar - Rajiv Gandhi: His Mind and Ideology, Gian Publishing House, Delhi, 1991.

Chander Harish and Padmini - Rajiv Gandhi -Many Facets, Noida News Pvt. Ltd., New Delhi, 1992.

Chidambaram P - He Lived too Dangerously, The Times of India, New Delhi, 26 May 1991.

Crosette Barbara- We have to do Much More, The Times of India, New Delhi, 26 May, 1991.

Gandhi Sonia - Rajiv, Viking, Penguin Books India (P) Ltd., New Delhi, 1996.

Gill S.S. - The Dynasty, Harper Collins Publishers India, New Delhi, 1996.

Goenka Shyam - Eternal Rajiv: Epitome of Humanity, Resurgent Publications Pvt. Ltd., New Delhi, 2006.

Healy Kathleen- Rajiv Gandhi: The Years of Power, Vikas, New Delhi, 1989.

Merchant Minhaz - Rajiv Gandhi: The End of a Dream, Viking, New Delhi, 1991.

National Herald - Remembering Rajiv, New Delhi, and 21 May 1992, 21 May 1993.

Nugent Nicholas - Rajiv Gandhi: Son of a Dynasty, BBC Books, London 1990.

Raju Jagmohan Singh - Quotes of Rajiv Gandhi, UBSPD, New Delhi 1994.

Rasgotra Maharaj Krishan - Rajiv Gandhi's World View, Vikas, New Delhi, 1991.

Roy Sekhar Basu (ed.) - The Legacy of Rajiv Gandhi, New Approach, Kolkatta, 2006.

Singh K. Natwar and Sharda Prasad, H.Y.- Rajiv Gandhi: A Political Study, Konark, Delhi, 1989.

Sikka Pawan - Rajiv Gandhi: Environment, Prime Concern, The National Herald, New Delhi, 20 August 2003.

Sikka Pawan - Rajiv Gandhi: He Wanted to See India Proud, The National Herald, New Delhi, 21 May 2005.

Sikka Pawan - Rajiv Gandhi: His Vision of the 21st Century, Science, Technology and National Development, Kalpaz Publications, New Delhi, 2007.

Sikka Pawan - Rajiv Gandhi's Modern India: Development with Science and Technology, Uppal Publishing House, New Delhi, 2007.

Verma Shrikant - A Portrait of Rajiv Gandhi, Arnold Heinemann, New Delhi, 1985.

Zaidi A.M. - Rajiv Gandhi: Towards Peace, Progress and Prosperity, Indian Institute of Political Research, New Delhi, 1987.

Index